MW00886408

CHARACTERS *of the* BIBLE

Finding My Stories in Their Stories

Enjoy the stories!

David Waddell

DAVID WADDELL

WestBow Press books may be ordered through booksellers or by contacting:

WestBow Press
A Division of Thomas Nelson & Zondervan
1663 Liberty Drive
Bloomington, IN 47403
www.westbowpress.com
1 (866) 928-1240

ISBN: 978-1-4908-6774-8 (sc)
ISBN: 978-1-4908-6775-5 (hc)
ISBN: 978-1-4908-6773-1 (e)

Library of Congress Control Number: 2015901136

Printed in the United States of America.

WestBow Press rev. date: 02/12/2015

This book is dedicated to my family and friends.
You invited me into your life.
You inspired me with your stories.
You encouraged me with your words.

When I think of the people God used in the Bible, I find peace. Those guys and gals were just like me! As I started to see them and their situations through the eyes of my own experiences, they started meaning a lot more to me.

The idea of studying particular people in Bible stories came to me after a period of restoration following some darkness and sin in my life. I was given an opportunity to speak to the church I had once served. I structured the message around the people involved in the story told in John 8:1–11.

As I reviewed the story, I saw myself in a crowd of people wishing punishment on a lady for committing the same sin they had done or wished to do. I held my stone, ready to throw. I saw myself as a Pharisee bringing one to "justice" in the guise of image protection and seeming to be holy. I played that game of pretending to be better than I really was. I saw myself as the woman who was looking for love in all the wrong places. I was the woman that basically was at the mercy of Jesus regarding her punishment and who, despite remaining quiet, was forgiven of her sins. At that point I began to see the connection I had in my life with the mistakes, sin, stupidity, and rebellion of Bible characters.

These writings deal with characters of the Bible. But these are not just characters as in actors or people in a story. My writings do not deal with character as a description of positive traits. No, these characters of the Bible are real characters, as in "He's a real character!" These characters are mean, lying, deceitful, cheating, conniving, and abusive. Isn't it great to have such wonderful role models? Some of these stories might also be a surprise to people I know, in that I've never confessed some of these aspects before. I ask family and friends and former churches to offer grace in matters I might have gotten away with up till now.

It amazes me that some of the people who got their names and stories in the best-selling book of all time were some of the most flawed characters in the world. I find comfort in the fact that I am just as flawed and goofy and wrong and misdirected as they are. It is through the lives of these characters that I see so much of myself. I have an idea you might find yourself in a couple of the characters as well. As I look at their situations, I see my life play out. Their story is my story. Their sin is my sin. I also know their victory will be my victory when I meet some of them in heaven. Oh, will we have some stories to share!

It is my hope you'll see yourself in some of the characters and realize you're not as bad as you may have thought. After all, a similar character got his or her name in the Bible!

CONTENTS

JOSEPH: THE ORNERY BROTHER (GENESIS 37–50)

As she set the clean clothes in my drawer, she saw something flicker. It was the reflection of the bedroom light on something wrapped in foil. The objects had the appearance of Christmas colors. It was the kind of foil that Hershey's uses to wrap their miniature candies.

It was Christmas candy.

Of course Mom was putting the clothes away near Valentine's Day, when new candy would be distributed. She thought nothing of it because it was normal behavior for me to stow candy away. You see, I was a brother. Born in the middle of three boys, we all set out to destroy one another with pithy statements, practical jokes, and an occasional all-out brawl.

"Ornery" is the word my grandparents and parents would use to describe me. When candy was given, my brothers would gobble theirs down immediately. I ate a little for the initial thrill but then would hide the rest of it. Later, sometimes months later, I would pull the candy out and teasingly and enticingly eat it in front of my brothers. Of course this would get a rise out of them, so I would get both chocolate and the satisfaction of irritating a sibling.

Talk about your win-win situation.

During the summers, because both Mom and Dad worked outside the home, we boys had the run of the house. I would usually rise before Allen or Mark and would read, play games, or watch TV until one of them was up. When they got up, they'd usually start something for breakfast. Normally it would be some kind of egg-and-toast combination. I'd wait a moment till they got started and ask if they'd mind tossing me in a couple. I mean, while you're cooking already, what's a couple more? I definitely was a brother. I had a good gig until Mom figured out what was going on and made me start cooking my own stuff.

Now, don't go feeling sorry for Allen and Mark. Believe me when I say they were brothers as well. I wonder often if the original Greek or Hebrew word for "brother" literally meant "obnoxious initiator for the purpose of inciting a riot." We would eat each other's leftover cake, drink the last Coke with someone else's name on it, and stuff each other's bed pillows with our dirty socks and underwear.

Sometimes we'd team up with one of the other brothers and pester the "outsider." Mark, whom I shared a room with from his birth until Allen moved out, was the youngest of the three. We'd often get together and bang on Allen's door, singing, "Coca-Cola is Coke, that's the way it should be"—a jingle from an old commercial. We'd hit the door to the tune of the song and sing it over and over again until he'd finally explode.

The phones back then were rotary dial, so if there was an extension, you could pick it up and screw up the dialing of the other phone. I'm not saying we did that, but I've heard of others doing it. I read a lot. Okay, it was fun.

In the story of Joseph in the book of Genesis, there is normally a reference to the evil his brothers did to him. The storyteller almost paints a picture of this "perfect son" that endures all sorts of unfair treatment.

I know better.

You see, Joseph was a brother. He was the eleventh son and twelfth child born to Jacob. He was the firstborn child of Rachel, the girl that Jacob loved more than his other wife, Rachel's sister. This makes him a middle child of sorts with the arrival of Benjamin, his little brother from the same mother. It also explains some of the special treatment his father gave him. The writer of Genesis tells us that Joseph was loved most by his father. His father gave him a special, richly ornamented robe. Further, it states that the brothers saw this favoritism and hated him. Talk about your sibling rivalry!

Being a brother, I don't believe Joseph was innocent in the growth of hatred toward himself. I have no doubt that Joseph took the ornamented robe and flaunted it in front of his brothers, much like I did my Christmas candy. No doubt Joseph pointed out how much more loved he was and how he was the favorite of their father. My brothers continue to claim to this day that Mom loved me best. Of course I didn't get additional chocolate from my mother; I just hid mine until later.

Later Joseph got a couple of dreams from God about how his brothers would someday bow down to him. Can you imagine the pride exuding from this boy telling this to his older brothers? It's as if he's requesting an additional couple of eggs to be tossed into the pan, making them his servants. *A piece of toast would be nice as well, if you don't mind.*

No wonder they wanted to kill him. I think Allen and Mark dealt with the same temptation. We did share one other thing with Joseph and his brothers: we could pick on each other, but if anyone else tried it, a fight would break out. Some of the best bus stop battles occurred when someone wanted to pick on one of us. Reuben, the oldest brother, didn't want to kill Joseph, so he convinced the others to throw him in an old well. Then Judah had the bright idea of selling him to a caravan coming through. Even in an evil act, his brothers were protecting him as best they could.

Of course we can read in the rest of the story how Joseph continued to experience new trials as God honed his pride by making him a humble servant God could use. God made him second in command in Egypt. A famine hit the land, which led his brothers to travel and ask him for food without recognizing who he was. Joseph recognized them, however, and proceeded to play with them a bit while taking care of their hunger needs. He put a little scare into their hearts before confessing who he was. One of the brothers even called out that they were getting payback for what they did to Joseph. In the midst of all this new conniving, the day came when the brothers did kneel before him. Don't worry, Mark and Allen, I haven't had that dream!

Joseph, after seeing the brother from his own mother, and in a spirit of forgiveness, pointed out to his brothers who he was and that what they meant for evil God used for good. I would imagine my brothers and I could all say the same thing. When I received what they perceived to be unfair treatment in an employment situation, they were greatly outspoken about it. When failure visited me, the brothers were there to pick me up and remind me of my worth. I do the same for them. Cain asked God if he was his brother's keeper. The answer for me is yes! Learning from my relationship with my brothers, I've added a host of friends to my life that I would consider my brothers. But not to worry, I'm not looking for any eggs to be cooked—that is, unless you're tossing a couple on the stove anyway.

So for those times when I harassed the daylights out of you guys, for those taunting and teasing exhibits of chocolate consumption, for taking you for granted and treating you like servants, I can only say that what I meant for evil, God has turned into good!

Chocolate anyone?

BALAAM: WRONG PLACE, WRONG TIME (NUMBERS 22:21–39)

She couldn't get around too easily. She used a walking cane, and it was evident to me, even as a first grader, that she could easily be outrun in the event that would be needed information in a classroom. I remember she had blue hair. I believe this is when senior adults were first called "blue hairs," because ladies at that time put something in their hair to get rid of the gray, only to have their hair turn blue. Despite her limitations, she was a strong lady. She did not accept anything from her class except their best behavior. I always struggled with those kinds of expectations in schoolwork, even at that young age. It was always more fun being the class clown.

My scariest memory of her is from one day after I returned from recess. I walked into the same room she was in. Upon my entrance I immediately felt her displeasure with me. *Of all the things I've done wrong,* I wondered, *which one did she catch?* I looked around, and the girls in the room didn't seem worried with her but were shocked to see me. She approached me, poked me on the arm with her cane, and told me, "Get out of this room, and never let me catch you here again."

Then she poked me again and stated the same warning: "Get out of this room, and never let me catch you here again!"

Can you believe this assault on an innocent child? The aggressiveness with which she dealt with me was shocking and scary. I immediately turned and ran out of the room, believing she would jab me with the cane once more. "Get out of this room, and never let me catch you here again!" Those words could still haunt me to this day.

Even at that young age, I was shocked at the violence demonstrated on me. *Is this what is meant by the board of education? Can a teacher actually get away with telling a student to get out of a room and never return? Isn't caning against the law in this country? And if not, shouldn't it at least be unlawful against first graders?*

Of course, there's part of the story I haven't shared yet. I was in the girls' restroom. And yes, I knew what I was doing.

It seems that I spent a good portion of my life in places where I shouldn't have been. Oh, more times than not I knew better. I just went there anyway—sometimes to flirt with sin, and other times to just flat out ask it out on a date! God always tried to communicate with me about better paths to walk, but I wouldn't listen. Throughout history God has chosen a variety of methods to communicate with us. Elijah once listened for God through a mighty wind, an earthquake, and a fire. Finally Elijah heard the Lord in a still, small voice.

While Elijah and other people respond to the gentle whisper of the Lord, I've always been a little hard of hearing and a slow learner. The whisper is exchanged for a heavenly two-by-four upside the head. If you look at my forehead close enough, you can actually see the "Yellow Wood" brand etched into my skin! I discovered wooden canes work too.

When I was growing up, there was a popular show on television called *Mister. Ed.* It was the story of a talking horse and the troubles he got into with his human owner. Perhaps I would have listened better if God had provided me a talking horse.

God actually used that method once, although it was a donkey rather than a horse. Balaam, a prophet of God, was guilty of the same thing I was. He tried going somewhere God had told him specifically not to go. The Israelites were making their trek toward the Promised Land. In the process, they had annihilated several societies on their path. Balaam had been summoned by his king to explore the coming Israelites and place a curse on them. The king, of course, was worried that he and his people would be destroyed as well. Balaam, after being told by God not to comply with the king's request, refused the king. The king then sent his servants again to plead and offer even greater riches for him to fulfill the king's wishes. When he refused again, he told the servants to wait until morning while he received another word from God. Isn't it funny how we keep asking God for things even after He says no? This time, however, God, giving Balaam over to his greed, said, "Go."

I have a feeling Balaam was trying the "Look at me, I'm the good guy" stance while also balancing the trip in the hopes of making a few bucks and satisfying some selfishness in his life. I've played that game too, Balaam! As long as I look holy, I must be holy, right? God, of course, could see he wanted to enter the girl's restroom, and He granted permission even though the trip made Him angry!

As Balaam was on his way, his donkey saw what was looming ahead. *No problem, it's just my first grade teacher with her cane.* Well, actually it was an angel from the Lord with a big sword aimed to kill them. The donkey, seeing with eyes Balaam had apparently closed in the girl's restroom, came to a stop and turned off the road, only to be whipped by Balaam and redirected onto the road.

On round two, out of fear, the donkey, seeing the angel of death again, ran Balaam into a wall, smashing his foot. I've always heard you shouldn't give children spankings when you're angry. Balaam apparently hadn't heard this regarding donkeys. The smashing into the wall got the donkey another whipping. Balaam apparently had a cane of his own.

Finally, on the third attempt, the donkey just laid itself down out of fear of the angel of the Lord. Balaam started beating the poor animal with his staff. That's when the donkey began talking. He questioned why Balaam was whipping him. It was during the conversation that God opened the eyes of Balaam and he saw the teacher with a cane in the girl's bathroom. Well, sort of—he was finally able to see the angel of death for himself. The angel questioned him on the beating of the donkey as well as why Balaam had decided to go into the girl's restroom, or defy God's wishes in going to a place God had forbidden him to go to. Balaam, realizing his sin, admitted he shouldn't be in the girl's bathroom.

So what does it take to keep us out of the wrong place at the wrong time? Can we avoid the flirtation with devastation? Can we defy the lies that lead us to desire something God is not in favor of? I would hope we can learn to listen to the voice of God in the gentle nudge, whisper, or still, small voice. If not, there are always walking canes, two-by-fours, and talking donkeys.

So "get out of this room, and never let me catch you here again!"

CAIN: DIDN'T GIVE HIS BEST (GENESIS 4:3–8)

Math was never really my strong suit. I'm not sure I can say any school subject was really my strong suit, unless you want to count comedy or being a class clown as a school subject. My reading skills were poor, and other than Superman and Batman comics, I didn't read much. My parents, being the wise folks they are, subscribed to *Sporting News* for me because they knew I'd read it. To this day I have no idea who Silas Marner was, but I know Paul Silas played in the National Basketball Association!

I could handle the basics of math in elementary school with minimal success. Baseball statistics helped me learn addition, multiplication, and division in figuring out batting averages and earned-run averages, but it didn't advance much further than that. As I started junior high, I realized that I could handle basic math, but when I got into algebra and geometry, I figured I might as well have taken geography, because I was lost. The feeling of inadequacy was not helped by having a smarter older brother to be compared with.

Recognizing a weakness for the subject, I gave myself permission to not do well. If it isn't hard enough to learn in the first place, then allowing for average success makes it all the more difficult.

Entering my freshman year, I had a choice between Math 1 and Algebra 1. My parents and advisors felt it was best to put me in Algebra 1. If only the guy Tom Hanks played in *Big* could have explained things to me. Mr. Jones, my teacher, was no Tom Hanks. It didn't start out well either. He asked if I was Allen's brother, and because I was, he assumed

I would have the same level of intelligence he did. That's just not going to happen. I did, however, notice one thing that could be used to my advantage: the answers to all the odd questions were in the back of the book. I did not realize those were there so you could make sure you had done the problem accurately. I submitted my homework of items one, three, five, and seven that day fully confident each one was correct.

In discussing the homework, Mr. Jones called on me for number one. I proudly called out the answer. I could sense the pride exuding from his smile. "Another Waddell" was his thought, I'm sure. He then asked me to come to the front of the class and demonstrate how I had gotten the answer. I grabbed my textbook, walked to the front, turned to the answers in the back, and pointed to the correct answer.

The class let out a roar of laughter. Mr. Jones was not joining in. It was the first of many high school journeys to the office caused by my sense of humor.

Not being one to expand my mathematical mind (unless you count baseball batting averages and earned-run averages), I began my college years with the knowledge that I had to take one math class. Having learned my lesson from high school, I registered for the college-level Math 1 instead of college algebra. I was cruising through, thinking I had it made with this class. Then it happened.

While I was working the recreation center at First Baptist Church, a third-grader asked me if I could help him with his homework. I agreed and asked what subject it was. He stated it was math and that he couldn't understand what they were trying to do. Despite my mathematical inadequacies, I sat down with the young man and he showed me the list of problems in his textbook. They were working on clock arithmetic. In other words, in clock arithmetic ten plus three would equal one. You just keep going round and round the clock with the numbers. Ironically, that was the very assignment I was working on for my college class. I started poring through this child's textbook and found an incredible number of items similar to what my college textbook was covering.

The sad part is I made only a B in the "third-grade" college-level math class.

Not doing one's best has been a problem for a long time. We've seen teams lose games because of it. We've experienced relationships ending prematurely as a result of this phenomenon. Overall we find numerous people giving up a cause because of it.

That's how Cain was. He was the firstborn child of the first couple in the world. Can you imagine not having anyone else to be compared to? No smarter brother. No one that was cuter, funnier, or more adorable. Then, as all oldest siblings would complain, here came his little brother, Abel. Poor Abel—can you imagine being compared to a brother that, before you showed up, had no comparison? Sibling rivalry was birthed in Adam's family!

Cain was a farmer, and Abel was a shepherd. When the time came to make an offering to God, Abel gave the very best he had, while Cain offered some of the mediocre grains. God was pleased with Abel's offering and upset with Cain's. Some Bible scholars feel this is because one was grain and the other was blood, the latter relating to the later "blood sacrifices" offered for people's sins in Israel—a point that directly relates to the sacrifice of Jesus in His death. I tend to believe God's displeasure was a result of Cain not offering his best, rather than the substance of the gift. Too many other verses in the Bible talk about giving what one can and doing so in a spirit of hilarious generosity. If it were the blood offering theory instead of grain, then Cain could argue he'd give blood if he were Abel!

Cain, like me, knew better. He knew, as I did, how to offer the best, but he chose not to try. It became easier to offer the second best. I offered excuses that some might buy, but inside I knew that if I tried doing better, it could have happened. I'm not suggesting I could have handled calculus, but I am saying I could have shot a little higher in my attempts at math as an offering to God than I did.

This situation with Cain and Abel caused more than just the normal sibling rivalry of having one brother better than the other. This one ended up with Cain killing his little brother. Luckily my older brother was smarter in math, eliminating the temptation to kill me. That temptation came to Allen for a variety of other reasons. The murder occurred simply because Cain wanted to hold out and not offer his best. Instead of dealing with God about the problem and revising his offering, he chose to remove the brotherly standard. I attempted the same through sarcasm, but Cain did so through murder. The problem is that the standard of being our best is held by God and not our brothers. Trouble came upon Cain because he chose to point to the correct answer in the book and not figure out and solve the problem. Cain did not have to go to the office for his "easy answer." Instead, God placed a curse on him for the rest of his life. That's similar to having the principal shadow you for the rest of time.

So what are you depending on the answers in the back for?

PETER: DID I JUST SAY THAT? (LUKE 9:28–36)

I had the mixed blessing of serving on the Pastoral Leadership Team at Germantown Baptist Church. I say the blessing was mixed because of the story I am about to tell. The senior pastor put together this team, which was basically like having department heads on the crew. Being the recreation pastor gave me the opportunity to sit in with the leaders of music, education, administration, missions, and the "top dogs"—executive and senior pastors.

During one of the meetings, our media pastor gave word that the local ABC affiliate wanted to do an interview with someone on our pastoral staff. Suddenly calendars became full and meetings came up, leaving no one available for the interview except me. Having had years of speech and debate experience, I looked forward to the opportunity. Plus, who knew but that this opportunity might be my fifteen minutes of fame? Didn't Walter Cronkite and Tom Brokaw basically start this way?

I quizzed the media pastor as to the topic of the interview, but he stated he did not know. The reporter wanted to get the "off the top of the head" type of response from one of us. *Not a problem,* I thought confidently. *I used to have to make up stuff on the spot for the debate team in high school.* Those on that squad were taught and well equipped to organize thoughts quickly. I had used this skill on numerous occasions when a pastor couldn't lead on a Sunday- or Wednesday-night service. One time, I was told just as the service was beginning that I was going to speak. Using the back of the offering envelope found in the back of a pew as a notepad, I proceeded to pick out a three-point message. Churches are notorious for leaving offering envelopes in case the spirit of generosity should overcome the people in attendance.

This interview was going to be my path to greatness! Besides the public speaking training, I had learned years ago how to speak off the top of my head in responding to questions about my misbehavior in dealing with my parents, in which I believed the truth would not set me free. My thoughts were *I got this!*

I made a dash home during the lunch hour to change shirts and put on a tie. If I was going to make my network debut, I wanted to look good. One never knows who's watching the ten o'clock Memphis news. Plus it would repeat the next morning on their early news broadcast.

The reporter came in and, keeping to the theme, didn't share the topic with me. The crew put makeup on me, which supposedly made me look better. I still feel I have the perfect face for radio! They did some preliminary taping of me walking to and from the recreation center for their promotion of the news story. Finally, the reporter sat me down on the steps at the front of the auditorium. The cameras were on and rolling. The lights of the camera shone in my eyes, making the reporter nothing but a shadow. Then she posed the question "Why is it so many Christians are so easily marked as targets for scam artists?"

Whoa! I thought to myself. I had no idea what to say. I used a technique that John Kennedy used in the 1960 presidential debates—pausing as if to gather my thoughts. The only difference was that nothing intelligent was coming to mind.

Feeling the pressure of the lights, the call of "Action!" to get the camera rolling, and the question, my quick wit decided to make a quick exit. Realizing I couldn't just stare blankly into a camera, I gave my answer. "Three things," I stated, not knowing where the next two would come from. "One is Christians are very trusting. They tend to believe the person perpetrating the scam." Making it up as I went on, I said, "Secondly, Christians are somewhat naive. They can't really see how someone would want to take advantage of them." Then, because I had said "three things" and had to create something else, I said, "Finally, some Christians are just borderline stupid."

Yes, I said it. And they had it on film and later that evening ran it on the air, with a repeat performance of my stupidity the next morning. When given a follow-up question on how we should deal with the scammers, I, in the hope of saving face, stated that "Christians, in dealing with people like this, need to become sheep in wolves' clothing."

I didn't have much left to say for this "off the top of the head" type of interview. Where was all my speech and debate training? Why did it leave me? Why, in not knowing what to say, did I speak? Despite my begging, the reporter was certain the interview went well and invited me to watch myself on television during the ten o'clock news. She offered that it would rerun the next morning in case I missed it that evening.

Well, the aftermath and the fallout were to be expected. People in the church thanked me for painting such a good picture of what it meant to be a Christian. Others poked fun at me for my obvious mistake in judgment. Finally some of the staff tried drawing pictures of what a sheep in wolf's clothing would look like.

It's no wonder one of my favorite verses regarding the apostle Peter is Luke 9:33, where it states, "Peter, not even knowing what he was saying, blurted out ..." If only Channel 24 could have run that Scripture as a personal disclaimer while showing my interview on TV. I didn't quite know what to say, so I said it! Peter was known for speaking up, sometimes before thinking.

Peter, like me, never seemed to be at a loss for words—for a lack of timing and tact, perhaps, but never for words. Often his boldness for speaking first and thinking later would come out with a confession of faith. Other times Jesus had to rebuke him or remind him of the overall mission.

How many of us have ever found ourselves in Peter's situation? I know I seem to make a habit of it! Why is it I feel compelled to say something in certain situations? The writer of Proverbs stated, Even fools are thought wise when they keep silent; with their mouths shut, they seem intelligent" (Proverbs 17:28 NLT)." Abraham Lincoln said, "Better to remain silent and be thought a fool than to speak out and remove all doubt." I usually remove the doubt.

James, when writing his letter that appears in the New Testament, talks about the tongue. He explains how we've learned how to tame wild animals and control large ships, but no one can tame the tongue. In fact, James points out that the little membrane will cause all sorts of trouble. The same body part praises God and then curses His creation. He goes on to say it is "restless and evil, full of deadly poison." (James 3:8 NLT) This happens when we don't know what to say and speak anyhow. I understand James! My tongue seems to run much quicker than my brain!

When I was a small child, my grandmother was talking about a brother that she had not heard from in years. She talked about how they used to be close, but he had moved to California and she had not heard from him for a long time. This knack of not knowing what to say and speaking anyhow must be in my blood. I popped off with a statement I had heard on a commercial without even knowing the meaning of the statement: "Well, often truisms are not true."

Grandma's eyes puddled up with tears. She excused herself from the room with her voice cracking from emotion. I asked my dad what I had said wrong, and he replied, "Something stupid, as usual."

What is it in the makeup of me and other human beings that makes us feel we have to say something? I've heard from grieving people that the thing that makes them feel best is just having someone cry with them or give them a hug.

So when the situation arises and I feel as though something needs to be said but I don't know what to say, I hope to put some reins on that tongue and hold it back!

The next time you don't know what to say, don't say anything!

SAMSON: THE TROUBLE WITH WOMEN (JUDGES 14–16)

She shared several classes with me in the eighth grade. Later we dated in high school. She started the suffering attributed to my attraction of redheads. I grew out of that sole attraction and instead learned to be attracted to any women that would actually talk back to me. I remember telling a friend about a girl that had smiled at me. I was pretty thrilled until she told me that when she first saw me she laughed out loud! It was early in my life when I realized my attraction to women was an affliction that would get me into trouble.

In science class she and her partner worked at one lab site, and my partner and I shared the other. We were always trying to do things to get the attention of these girls. Since I was not blessed with an eye-turning physique (unless Barney Fife or stick figures make you hot), I had to rely on humor and stupidity to get a girl's attention. Please don't judge me. I still rely on that same technique to this day.

Nothing seemed to be working on this particular redhead. I could get a couple of cute giggles out of her, but she would always go back to her work. We reasoned that if humor didn't get the girls, perhaps they were looking for a more worldly man. How does one express a sense of masculinity in a science class? I could pick a fight with an athlete, but then I'd have to hope the girl suffered from the Florence Nightingale syndrome and would want to nurse me back to health. I could pick a fight with a nerd, but I figured that although I could last a little while longer in that case, the bookworm would eventually wear me down as well. I knew I didn't want to fight with a girl, because the embarrassment of that inevitable loss would haunt me forevermore.

I noticed each lab had Bunsen burners for various experiments. There were also plenty of brown paper towels. Now mind you, this was a time when you had to actually pull a towel out of the dispenser. When I was in eighth grade, there were no hand dryers or automatic dispensers. The texture of those towels was very rough. They not only dried your hands, but they also removed the top layer of skin. Joking around, I rolled one into a cigarette and lit it with the Bunsen burner.

Now, I had always sworn to my dad that I would never smoke. This was before the days of "not inhaling," but I didn't. I just wanted to play with the paper towel cigarette. I held it to my mouth, pretending to smoke it and feeling really cool. While it didn't actually get me the girl (I'm assuming my overwhelming charm did that), it did make her smile, so I won! This particular behavior also led to my nickname of Pierre, as David is just not worldly enough for a man of my caliber. My older brother and several high school friends still refer to me by my "worldly" name.

Women can be a source of trouble. I'm not just referring to sexual trouble; it's all sorts of other stuff. I've noticed a genetic trait found in all women that they use to their advantage—that eyelash blinking thing. When I do it, I just look stupid. When they do it, I want to buy them dinner, take them shopping, or bring them flowers. Since I had only sons, I didn't realize this is an inbred trait common to all girls. My little granddaughters didn't even have to be taught this move; they just did it and got ice cream. They'd blink again and we were getting candy. I don't know that little girls know of this power they hold over men, but I'm pretty sure they learn it early on. I apologize to men everywhere for revealing one of the secrets to our weakness.

There's also a good bit of power in the female voice. A friend once stated, "You men are supposed to be the stronger sex, but the words from a woman can turn you into Jell-O and mush." She is absolutely correct. Once in my life, while I was seeking counsel for some issues in my life, my therapist was trying to convince me that God affirmed who I was. I told him I knew God affirmed me but I wanted to hear it from someone with curves. There's incredible power in the affirmation or intense devastation bestowed upon men in the words of a woman.

Don't even get me started with tears or a woman crying and the effect that has on men!

Samson was a sucker for the eyelash thing and a woman's voice. He fell once for the trick in marrying a woman that he wasn't supposed to. It wasn't a Romeo-and-Juliet thing; it was in following the wishes of the Lord. God wanted the Israelites to remain pure in their bloodlines. Marrying someone from another nation or people group would destroy the people, as they would start worshipping their spouses' gods instead of the true God. He married her anyway.

In one skirmish with the Philistines, Samson's enemies went to his wife to coax him to tell them the secret to a riddle with which he had puzzled them. She used the eyelashes and some tears to coerce Samson into telling her the secret. When he realized she had lied to him, he killed thirty of the Philistine men. At that point his wife was given to his best man. Must have been different customs back then, because I was a best man once but didn't get a wife in the deal.

Now, if that wasn't lesson enough, Samson went after another Philistine woman. She was a prostitute and part of a plan to murder him. He was able to escape the threat.

Then into his life came yet another woman. Her name was Delilah. She was from the Valley of Sorek. In art and the movies she is usually depicted as a redhead, although there is not biblical proof of that. Delilah, with her voice and eyelash thing, tried to get Samson to reveal the secret of his strength. Delilah accepted an offer from the Philistine leaders to sell out her husband to them. Is that not a great demonstration of love? Can you feel the heart of this wonderful woman? She asked Samson the source of his strength, and he fed her some line. The Philistines used the information to try to capture Samson, and he broke free. A similar scenario was repeated twice, and each time Samson broke free.

Does the phrase "Once bitten" come to mind? Despite being lied to three times by Delilah, Samson finally told her the source of his strength, if for no other reason that to quiet her. There was power in her voice when she said, "How can you say, 'I love you,' when you won't confide in me." Really, Samson? I mean *really?* I have no doubt in my heart that Delilah was doing the eyelash blinking thing while asking him the last time. The truth from Samson eventually led to the end of his life.

While I'd like to think that Samson is stupid, I realize I've made the same mistakes in creating "train-wreck" relationships with the opposite sex. I have accepted the lies. I have let the voice put me in situations I shouldn't have been in. I have caved in to crying when I should have remained strong. The eyelash blinking thing has influenced me in wrong directions.

I think the problem most men have with women is that they look to them for things that only God can provide. I've never been a woman, but the opposite is probably true for them as well. If we place our emphasis on the source of love, then loving others falls into line much more. Unlike the evil Delilah, a true lady will seek only our best. The same can be said for the ladies regarding the men in your life. That's who we should be listening to and falling for.

Follow the correct eyelash batting!

WOMAN CAUGHT: ESCAPING JUDGMENT (JOHN 8:1–11)

It was my last year at North Rock Creek Elementary. I was in fourth grade, and the next year I would move to the middle school, which comprised the fifth through seventh grades. I had climbed in my responsibilities and had become the stair monitor on the concrete steps leading from the school's sidewalk down to a lower-level street. I used these stairs when I walked to school, and yes, it was uphill both ways and sometimes it snowed!

It was the last day of the fourth-grade year. The teacher was taking us to Hill Park, which was located a few blocks from the school. I had been to Hill Park numerous times with my family. There were great big open spaces with grass, and the normal traits of a park with benches, walking trails, and picnic tables. The greatest thing about Hill Park, though, was the extremely climbable rock formations. The only bad part was, like the Tree of Knowledge of Good and Evil for Adam and Eve, the rock formations were deemed "out of bounds" by the teacher.

Being typical fourth-grade boys, we got bored with the regular games and activities and sneaked over to the rocks. We had a great time climbing and dodging the glances toward the rocks from our teacher. As the picnic time closed, we sneaked out of the rocks and got on the bus to go back to school. Once we arrived back at the school, our teacher asked to meet with all the rock climbers in the hallway. To this day I don't know if she saw us or one of the pesky girls tattled. Either way, we were busted. We had disobeyed and done something we weren't supposed to. I wish we could have claimed an accidental sin like Aaron did when he offered an explanation for a gold calf idol being made by saying, "We threw the jewelry in the fire and this calf came out." It was no good. We were busted.

Then the miracle occurred. The teacher asked me why I was in the hallway. I admitted my guilt and threw myself and my friends on the mercy of her court. She stated that she had not seen me with the group and offered how admirable it was that I was willing to take the punishment with my friends. She told me to get back in the room. I protested once, and she gave me that "teacher look," so I retreated into the room.

This was the last day of classes, but the guys had to come back the next day to face their punishment. They were made to draw three circles on the chalkboard and put their hands in two of the circles and their nose in the third one. I'm sure the Nazis used similar tortures in their concentration camps. Despite my confession and continued efforts to make her believe I was a part of the disobedience as well as partly the leader of such a movement, she wouldn't believe me and therefore released me from the punishment. The other rock climbers suffered the punishment, but I was set free. So I did the crime but didn't have to do the time. I escaped the consequences. That doesn't happen very often outside of God's grace.

John, in his gospel, tells the story of a woman in a similar circumstance. She knew not to do something and did it anyway. When caught, she had to meet the Pharisees, the religious leaders of the day, out in the hallway to have them decide on the punishment. In this case, they referred to the law of Moses, and what she had been caught doing would require a death penalty by stoning. I think I'd rather stick my nose on a chalkboard!

The Pharisees saw this as a great opportunity to trap Jesus. This was more than a hobby for these guys. It was more of a vocation. On numerous occasions the Pharisees tried to ask Jesus particular questions in order to trap him. Somehow Jesus always got out of the trap, usually by answering their questions with questions of his own. But this situation was the most beautiful trap that could ever be created. Bringing her to Jesus set Him up in a lose-lose situation. If He didn't stone her, He would violate the law of Moses and ruin his credibility. If He did stone her, He would go against His own message of love and forgiveness of sin.

When the woman was brought to Jesus and the situation was explained to Him, He didn't respond to the accusers at all and instead began writing in the dirt. No one knows what was written, although there are some fun guesses and speculations. I've heard Jesus might have been writing out the sins of those with stones. Can you imagine standing in a crowd and all of a sudden seeing "David Waddell—lied to parents, cheated on school exam, stole candy from the local store, and climbed forbidden rock formations." (Those are the sins I'll list here. Unfortunately Jesus would have been writing worse things in my dirt). I heard another time that He was writing down the names of people and including the names of the people with which they had committed the same sin they were accusing the lady of. I also heard that Jesus was writing down the names of the guys in the crowd that had committed the same sin with the lady they had brought before Him. I suppose it really doesn't matter what He wrote, because of what happened next.

When Jesus popped back up, He declared, "If any one of you is without sin, let him be the first to throw a stone at her." Then He knelt back down and started writing in the dirt again. Can you imagine the roller-coaster ride of emotions you would experience in thinking you are to stone someone justly because of what she has done, only to discover you're not qualified to participate? It's like being just a little too short for the fun rides in amusement parks. The unbelievable joy of righteous lynching becomes a DVD version of your own life. I don't like to talk about my sin; I'd much rather punish you for yours. John, the writer, declares that one by one they dropped their stones and went away until only the woman was left with Jesus. It had to be a frustrating day for a Pharisee. It would have taken me a bit to drop mine, because I'm good at rationalization. But I tell myself that, once I got through the lies, I'd drop the rock and hope Jesus would offer me the same love He offered the lady.

Jesus asked the lady where those who condemned her were, and she stated no one remained. I want to point out what may be obvious to some but was hidden for me until recently. *He then forgave her of her sins without her asking for it.* This is a crucial point in grace.

I escaped chalkboard punishment while claiming guilt. The woman escaped condemnation while still in the middle of being caught in her sin. Forgiveness from God is present whether we seek it or not. It is not earned. It is not something we work for. It is given. Just like the freedom of not coming back to school for chalkboard punishments, it is awarded to us because God wants us to have it. We simply have to accept it or reject it. Jesus gave the woman some good advice on living in the future and sent her back to live life. It was advice that is good for all of us: "go and sin no more."

Despite doing the crime, she was not going to serve the time! She earned death, and she gained life. She sought lust with strings, and she was granted love without conditions. She sneaked away to the part of the park that was off limits and escaped the chalkboard punishment. She was scheduled for stoning and came away with salvation!

What rock climbing experiences have you had, only to escape the chalkboard punishment?

WOMAN AT THE WELL: RULES ARE MADE TO BE BROKEN! (JOHN 4)

I was always looking for a way to get out of work. We had certain rules when I was growing up. I think my ability to avoid work was my introduction to something that has served me well in my life as well as gotten me into trouble. I found out about loopholes.

One of the rules growing up was that I was responsible for doing the dishes on Monday and Thursday evenings. Mark, my younger brother, got Tuesday and Friday, and Allen, the eldest, took Wednesday and Saturday. Mom got Sunday. None of us, including Mom, ever figured out how Dad got out of the rotation. He'd say something about earning a living and being able to whip all of us. When the whipping was brought up, we would drop the subject.

All three of us got particularly good at finding the loophole in dish washing. Let's say, for example, there was a teaspoon or so of mashed potatoes in the pot. It could be argued that someone might eat that as a leftover, if not as a small potato pancake the next morning. Perhaps there were two or three noodles left in the macaroni and cheese casserole dish. Was it our fault that no one would touch it until it started growing green stuff? If it was timed just right, the pot would be discovered on a night that was not my night to wash the dishes. Before you feel sorry for my brothers, please note they played the game just as well as I did.

Another rule we lived by was this famous one: "If Momma ain't happy, ain't nobody happy!" I know the English is atrocious, but that doesn't make it any less factual. I remember Dad always got mad at us for upsetting her or frustrating her at certain times. It was something about moods, although I didn't catch all that Dad was cursing about. The worst whipping I ever remember Dad giving me (and I've blocked many out of my memory banks) was after I sassed Mom when she was telling me to do something. I carried on the tradition with my boys and their mother.

I had just two rules for my children when they were growing up. Rule one was "Dad is always right." Rule two was "If Dad happens to be wrong, refer to Rule number one." These rules led to numerous discussions and enjoyable arguments with my children. Like me, my sons were active in finding the loopholes.

The woman Jesus met at the well was in the loophole business like me. She went to draw water at an odd time of the day. This loophole was discovered, no doubt, to avoid the leering eyes and verbal jousts of a judgmental crowd. I'm sure she was the topic of conversation among other well dwellers. One of the things we do best as Christians is offer our arrogance "in love." We love to shoot our wounded! In the South you can say whatever ugly comment you want as long as it's followed by "Lol" (laughing out loud)" or "Bless his heart!" This poor woman had been divorced five times, so to avoid breaking that rule again, she chose to live with a man outside of marriage. Bless her heart!

The problem with rules is if they are broken, we generally deal with it by making more rules. The Pharisees at that time were good at it. I think I turned it into an art form! I fell into the habit of dealing with sin by establishing more rules. If someone came to me about something bad happening in his or her life, my advice was always that the person should follow more rules. As methods of dealing with sin, I recommended that people get more active in church, start tithing or giving more, and coach junior high boys' basketball. I taught a gospel that stated you could make a rule, do the right things, and cover your sin.

Now, I didn't just offer this to other people. I practiced it myself. Once, as I was leaving a period of darkness in my life, I, along with an accountability team, decided to set up more boundaries and rules to make sure I never fell back into the old way of thinking or behaving that led to my sin. We created an entire 8.5" × 11" sheet of paper full of bullet-pointed items I was to do or not do. It doesn't work. I couldn't keep the one rule God gave me, so how was making fourteen more going to help?

You see, by talking with this woman, Jesus was already breaking a rule. She was a "despised Samaritan." This grudge between Jews and Samaritans was centuries old by now, and it related to part of the separation of Israel back in the period of rule-breaking kings. The mixing of peoples of Assyria and Israel made them a "less pure people" in the eyes of the people of Judah. So you had the Samaritans versus the Jews. UFC fighting and deep southern prejudice had nothing on these two groups of people. These were the original Hatfields and McCoys! Jesus, as we know, created the loopholes in rules that were created by man and didn't really matter to God. He healed people on the Sabbath, touched unclean people, and didn't give in to Pharisee peer pressure. Jesus was more worried about the boy knowing his Father than in his doing the dishes and cleaning out the pot of miniscule leftovers in the fridge. Similarly, Jesus pointed out later that Mary, in listening to Him, chose the correct path over housework. I know that thrills a good number of us!

When the concentration is on the rules, I never receive the grace. I end up cleaning my pan of leftovers as well as Mark's and Allen's. When I think about how not to sin, then sin is still what is on my mind. It's like me telling you not to think about purple frogs. The more you tell yourself not to think about purple frogs, the more they appear in your head. The only way to make them "croak" is to replace them with red elephants. As Paul said, "And now, dear brothers and sisters, one final thing. Fix your thoughts on what is true, and honorable, and right, and pure, and lovely, and admirable. Think about things that are excellent and worthy of praise." (Philippians 4:8)

Sin cannot be managed. It won't work. The more you concentrate on managing it, the more it controls your thoughts. The reason the book of Leviticus is so difficult for us is that it's full of rules we don't understand or find impossible to follow. The expectation is obedience. The reality is sin. Even if the "Leviticus list" could be kept, Jesus pointed out that our attitude and thoughts weigh in just as much as do our actions. You see, sin can't be placed on a list of rules and expect compliance. The nature of sin won't allow it. In fact, Satan loves it when we try to rule or manage ourselves into God's favor.

Jesus knew that relationship is the key. Establish a loving relationship and obedience becomes a want rather than a need. In fact, once He established the sin of the woman, He allowed her to change the topic to worship and then proclaimed Himself the Messiah to her. Jesus wasn't bound by rules that interfered with Him reaching people with love. He not only talks to a "forbidden" Samaritan woman; He invites her in the same way He did another "approved" Jew.

The woman went to the well looking for a loophole to find water for living. Instead she was given some Living Water—without any loopholes! That's better than getting to leave leftover mashed potatoes!

What sin are you trying to rule and manage? Find any good loopholes?

GIDEON: SIGNS, SIGNS, EVERYWHERE ARE SIGNS (JUDGES 6–8)

My family and I were on the way to make a drive to Springfield, Missouri, from our home in Natchez, Mississippi. I was going to the First Baptist Church, my home church, to be considered for their position as recreation minister. I had worked there in college and was excited about the possibility of serving there again as their leader in that department.

Not two blocks from our house was a three-way stop sign. The road to the right was a short cul-de-sac. The reason for the stop sign was not the incredible traffic load from the four houses in the cul-de-sac, but rather to slow down traffic in the residential area.

I was in the habit of slowing down for the sign but not coming to a full stop. This particular day, with wife and sons in tow, I rolled through; but as I hit the middle of the intersection, I saw a police officer sitting just beyond my view to the right. I came to a complete stop, but that was after I'd pulled through the intersection. I found out that doesn't count the same.

The officer came to my window and got the information on my license and insurance card. He asked if I knew why I'd been pulled over, and I told him I saw the stop sign and slowed down but didn't stop. Then, for some weird reason, I decide to tell him a joke. The joke is about someone slowing down for a stop sign. He is pulled over by a police officer who tells him he didn't come to a complete stop. The man states that he was slowing down and that it is the same thing as coming to a complete stop. The officer then pulls out his night stick and starts hitting him with it. Then the officer asks the man if he wants him to stop or slow down.

It's hilarious, right?

My police officer glances up from the ticket pad, looks me square in the eyes, and without so much as even a bit of a smile on his face says to me, "Yeah, I've heard that one." It was all my boys could do to keep from laughing out loud. I think their mom might have snickered out loud just a bit.

When I was a freshman in college, I served as youth minister at a church in Ava, Missouri. It required me to drive to the church from Springfield every weekend and Wednesday night. So twice a week I was driving sixty miles one way. This was late in the year 1975, and the speed limit on the road was still fifty-five miles per hour.

On one particular journey I was zooming along when the highway patrol decided they were lonely and wanted to visit. I pulled over and was told I was doing sixty-two in a fifty-five zone. I knew I was guilty; in fact, his radar might not have gone off until I was actually slowing down some! I looked him right in the eyes and claimed I thought the speed limit was sixty and that I had been confused by the signs for Highway 60.

He didn't buy it.

Signs are provided to us to help give us direction. They are also used as warnings. They tell us what we can and can't do. At times, they give us guidance on the correct path. Gideon would not have made it without signs.

Gideon was one of the early rulers in Israel. The neighbors of the Israelites were called Midianites. This group of people took over the land and oppressed the Israelites enough that as a nation they called out to God. So God recruited Gideon to lead the people out of oppression.

Gideon wasn't "hopping" to get into service. He asked for a sign that the messenger was really an angel. A sign appeared on the road when the angel made a meal that had been cooked for Gideon burn up with just a touch of his staff. Gideon thought he was going to die for being face-to-face with God. Gideon was given orders to destroy the worship altars of the false god Baal. He waited until nighttime to do so because he was afraid of his own family.

Later he asked God for another sign he was the man to lead Israel. He would leave out a wool fleece on the ground. If it became wet with dew and the ground remained dry, then he would lead. When that happened, he asked for another sign, this one being the opposite—dry fleece with wet ground. When that occurred, the sign was "55 mph" and obviously not "Stop." He knew at that point he was to lead the army.

So somehow an army was recruited. I figure they blasted the city with "Gideon Wants You" signs all over the place. Billboards and chariots carried the advertisement. What with his popularity from his Baal temple terrorism, he must have been quite the hero! When the count of all the recruits took place, thirty thousand men had signed up to fight with Gideon. God, knowing the people would say it was won in their own power if he attacked with that many men, told Gideon to send home anyone that really didn't want to fight. Twenty-two thousand men took off, and I would have been one of them! Still having too many, God reduced the group even further by asking Gideon for a sign in his men's drinking habits. Those who cupped water in their hands and brought it to their mouth were in, and those that lapped the water like dogs were sent home. God knew a soldier that cupped the water to his mouth was still on the lookout. It's hard to see an approaching enemy when your mouth is buried in the pond.

Three hundred men were left to take on the Midianites. That's not a very big sign to show before war! So Gideon requested one more three-way stop sign. God told him to listen to the Midianite camp as one man was talking about a dream he had. In the dream, a loaf of bread came rolling into camp, killing all of them. Another Midian man claimed, "It's the work of Gideon!" I'm not sure where the connection was for them between bread and Gideon. That is, unless he was a crusty old fellow. Or maybe it was because he always rose to the occasion. Perhaps the battle would come from the yeast instead of the waist. This may have been the first time little loaves were called rolls! Regardless, Gideon was not planning on being toast anymore.

The Israelites fought with clay jars, torches, and trumpets. It was another sign. Of course a similar method had worked in Jericho some years back. The men marched around the encampment, blew the trumpets, and broke the clay jars. They took up the torches, screaming, "A sword for the Lord and for Gideon!" The Midianites, hearing and seeing the commotion, ran around killing each other with their own swords. God gave them the victory.

God was extremely patient with Gideon. I feel the same about me. I want to do the right thing most of the time and feel frustration not knowing which way is correct. So in asking for a sign, what is the difference in clarifying God's direction and testing His direction? I think that if a sign is requested that His commands already cover, that is more of a way for us to do as we wish rather than His path. If I say I will do a particular thing if the clouds part, traffic dies down, or the phone rings is ludicrous. However, if I feel a particular emphasis in my heart and during that span God shows me several things associated with that emphasis, then I assume I might have put the correct fleece out for a sign.

Or perhaps instead I should read the signs that are already up and get busy doing what I already know He wants.

What are your signs saying? "Yield?" "Stop?" "One Way?"

ADAM: PASS THE BUCK (GENESIS 3)

The ability to blame others for your own failures is not necessarily a learned trait. It comes early on in life. I think it's ingrained in our DNA.

In my first year of seminary, I was blessed to be given a job as a recreation minister in a local Fort Worth church. The church at the time was called the Polytechnic Baptist Church; the name was later changed to East Meadows. The name Polytechnic came from that particular area of Fort Worth. The church had its main campus in the Polytechnic area and had built a satellite location on the east side of the city. The east campus was a "gymnatorium"—a gymnasium that also served as the church's auditorium. This was a popular architectural style for churches in the '70s and '80s.

While I was on staff, the church also hired a man to work with the teenagers in the church. We were to share an office. At our stage of wisdom and maturity, this was the worst possible move to make. The first thing we did was to hang a Nerf basketball hoop in the office. Numerous games of one-on-one and horse were played both on the gym floor and in our shared office. Racquetball was another pastime during office hours. The gym was open each afternoon under my leadership and was handed off for the evening to one of the church volunteers. A group of teenagers soon started making the church their after-school hangout.

When you combine teenagers and building structures, something usually gives. When it was decided to open the recreation center to the community in my church in Springfield, Missouri, the main concern was possible damage. Some of the people said, "What if they paint graffiti on the walls?" The pastor replied, "We'll paint over it." They asked, "What if they break the toilets?" The pastor said, "We'll fix them."

Sometimes we have to be reminded that people are more important than things. The funny outcome of the Springfield move was that more damage was done to the facility by "good church kids" than by the alleged hoodlums of the neighborhood.

This group of Fort Worth teenagers was no different. They knew how to have fun, and they knew how to destroy things. Light fixtures, Sheetrock walls, and doorknobs seemed to always come up with troubles.

This brings me to the story at hand. One day, during our normal misbehavior in the office, my officemate and I got into a running tag game. As I was trying to catch him, he stepped through and partially closed a door to a classroom. I grabbed the door and swung it open in order to continue the pursuit. Somehow the door went through the rubber doorstop on the wall, and the knob made a huge hole in the Sheetrock. At that point I knew exactly what to do: blame it on "those" kids.

I was once given this poem by my brother-in-law:

> Yield not to temptation
> For yielding is sin
> Find someone to help you
> Then blame it on him!

I had hidden a sinful and dark part of my life for years. After my hidden sin had come to light, I was placed in a group with men that dealt with similar sinful behaviors. Part of the process was a twelve-step sort of approach to the sin. In this process, a look back in our life was made. I found it easy to start blaming all sorts of people and situations as I reviewed how I went so deep into such a sinful life.

I've played the blame game all my life. It was easy to blame things on being bullied in junior high, having poor potty training, or suffering from middle-child syndrome. A good excuse seems to grease the wheel toward a downfall. What is it that makes me say those kids did it? Why have I always been quick to point out how things are someone else's fault?

I come by it naturally.

The first man ever to live on the earth was created by God. He got to live in a lavish garden where all his needs would be cared for. God even gave him a woman to hang out with. Life must have been good. Then a serpent convinced them to eat from a tree that God had said was a no-no. Once they bit into the fruit, they knew that they had blown it and the party was over. Everyone had to get out of the pool.

When God chased Adam down, He asked him what had happened. Adam said, "The woman you put here with me – she gave me some fruit from the tree, and I ate it." How convenient. "It wasn't me; it was thee!" In one bold sentence, Adam shifted the blame to the woman as well as to God for "the woman [He] put here."

When the woman was questioned, she immediately blamed the serpent. The serpent probably looked around and couldn't find anyone else to blame and thus remained quiet.

What most folks miss in this story is that it is earlier stated that while the serpent was having a conversation with Eve, Adam was with her. He had every opportunity to say, "Uh, Eve, we're not supposed to do that." The excuse given was in hope that God might not be all-knowing and somehow missed Adam's part in the story. I'm sure Adam also felt that perhaps God would cut some slack on his sin, in that it was more "that woman" that was at fault.

As much as Adam had hoped to lay it all on Eve and God, he also knew himself he had done wrong and tried to cover his nakedness with a leaf. The problem with sin is that it exposes our nakedness. The problem with blame is that we feel justified with our leaf and feel it provides full coverage of our sin.

Blame is not something that dies easily. Even though I know the myriad events and people I would like to blame are not at fault, I find myself from time to time blaming them all over again. I would imagine that years later, after a hard day of "toiling the earth," Adam still held a grudge against Eve for the serpentine decision. The blame game does not end easily. On the other hand, Eve may have threatened murder and maiming during the first labor pains ever. Instead of owning up to the sin, Adam, like me, found it easier to blame someone else.

Until I own my mistakes in life, I will not learn from them.

So, to those who remain at East Meadows that might know me: the patched place in the Fireside Room wall by the northern door right next to the kitchen entrance was my fault and not the fault of "those kids."

So who are you blaming?

JOB: WITH FRIENDS LIKE YOU, WHO NEEDS ENEMAS? (JOB 2–32)

I have been blessed with some of the greatest friends in the world. Generally, my friends offer great advice and wisdom. Occasionally, they do not.

I had some reconstructive surgery on my left foot back in 2009. I suffer from a condition called Charcot-Marie-Tooth disease, or CMT. It causes atrophy in muscles and tendons and causes deformity in legs, feet, and hands. Surgery is not suggested except in the most extreme cases. Prior to the surgery I wore an AFO device, or "brace," to keep the ankle from turning. I had come to the point where the foot hurt when I walked on hard surfaces without the brace and shoes on. Still, the doctors did not recommend surgery at that time.

In 2006, when I first started teaching at Ole Miss, the department was going to the National Recreation and Parks Association meeting in Seattle, Washington. This would be my first conference like this that I had attended since leaving church work four years earlier. I knew of one church recreation minister friend that would be in attendance, but I was surprised to run into a couple more while there.

Prior to the flight my foot really began hurting. I had just seen the doctor regarding my condition and got fitted for a new device. The foot was at the point where it hurt to walk on it at all, causing a bit of a limp for me. My friends at the conference were concerned for me, and I know that's what drove the game of twenty questions. Despite me saying nothing could be done, my friends continued to offer bits and pieces of medical advice. Each offer was refuted until finally instead of refuting I chose rebuking. In a fit of rage, I explained once more there was nothing that could be done and pointed out sarcastically that they must know more than medical professionals. At some point you have to recognize your limitations and admit that, despite having stayed in a Holiday Inn Express, you are not a medical professional. The offers of advice ended with the outburst.

Six years later my heart decided to go back into atrial fibrillation, or "a-fib" as it's called by medical professionals. This had happened to me once eleven years prior, and it had been shocked back into rhythm at that time. This time around was a bit more serious, and I was placed on a low-sodium, liquid-limited, and no alcohol diet. I found out later that people with a heart in the condition mine was in have about a 5 percent chance of survival.

Despite the medical advice of people that know what they are doing, I had certain friends always trying to tell me to enjoy life and stating that "one won't hurt you." I'm afraid the graveyard is full of stories where one *did* hurt them. I know of a couple in my own family. Later, in the process of a miracle in which God renewed the strength of my heart, it was determined a follow-up procedure was needed. Despite a decision already having been made with consultation of the cardiologist, I had friends telling me about other options. Holiday Inn Express must know what they are doing. So many budding medical professionals, and I'm blessed that they are my friends!

What is it about friendship that makes us doctors, lawyers, and preachers? Why should I even attempt to listen? It's not like peer pressure is going to control me at fifty-five like it did when I was fifteen. Yet I'm no different than my friends. I have tried to communicate the same things to different people in a way of explaining things that have no explanation. I tried to get the situation to a point at which someone could understand where there was no understanding.

Job had the same kind of friends. Job was facing some awful tests being thrown at him from Satan. God kept resetting boundaries and allowed Satan to run right up to the border. Job cried out about the injustice of his afflictions. He questioned why it was happening and even cursed the day of his birth.

How did his friends react? The same way I might have. The first friend, Eliphaz, claimed there must be unconfessed sin. This is a popular argument for the things that go wrong in our lives. Get a flat tire? You must have said a naughty word. Got fired at work? You shouldn't have lusted after that lady at lunch. This notion continues in wrong theology to this day.

Now, my diet certainly didn't help my heart situation, but that's not what this belief refers to. This belief lines itself up with the depravity of man rather than the saving grace of Christ. This theology would claim that God is limited by our confession of sin. Eliphaz would tell me it was unconfessed sin that caused me to have a hereditary disorder such as CMT. This is in line with the thinking of the disciples when they asked Jesus if a man was blind because of his own sin or the sins of his father. This thought would tell me that the a-fib occurred because of a fib I told while growing up.

A second friend, Bildad tried telling him that if he was truly righteous, then he would have riches and victory over his enemies. This is a popular belief in the health and wealth prosperity messages. Bildad was pointing out long before television evangelists that following a proper call meant finding plenty of cash. So apparently Job was not as innocent as he was claiming. If he were, he wouldn't have lost his family, his farm, and his fitness.

I've followed the Bildadian philosophy before. Devotion to God is always rewarded by dollars from God. I would employ my own definition of what was to be considered a blessing from God.

A third friend, Zophar, accused him of not placing true belief in God. This is one of those easy outs. In this thinking, if something happens or doesn't happen, it's because you didn't exhibit enough faith. I know a man, thinking he was doing the right thing, who told the widow of a cancer victim that the reason for death was his "taking his eyes off of Jesus." What kind of "friend" does this? We create our own litmus tests as to what true belief is. More times than not, our list of things is man-made and not God ordained. This thinking would label the apostle Paul as a bad guy because he had a thorn in his flesh that God wouldn't remove. Apparently his faith wasn't strong enough. The problem with this thinking is that it gives us too much power.

Yes, our faith can make us well, but our faith mainly gives us strength depending on how God chooses to deal with our situation.

Job answered each one of his friends. For the next few chapters in the book, the three friends and Job are involved in a verbal jousting match. Finally Job responds with his own rage in sarcastically answering their comments.

When Job needed comfort, grace, and understanding, he was greeted with judgment and poor theology! The very friends that came to reassure Job were the ones trying to drag him down. It reminds me of the phrase "When I'm at death's door, you are there to pull me through!" Or, translated even more, one could ask, "With friends like this, who needs enemas?"

Far too many of us forget that true friendship means laying down your life for others. Sacrifice has nothing to do with advice containing no facts. Sacrifice means doing what you can to help your friend. Sympathy and empathy, listening without feeling the need to offer your two cents, and discovering and tending to your friend's needs are more important acts of friendship. God forgive me for those times I have stayed in the Holiday Inn Express and offered advice I know nothing about.

What are you telling your friends?

DAVID: COCKY OR CONFIDENT (1 SAMUEL 17)

It was freshman year, and I was in biology class. The varsity football coach was the instructor. In most high schools in that era, having one of the coaches as a teacher meant you could ask football questions and "chase that rabbit," neglecting some of the teaching for the day. This coach very rarely fell for that strategy.

During my freshman year I stood four feet ten inches tall and weighed ninety-five pounds. I could have been the Barney Fife of my high school. I was skinny and scrawny enough that some could have thought I had anorexia. Being that size opened me up for all kinds of teasing and abuse in junior high. Out of that pain, a most amazing gift of sarcasm and humor was created. Through humor I found a weapon to use against the most bullying of people. It was actually more damaging than hitting back. Whoever said "Sticks and stones may break my bones, but words can never hurt me" never had to deal with really hurtful words. I've had my share of both types of beatings, and I can assure you I've forgotten the physical beatings. The verbal ones, however, pop their heads back up every so often, as if they are life's version of Whac-A-Mole.

The win-win aspect of sarcasm also served me well. Not only could I cut away at someone's heart, but other people would laugh, thus giving me two victories in one contest. The ability of quick wit and hurtful sarcasm gave me what I thought was a sense of confidence. It can be better defined as a sense of cockiness.

As we were studying frogs in biology, we were preparing to dissect the suckers, and the coach was giving us the last-minute rundown on terminology. He found it easier to use the actual words for body parts rather than, say, "that thingy coming out of his chin." That's when my moment of glory arrived.

One of the senior cheerleaders asked the coach a question. To this day I figure she knew the answer and just wanted to chase a rabbit or see his reaction. She popped her hand in the air and, when recognized, asked him about a certain part of the frog's anatomy.

The coach, without batting an eye, and no doubt a veteran of this kind of game, explained to her that her question referred to a part of the male frog's reproductive system. The senior offensive lineman from the football team was sitting next to her. He leaned over and offered to show her his version after class. I poked him square in the back and said, "You can't. You don't have any."

I have never seen a man turn that red before or since. During the rest of the class, he turned and glare at me. I could feel the anger rising out of him as if it were the heat coming off of an asphalt road in the middle of a hot summer day. He kept mouthing that he was going to get even with me for my comments. After the class, he was able to find me, and I was placed headfirst in a hallway trash can. What the lineman didn't realize was that my garbage shampoo gave me the opportunity to tell the story over and over again. He may have been larger than me and put me in the trash, but I won the battle that day! So was I confident or was I cocky? I have to admit, I was a tad bit cockier than I was confident.

When King David was just a four-foot-ten, ninety-five-pound shepherd, he had been sent by his dad to deliver some food and supplies to his brothers, who were fighting with King Saul. While he was with his brothers, he noticed a gigantic offensive lineman screaming at the Israelites. In a bit of cockiness, David asked about the senior lineman and all the braggadocio coming out of his mouth. "Who is this pagan Philistine?" David asked sarcastically, pointing out the godly inadequacies of the giant. I love the biblical trash talk used here! It is not all that different from my sarcastic offering to the lineman. Even David's oldest brother, Eliab, pointed out how conceited he was and expressed anger at the young David. Eliab wondered who was taking care of the few sheep assigned to his younger brother.

The Philistine lineman offered for each camp to send their best warrior out for a "winner-take-all UFC-style battle." The battle would feature the best of the Philistines versus the best of Saul's army, with the loser serving the victors. It would be a classic one-on-one battle to determine the winner. The winner would get to rule over the losers. This would be like two teams from the National Basketball Association determining the champion based on a one-on-one contest rather than the teams playing it out.

David got involved with the verbal jousting and told the offensive lineman named Goliath, in true cocky fashion, that on this day the world would know there is a God in Israel and that he, Goliath, would become buzzard bait. The actual words were "Today I will give the carcasses of the Philistine army to the birds of the air and the beasts of the earth," but you get my point.

Goliath was dressed in armor, and the storyteller describes it in detail. He was over nine feet tall and outfitted for battle. David, on the other hand, was fitted for Saul's armor, but it swallowed him up, so he prepared for battle without armor or heavy weaponry. His cockiness turned into a heavenly confidence as he explained that the same God that saved him and his sheep from the mouth of the lion and the bear would help him destroy "this Philistine." He cried out to Goliath, "You come against me with sword and spear and javelin, but I come against you in the name of the Lord Almighty, the God of the armies of Israel, whom you have defied." Then, in classic cockiness-transformed-into-confidence manner, he finished, "This day the Lord will hand you over to me, and I'll strike you down and cut off your head."

David pulled five small stones out of a brook and took his sling with him. He slung a rock, which literally stuck in the forehead of the lineman. It must have been a great shot, because Goliath fell facedown on the ground. David then took the huge sword of the lineman and removed his head from the rest of his body. The rest of the lineman's team ran for their lives.

I know David was the hero of this story, but I also know the humanity David had in his makeup. He was a little conceited. His own brother saw that. He was a little cocky, but that cockiness turned into confidence when he remembered the other ways God had been with him in keeping the sheep. The switch from cockiness to confidence is what made the difference between victory and David finding himself upside down in a Philistine garbage can.

I find I am cocky when I trust my own quick wit and ways to get me through a situation. I find I am more confident when I trust God for assistance. In fact, I am usually at my wisest when I have no idea what I'm saying.

What offensive lineman are you dealing with?

ELIJAH: POST-MIRACLE DEPRESSION AND PITY PARTY TIME (1 KINGS 18–19)

No matter whom you talk with, the story remains the same. I make a prayer for a particular job or situation to occur, and when it does, I go into a pity party depression about the glorious thing God has done for me. What should be a moment of joy turns into a moment of depression. I often believe the person with the most difficult job in life is me. The person with the easiest job is everyone else. I feel as though God has deserted me. The only problem is that everyone else is saying the same thing about their job and mine. Well, that's how I see it anyway.

For several years I was in charge of a recreation ministry in churches. To serve in these particular places was a blessing for me. Each church had built an elaborate recreation center that would better or rival the finest city or county facilities. The YMCA had nothing on some church recreation centers I've worked with. Being in charge of a facility as well as a program can mean some long hours and extra trips back into work. The buildings and fields usually stayed open until 10:00 or 11:00 p.m. This was before caller ID and cell phones, so unknown numbers would call in to me from the center with issues of behavior, discipline, and building troubles, such as broken bowling lanes, leaky ceilings, and clogged toilets. Once a call came in, I was off and running back to the church. I never really relaxed in the evenings or on weekends until after the facility or field complex was closed.

That's when my pity party started. Instead of rejoicing in the blessing of the place I got to serve, I looked around at the others on staff and saw injustice. I thought it was unfair that they could go home and not have to worry about what was going on in the church building. Everything else was closed except the recreation center. Those other guys never had to run back up to the building. Plus, I was the lowest-paid person on the ministerial team, but I was doing most of the work. When I worked with children, one song that would pop up occasionally was the following pity party song:

> Nobody likes me
> Everybody hates me
> Think I'll go eat worms

It's easy to fall into feeling sorry for ourselves! I was often tempted to update my résumé and run away from home to a new church, where I felt things would be better.

What is it in our makeup that makes us think we have it worse than anyone else? What is it about answered prayer that places us in such a depression? I always felt abused as a middle child and swore it was harder on us than the oldest and the youngest in the birth order. It seemed, on numerous occasions that Allen, the oldest, was getting benefits because he was the oldest. When a year passed and I was the age he had been upon receiving his special bonuses, I was told it wouldn't be fair to Mark, the youngest, if I got something he didn't. The whole process made me want to run away from home to a place where I would be appreciated as much as I deserved. Well, that's how I saw it anyway.

In high school I joined the speech and debate squad. It was not an easy team to make; therefore, it was somewhat miraculous I was there. There was a lot of competition just to make the team. Had it been a fair fight, I would have been fine, but it seemed as though the speech and debate coach was elevating everyone but me and my partner. Even after a successful year, our name was left off the active roster list at the start of my senior year. Everyone called the coach by his first name, but he specifically told me that his first name was for his friends and that I should refer to him by his last name. Well, that's how I saw it anyway.

Numerous times in life, through a failed marriage, lack of salary increases, and a long period of getting back into my calling as a career path, I have thought to myself that everyone has it better than me. Am I the only one that sees how bad I have it? How come everyone else, even evil people, is doing okay? Well, that's how I saw it anyway.

Even when I find myself successful in an endeavor or in a relationship, the pity party mind-set kicks in. The applause and accolades die off, and I go back to being normal Dave. It's as though I specialize in "whine and geez" parties! It's pretty depressing, right? Well, that's how I see it anyway.

Elijah suffered from the same disorder. I like to call it post-miracle depression, or PMD for short. It generally strikes after a glorious moment or something good happening in life. It's a depression that brings us back to our previous state of normalcy while ignoring any of the changes God just instilled in our lives.

Elijah was the leader of one of the Bible's most interesting battles. God versus Baal was the main ticket! Elijah, as the prophet of the living God, was set against the numerous prophets of Baal, the false god of the Canaanites. Elijah set up a glorious battlefield with a wooden altar and a dead bull. The god with the power would light the wood with fire, and everyone would enjoy the barbecue. He allowed the Baal team to bat first, and they started crying out to their god to strike fire into the sacrifice. Nothing was happening. They started cutting themselves to appease their god, and still nothing. Elijah even asked if perhaps Baal had stepped away to use the bathroom. Talk about prophetic trash talk! Well, that's how they saw it anyway.

When the other guys failed, Elijah wetted the ground with several barrels of water during a drought in the land. Then he prayed, and God immediately sent fire from heaven that consumed the bull, and all the prophets of Baal were killed as well. Well, that's how everyone there saw it anyway.

That's a great victory, right? You'd think Elijah could live a while on the glory of that story. But he didn't. Queen Jezebel was ticked at the outcome of the game and put a price on his head. He retreated to a mountain and fell into a pity party of his own. Elijah, in a classic PMD action, felt he was the only one left in Israel serving God. He even said, "I have had enough, Lord. Take my life. I am no better than my ancestors." Elijah was actually scared for his life at this point and took off running away from home. I have a feeling he would have eaten worms had they been available. Well, that's the way he saw it anyway.

God sent some angels to Elijah to feed him and send him on a journey. When he arrived at his destination God gave Elijah a message to stand on the side of the mountain, for He, the Lord God, was about to pass by. There was a mighty wind, earthquake, and fire that came by, but God was not heard in any of this phenomena. No, the word from God came in a gentle whisper. Elijah heard the message in the "still small voice." Of course, I would have held out for the earthquake message! God told Elijah, "I reserve seven thousand in Israel - all whose knees have not bowed down to Baal and all whose mouths have not kissed him." In other words, "Snap out of it, Elijah. Turn out the lights; the party is over. Get over the PMD. You're not the only one out there, and there's no need to be in a pity party." Well, that's how God saw it anyway.

Rarely am I the only one suffering or working. Rarely do I actually have it worse than others. There may be moments that are extremely bad, but even if something kills me, I get to be with Jesus. Remind me how that's eating worms. Well, that's the way I see it anyway.

Are you sending out party invitations? How are you seeing it?

JONAH: INSTRUCTIONS? WE DON'T NEED NO STINKING INSTRUCTIONS! (JONAH 1–4)

I had learned the lesson in eighth grade, and it was confirmed my freshman year in high school. Physical education as a class was the coach's way of seeing if he or she had missed any possible talent that hadn't tried out for the team and could eventually make them state champions. During football season, we'd play flag football. A young man my size—I was four foot ten and weighed about ninety-five pounds—never had to worry about being discovered as lost talent in football. And if my size fooled you, then my lack of talent would confirm my destiny in sports. If I had played football, I would have ended up being the team's drawback!

The problem with this discovery process was that the guys that had already made the team on the offensive or defensive line were tired of never being the hero in the real game. So they became the quarterbacks and running backs of the PE league. I became a lineman. The difficulty came against the defense. On defense, the regular huge linemen still wanted to play on the defensive line. The mentality of defensive linemen is to destroy the quarterback and anything between them and the quarterback.

I was between them and the quarterback.

In an effort to save my life, and my mom was proud of me for this decision, I whispered the play to the defense. I would feign an effort at blocking to fool the coach and live another day.

Then it became wrestling season. My best friend and I were in the same PE class. Neither one of us wanted to have anything at all to do with grabbing and groping at another boy. Nor did we want to be grabbed or groped ourselves. The coach set up a tournament of wrestling competition. He gave explicit instructions on how the tournament would work and what he was looking for in the wrestling matches. Knowing that our innocence was on the line, my friend and I agreed to a strategy. We figured that when the whistle blew to begin the match, we could just flop. In other words, we would fall over on our backs and throw the match. We reasoned having a guy on top of us for three seconds beat the possibility of the other guy grabbing somewhere that will remain anonymous for this writing.

The first couple of rounds went without a hitch. I watched my friend with pride as he flopped himself over at the beginning whistle. He observed the same in me. We were getting away with our wonderful plan when something went awry. The coach noticed our game plan. Now, coaches are given an attribute from God about winning. Whether it's in a game or driving on a highway, a coach is focused on getting ahead. This particular coach was not going to let a couple of punk freshman make a mockery out of his educational expertise in PE. New instructions were given regarding flopping. Then he pitted us against each other.

The entire class, aware of our game plan at this point, gathered around to watch the match and offer their own instructions. He took the position on all fours and I was selected to take the other position, where I was on my knees with one hand on the floor and the other arm wrapped around my opponent. The coach told us specifically to wrestle each other or else there would be consequences.

I didn't know what he was going to do; nor was he aware of my plans. The whistle blew, and both of us flopped onto our backs. The class was laughing like crazy. The coach was screaming instructions at us to start wrestling. Both of us strengthened our resolve when the coach started yelling, "One of you get on top of the other!"

That statement made it sound worse than before. Despite moments of the coach screaming, neither of us moved. We opted for the running of laps rather than risk touching another guy. The coach was determined to have his instructions regarded, and we refused. Do you know how many laps you can run in twenty minutes in a regulation high school gymnasium?

Unfortunately I do.

Jonah would have been great in my PE class. He was given instructions by God to deliver a message to a group of people that were not living in a moral manner. God's instructions were simple: repent or die. Jonah did not particularly care for these people and opted to flop on his back—or, if you will, run away from the situation. Why do I think that avoiding a decision will make it go away? Jonah apparently thought the same way I do. Jonah's bad decision came back to swallow him, both literally and figuratively.

Jonah boarded a ship and set sail for Tarshish. While he was on the ship, a deadly storm took place. The sailors cast lots, and it was determined Jonah was responsible for their near-death experience. When he confessed the storm was his fault for not responding to God's call, he offered instructions, and they followed them by tossing him off the side of the boat. When they threw him overboard, the storm subsided immediately and the water became peaceful. While he was in the water, a big fish swallowed him, and after three days of flopping around in the water, the fish spit him up on shore. All of this so that Jonah could follow instructions to get into the wrestling match and deliver a message.

He finally relented to be the messenger and delivered the message to the people of Nineveh. I can only imagine the lack of inspiration Jonah must have exhibited in delivering a message. It might be similar to a request for a date that is never successful, such as, "You don't want to go out with me, do you?"

Then Jonah got a surprise from the message. The people actually repented! It was his hope that they would be destroyed by not following his instructions. It backfired on the judgmental part of Jonah, because the instructions were accepted.

God gave specific instructions to be delivered, and once again Jonah flopped on his back. In his dislike of these people, Jonah could not see them as God saw them. Jonah wanted them killed for not doing what God desired, while Jonah did not do what God desired. I'm right there with you, Jonah! I always feel others should live up to a higher standard than I should! When God allowed repentance to the people of Nineveh, Jonah went into a depressive funk.

So God put Jonah through some running of laps while he was pouting. It was hot, so God gave him a vine for shade. Then God sent in a bug to eat the vine, causing Jonah to wish himself dead. Jonah then began whining about the loss of his shady vine. God pointed out that Jonah was concerned about the vine but didn't give a rip about 120,000 people living in Nineveh. Through these interactions with God, Jonah finally got the lesson on following instructions.

The instructions are rather simple in life. If I follow them, life generally is easier and things are put together in a better fashion. I, like Jonah, have the most difficult time following instructions that I don't understand or agree with. Somehow my sin always comes back to my own selfishness rather than my following the instructions for the good of all people.

Are you flopping with any instructions?

JACOB: ROLL CALL! WHAT'S IN A NAME? (GENESIS 25–32)

I swear it was done as a way for my parents to get even with me before I caused any of their loss or greying of hair. My older brother was called by his middle name because he was named after our dad. Since Dad was Wesley Allen Waddell and went by Wes, the first son would be Wesley Allen Waddell Junior and would go by Allen. What overcame my parents at that point I'll never understand, but they decided to go with middle names for both me and my younger brother as well.

This decision has cost me in pain, correction, and what could have been thousands of dollars in therapy. Each year of school, when the initial roll call was made, I had to correct a teacher on the proper name to call me. I have great sympathy for the students now that I'm on the roll calling side of the desk. The problem was exacerbated in junior high and high school, when I had several teachers who had to make the change. Having a last name that was easy to mispronounce only made the situation even more difficult. "James Waddle?" the teacher would call. "Call me David, and it is pronounced Wad-*dell*." Or "'Wad' as in 'paper' or 'spit,' and 'dell' as in 'farmer in the'!"

I had heard that at one time my family name was pronounced "Waddle." The rumor was that one of my ancestors became a physician and his sister changed the pronunciation to "Wad-*dell*." I suppose nothing sounds more like a quack than a doctor named Waddle! Of course it's easy to get sidetracked and get down off duck jokes. They're not all they're quacked up to be! No charge for the duck puns, however;

we'll just put it on their bill. It's easy to see now why my mind is so "mallard-justed!"

My world history teacher would never make the change to call me David. He claimed that since the name James was in his records, he would call me James. I tried, I really did, but I just wasn't clued in to wake up or stop doing what I shouldn't have been doing upon hearing the name James. I took several trips through the hallways with a pink slip notifying the guidance counselor of my sins. The argument that I wasn't in trouble because "James" had committed the offense never seemed to work. Finally it got comical with the counselor, who would sign the notice, laugh, and tell me I would have to learn to wake up to my first name. Come to think of it, the students had an interesting name for the teacher too. It wasn't as becoming as "James," however.

The fun with names continues in life. I flew out to Phoenix once to visit two of my sons and their families. I flew out of Little Rock, Arkansas because I didn't have a kidney to spare in flying out of Memphis, Tennessee. This was before Southwest Airlines flew out of Memphis. Even with mileage, it was cheaper to fly Southwest Airlines out of another city than to be robbed at the Memphis airport. Going through the Transportation Security Administration's (TSA) security check, I offered my driver's license and my "David Waddell" boarding pass. There was a slight hiccup in that I was wearing a defibrillator vest for some recent heart trouble that God miraculously took care of. Other than that, there were no problems in getting through and boarding the plane.

It was the return trip where my name difficulties began again. Let me preface this part of the story by saying that security companies and groups like the TSA at times hire people for positions of authority who don't need to have authority. I call it the Barney Fife syndrome. Barney was the skinny, inept deputy sheriff on *The Andy Griffith Show.* He kept a bullet in his pocket because the sheriff didn't trust it in his gun.

I approached the lady working the first part of the screening. She looked at my license and boarding pass and then handed both of them back to me. "I can't let you in. Your name on the boarding pass is

David, but the name on your license is James David." I asked if she was serious, and she gave me a look that answered the question without words. I believe a lack of a sense of humor in the job is a requirement of TSA employment. She asked if I had any other pieces of identification. So I showed her everything in my possession. My Ole Miss ID had the name James D. Waddell on it. My credit card read "J. David Waddell." My voter registration showed "James David Waddell." I didn't offer my Cap'n Crunch decoder ring membership card. Of course, my name on that ID was either Otto Mobile or Jim Naysium. Perhaps I should have done that, because nothing else was going to allow me to pass. Despite the name David appearing on both license and boarding pass, I was not allowed in.

So I was sent back to the long line of people flying Southwest on the Monday of Labor Day weekend so that I could change the name on my boarding pass. In so doing, I had to change my name on my Southwest Airlines Frequent Flyer membership to James David. I finally boarded the plane after more thorough checks of my defibrillator vest and backpack, and an inspection of the insides of my pants around the inside of the waistline.

In ancient Israel, names were given as a description of personality. Native Americans did the same thing. A good friend renamed me Pierre after I lit a paper towel cigarette in science class to impress a redhead. He said the name David just wasn't worldly enough. I'm called Pierre by my older brother and some high school friends to this day. I once sent a list of made up names to a friend trying to make the point about her personality traits in a name. Examples included Itbee Lawngtoo Yoo, girl who captured my heart; Wanna Dioux Mofohir, girl who deserves the best; Lotta Grenns, girl that makes me smile; Hartbeet Fassa, girl that excites my spirit; and Connat Stah Pe-king, girl with incredible beauty.

Because of the personality descriptions of names in the Bible, there are many cases of names being changed, such as Simon to Peter, based on personality or calling. One of the most famous changes happened to Jacob. The name Jacob means "deceiver" or "cheater." When you look at his life up to a point, you have to say, "Yep, that's him!" He wrestled with his brother in the womb for positioning as the firstborn. He ended up coming out second with his hand holding on to his brother's heel. He later cheated his brother out of the birthright of being the firstborn by having a stew ready to eat when his brother was famished after a long hunt. His brother did most of the hunting while Jacob hung around the house. Jacob used anything to his advantage that he could.

With the help of his mother, he was able to get the blessing from his father reserved for the oldest son. He dressed up in fur so he'd be as hairy as his brother. Isaac, his father, had very poor eyesight near the end of his life, and Jacob used this to his advantage to deceive and cheat his brother out of the firstborn blessing.

He deceived his father-in-law, who was a pretty keen con man in his own right. His matches with his father-in-law were classic, as they were both pretty deceptive. Jacob worked for seven years to gain the woman he loved in marriage, but his father-in-law sneaked the older sister into the marriage bed instead. He ended up working seven more years to get the love of his life as well.

But God got involved in Jacob's life, and his name was changed to Israel, or "God perseveres!" God renamed him based on what he was going to become rather than on who he was at that moment. God reminded Jacob of the promise He had made to Abraham and Isaac, and He promised to carry out the creation of a nation through Jacob. God saw who Jacob could be and named him accordingly rather than continuing to see him with his current label. I am glad God does this for us!

One of the beautiful aspects of following Christ is that God has renamed us "sons and daughters." He literally looks at us and sees the righteousness of His Son. So, in making us a new creation, He has also given us a new name to fit in with His adoption. Like Jacob, we have been given a new name that better fits with our new creation personality.

So what's in a name? What's up with the TSA being so particular? "James" literally means "brotherly." No doubt I gave a brotherly appearance. "David" means "beloved." I started off in a loving mood with the TSA, but soon my name was going to be changed to "Ticked-off"! The name Waddell, as I learned from my studies in Freshman English 101 in college, was either for the "ward on the hill" (law enforcement) or for a mustard plant named Wadel. It didn't gain me any points in English, but since then I've pointed out my name means "I'm brotherly beloved hot stuff!" I would like to think my life matches up to the name definition. I know it doesn't, but I'd still like to think it does.

I'm sorry; I didn't catch your name ...

KORAH: THAT'S SO BENEATH ME (NUMBERS 16)

I was not blessed with musical talent. My younger brother has loads of it. People in our church would get us confused from time to time. If they ever told me, thinking I was Mark, that my solo was very good and complimented me on having such a great talent to use for the Lord, I would just say thank you.

During my senior year in high school, the Choral Department and the Drama Department gave auditions for the musical *South Pacific.* Knowing my musical abilities, I went to the audition to try out for the part of Captain Brackett. It was a smaller acting part, but there was no singing attached to his role. I approached Ms. Walker and Ms. Gillihan regarding the part. I read a few lines and was instructed to turn to a certain page for a sample of my singing. I reminded the ladies I was trying out for a speaking part, and Ms. Walker, the choir director, stated, "It's a musical! People sing!"

As she started playing the piano, I gave my best efforts at the song "There Is Nothing Like a Dame." About one line into the song, Ms. Walker stopped playing the piano, looked over the top, and asked me, "You're trying out for a speaking part, right?"

While serving at First Baptist in Port Neches, Texas, the music minister had a special event and called for a men's choir to lead the service one particular evening. I joined to show him my support. While we were practicing, he called out that someone was not on key, but he wouldn't mention a name. I demanded that he point the person out, but he chose to let it remain anonymous. I thought it was nice of him not to embarrass whoever was off-key.

I had the joy of observing my sons in numerous choral endeavors. One event was an annual Christmas carol sing at the Peabody Hotel in Memphis. In the middle of the run of songs, the ducks would make their appearance. At the conclusion of the last concert for my youngest son, I pointed out to his friends that it was indeed my singing that gave each of my sons the inspiration to learn good music. Adam pointed out that while the statement was true, it wasn't meant the way they were taking it.

In fact, when I sing I get a lot of requests. "Stop," "Don't," and "Quit" are among the favorites. I carried on the tradition of singing off-key for family birthdays established by my father. Only later did I realize he wasn't trying to sing that badly off-key. My sons would make funny faces at my singing in church. Their mom used to cover the notes on the hymnal page, claiming something about pitch. What's baseball got to do with music?

Just a few years ago, I finally got the message. A friend and I were at the bowling alley for karaoke night. She was a tall, good-looking brunette, and I am a short, wimpy-looking older guy. So we decided to offer the Sonny and Cher hit "I've Got You Babe" to the crowd. I had done this once before with another tall, good-looking brunette when I lived in Natchez. We began the song. I realize now the words are supposed to be sung when they pop onto the karaoke screen. The performance was horrible. Luckily the audience was partially inebriated. The next day, the message came to me loud and clear regarding my singing career when the bowling alley burned down. Investigators to this day do not know what happened, but the karaoke guy still avoids me in public.

Flashback to my high school years again. As a teenager in that day, if you were to get any stage time or "use your talents," you had to be able to sing. They didn't have a lot of speaking engagements, writing opportunities, or dramas in which to act. So if you didn't sing, you didn't get used by God. I remember that on several Wednesday nights, my guitar playing friend would have all the girls our age huddled around, oohing and aahing at his music. I, on the other hand, would be surrounded by second graders desiring me to tell them another story. I enjoyed the attention, but it's not wise for a high school boy to date second-grade girls.

This emphasis on singing caused a great deal of frustration. It's not a good feeling knowing you can do more but not being given a chance. I felt the same way when I was in church leadership watching "less talented" people get jobs while I just trudged away as a "dumb ol' recreator."

Korah, in the book of Exodus, had the same difficulty. Even though he fulfilled an important role, he kept seeing Moses and Aaron getting all the glory of their work with the Lord. Korah decided he wanted his piece of the pie. It was time this world met the "real talent." He gathered 250 leaders from the community and demanded that the two boys share the limelight. Korah claimed that he was just as holy and just as much a leader and could see no reason why Moses was still in charge. Korah couldn't understand why Moses was getting all the solos and attention in the scheme of things. Instead of taking his responsibility and doing the best with it, Korah wanted to have Moses' job. At times, I'm right there with you, Korah!

I remember hearing from a music director friend that he had a very talented lady volunteering in his music program in this particular church. The lady seemed to spend a lot of time with my friend and was always seeking to help in any way she could. The music director's wife, who served as the church's pianist, once commented that she was nervous about the attention this particular lady was giving to her husband. She made the comment that she was afraid this lady wanted her job. My music director friend stated that there was no way that would happen, as his wife was far more talented musically. When told this, his wife said, "It's not the pianist job that I think she's after."

There are times in my life when I am just like the lady. I manipulate and work the system to get where I think I need to be rather than wait on God. Even if I were more talented or somehow came up with some singing ability, I should still wait on the Lord to put me where I need to be. Korah, wanting more attention and recognition in his work, fell into the same trap.

I suppose I should be glad that God chooses to humble me when I think I'm better than I am. It beats the method he gave to Korah. God had the earth open up and swallow Korah and his followers in his disobedience to God's appointed leader. Okay, maybe I'm not as good as those others who were getting the work.

Reading about Korah helps me recognize my place. Whereas my ego wants to be the guy that everyone looks to for help, I have found that my place in life is helping one or two people at a time figure out life. Perhaps God has rearranged my life simply because one person needs what God has gifted me with in "speaking parts" rather than for me to break out into song for them. When I was climbing the ladder in church recreation work, I always longed for a program and facility like those other churches had. I never learned the secret of contentment and working where God had placed me. I suppose I always wanted that lead singing role of God's ministry.

Find out what you can do. Figure out where your gifts and abilities play into God's work. Don't compare yourself to others. Remember the words of Homer Simpson when Bart did something remarkable: "No matter how good you are at something, there's always about a thousand million people better than you."

Trying out for the speaking part?

DANIEL: KILLER B'S DIET PLAN (DANIEL 1)

Diets and I have never been formally introduced. When I was thirty years old, I weighed only 125 pounds. I could have been selected as a Barney Fife look-alike. I made stick figures look heavy. Then, at thirty, something happened. Food started sticking around longer than it used to. Several pounds later, and a few years as well, my diet was still one of the least disciplined aspects of my life.

Then news came from the doctor that was as shocking as the procedure to put my heart back into rhythm. I was in the hospital following the wonderful news that atrial fibrillation, which I had survived once already in my life, had returned. The first go-round was due to a viral infection. This one was caused by a bad electrical signal and compounded by a diet laden heavily with sodium.

Prior to receiving the cardioversion, a procedure in which the heart is shocked back into rhythm, an associate from the doctor's office shared with me the diet plan. Liquids would be limited to sixty-four ounces a day. That's any liquid. Water, juice, soup, and leftover milk from my cereal were all included in the limited amount. Then I was told I had to limit my intake of sodium to 1,500 milligrams a day. Normal healthy limits are around 2,000. Prior to the difficulty, I may have been averaging around 5,000. My diet up to that point was based on what sounded good at the moment. Nachos, ribs, nachos, fried chicken, and nachos were the staples of my diet. Then the final word on the diet came to me. No alcohol. None, nada, zip, zero. I even had to refrain from taking cough syrup that might contain .01 percent alcohol.

I called the diet my "Killer Bs." No beer, no bacon, no barbecue. Following the procedure I took a trip to Georgia to see one of my nieces get married. My Florida daughter-in-law posted the names of some of the restaurants on Facebook where we were dining. I had a friend back in Oxford, and noting the sites, she asked if I was complying with the Killer B diet. My response was as follows: "Yes, I am Being a good Boy with my Bs! I have three new ones in my diet now; Boiled, Broiled, and BORING! I B-lieve if I stick with it I will B-come B-nign to the B-fuddled and B-wildered feelings about this new lifestyle. I do B-lieve it B-hooves me to B-gin so that I can B a B-con of hope without having to B-little or B-moan others. Some might ask, 'Why?' I will reply, 'B-cause!'"

My brother Mark and I had quite the laugh on Facebook making several puns about healthy eating. A few of them are listed below:

> David Waddell:
>
> Beginning Week 3 of the Killer B diet. That being no BBQ, no beer, and no bacon. Low salt, limited liquids, and no alcohol. I honestly don't know which one I miss the most. Ha ha!
>
> The new diet is making me feel squashed! If I give a carrot all I'll stick with it! Today I will turnip a new leaf (spinach) and snap to it. I've bean dedicated to make the changes! I'll get my peas in a row! Orange you glad I posted this? I know you are saying, "Please asparagus of any more puns!" Artichoke up when he saw it!
>
> Lettuce pray ...
>
> Mark Waddell:
> When you can beet this, you can say I yam the greatest.
>
> When he's better, he can teach more classes and earn a better celery. But we still love him cumquat may.
>
> And he shallot last be healed

David Waddell:

> It would appear persimmons, that I have been impeached as the family punster. Mark, you may call Mom in Cauliflowernia and boast.

The diet worked! After a period of three months, God performed a miracle and gave me a stronger heart.

Right after Judah was taken over by the Babylonians, Daniel and some of his friends were made a part of a training group by their new king. The idea was to kill off the Jewish culture by indoctrinating the youth with their way of thinking. Part of the plan was to fatten the boys up with all sorts of rich food. Some research indicates a "Killer B" diet in Babylon. Their main source of food was barley, which was used to make bread and beer. They also enjoyed beef, barbecue (pork), butter, bulbs, and buffalo. It's easy to see why Daniel wanted to set his own diet plan. Myself, I'm thinking, *When in Babylonia, do as the Babylonians do!* I'll be glad to trade one set of Killer Bs for another one. Anything with butter can't be bad, right?

Daniel and his friends created a contest with the leaders. In the present age it would have been set as a reality television show. The boys of Judah would maintain a healthy diet according to their beliefs, and at the end of ten days the Babylonians could see which group was more fit. This *B* diet probably included things like broccoli, brussels sprouts, and beans. I smell a TV contract in this one. *The Fastest Fittest.* No? We could also sell a great fitness plan with an infomercial about being fit in ten days or getting your money back!

Of course God was with Daniel and the boys, and at the end of the ten days, God received the glory, as the boys were in much better shape than the others. I know God was involved because I've never had a successful ten-day diet! The boys looked healthier and better nourished after this short time. This might be the very first version of Veggie Tales! While the king wished to remove the Jewish culture from the boys through a new diet, the tide was turned and the boys became influential leaders in the new government. Out of this experience the king leaned on these young men and their wisdom. God used all of this to keep His people worshiping him while they were in exile. A strict compliance to diet might actually help people see the miracle that takes place in our bodies.

I have discovered that when one area of my life is disciplined, the others tend to fall in line as well. Why not honor God with the food I put in my system as Daniel did?

Can you please pass the broccoli?

SHINAR, SHINAR SILVER MOON UP IN THE SKY: SPRECHEN SIE DEUTSCH? (GENESIS 11:1–9)

I sat in the guidance counselor's office trying to determine the schedule for my senior year of high school. He noted I had not taken a foreign language yet, and I needed one in order to graduate. I have difficulty communicating in English, let alone another language! Throw in different accents and I'm even worse! The choices in our school were Latin, Spanish, French, and German. I ruled out Latin because it always sounded too hard. French was too hard to pronounce without actually choking on your throat when making guttural sounds. When it came to Spanish, I thought to myself, *Who in the world will really be speaking that in our country?* So I signed up for German. The guidance counselor looked at me puzzledly, but knowing I was going into church work, he reasoned I could look up the writings of Martin Luther. To this day, I have no idea why Martin Luther made an appearance in a bad decision. So I skipped taking Spanish. I know; you don't have to remind me. I don't know how I've made it in this country without knowing Spanish. Not only have I run into Spanish-speaking people in my work, but just about every mission endeavor I ever took required some Spanish.

So by having taken German I during my senior year of high school and German 101 (basically a repeat of the high school course, only slightly harder) during my freshman year of college, I had a small bit of a foreign language I could speak. I had learned just enough to get me into trouble.

During one of the trips I took with the teenagers from the Natchez church involved a day or two of playing at Disney World. Standing in a checkout line, I overheard a couple of ladies speaking in German. "Guten Tag," I said to them, which means "Good day." The two ladies turned to me and asked, "Sprechen sie Deutsch?" (Do you speak German?). I said, "Ja" (yes), after which they blasted me with a litany of words that I did not understand and had never heard before. I have a feeling they were saying, "Let's just say a bunch of words and watch what the nut does."

I just nodded my head, unsure of what I was agreeing to with the visitors. Paul, one of our trip sponsors said, "We need our own foreign language while we're here."

The flashback hit me. In my senior year of high school, not only did I learn German, but a language made famous on *Hee Haw* got indoctrinated as the "class language." It was called "alfalfa." The process of speaking alfalfa is to place an "lf" in between syllables and then to repeat the syllable sound. So, in alfalfa, "How are you? Isn't that a lovely moon out tonight?" would actually be said, "Holfow alfare youlfou? Ilfisn't thalfat alfa lolfovely moolfoon tolfonilfight?" Good luck getting that through spell check!

The language had caught on quickly throughout the high school, and now it did so with our teenagers and youth workers. It became a way of communicating that would leave others wondering what all the muttering was about. I would speak it when I didn't want my sons to know what I was asking their mother. It came in handy in discussing gift ideas with the birthday boy in the room! One particular case of the use of alfalfa was when one of our workers was serving as a substitute teacher at one of the Natchez schools. One of the students decided to sarcastically respond to her request in alfalfa. Was he ever surprised when she answered him!

The Bible tells us that at one point everyone was speaking the same language. The ability to communicate without any barriers could have been a good thing in sharing how the God they worshipped was the true God. Instead, like I do with all good things, the ability to communicate was perverted into a method of making us equal to God. Or, in other words, we began to think, *I don't need you!*

The folks in a town called Shinar decided to get together on a project. It was not to create Shinar Bock. That beer is actually brewed in the town of Shiner, Texas. It's a lovely city, but no tall towers have been built there. No, this community decided to build a building that would be tall enough to climb it and get to the moon and the heavens. This shouldn't be so hard to put together, since the designers spoke the same language as the construction contractors. They wanted a structure where they could see God face-to-face and make a name for themselves. The root of sin seems to always be the same. I tend to think I don't need God or I can control God. In the same way as these people, I've done similar things without the big building project. I've tried to do things without asking God, as if I were at the top of a tall structure and could direct God. Oh, the trouble my ego gets me into!

God, knowing how man thought, thwarted the plans and gave the people of the earth different languages to speak so that our differences in language would serve to confuse us and keep us from getting together and trying to make ourselves equal with God. Not only did He confuse our languages, but He gave us different accents as well. Having lived in Missouri, Texas, Tennessee, and Mississippi, my dialect is messed up to the point that I'm not welcome anywhere! It's difficult to understand me with my southern/Texan/Midwestern drawl the same as I might have difficulty listening through a Boston, New York, Irish, or Scottish brogue. I was on a senior adult tour through New York once, and I was holding an elevator door for a couple. As I held the door back, I said in my accent, "Y'all, come on in."

They stopped, looked at me, and said, "Say that again!"

On a mission trip to the London area, I met a man who told me his name. It sounded like he said "Dial," so I asked him if it was like the soap. He said, "Not Dial, Dial." I asked him to spell it, and he told me, "It's spelled d-o-y-l-e, Dial." We spoke the same language but still couldn't understand each other.

Oddly enough, the different languages came into play again in God's redemptive plan. From the days of Babel until this time, languages served as a way to separate people. There could be no understanding because there could be no communication. Shortly after the resurrection of Jesus, the disciples were hanging out when the Holy Spirit worked an amazing miracle. The followers of Jesus were given the ability to speak in the languages represented by people from all over the world. Mere Galileans were speaking to Parthians, Medes, Elamites, and more, telling of the wonderful love of Jesus. There's no reference for the Alfalfians, but I'm sure someone must have been speaking their language as well.

So different languages were created by God in Shinar to confuse us and keep us from the sinful thinking that we are equal to God. Then, at Pentecost, God used the different languages to communicate the sacrifice to us all in order to make us equal to His Son. Wow!

Let me translate that line for you in a variety of languages.

> English: This is good news.
> German: Dies ist eine gut nachricht.
> Spanish: Esta es una Buena noticia.
> French: Ce sont de bonnes nouvelles.
> Pig Latin: Isthey isay oodgay ewsnay.
> Alfalfa: Thilfis ilfis goolfood nelfews.

What have you got to say?

THE PRODIGAL'S OLDER BROTHER: HOW COME HIM? (LUKE 15:11–32)

My career in church work seemed to last about six or seven years in one particular place before another door would open and I would start in a new place. Some of those moves were warranted by what was going on in the church, and the others were warranted by what was going on in me.

I was serving in one church and felt quite comfortable until a political battle grew in size and our senior pastor took off for greener pastures. Suddenly a secure place didn't seem like heaven on earth anymore. When times get tough, some people pray. For church staff members, we tend to update our résumé and send it out to friends for recommendations. Oh, then we pray. Usually when we do this, nothing really comes up and we survive where we are or God moves us when He is ready.

Such a move was brewing for me. I returned from a mission trip to find a pink slip with a phone message on it. Please note this was before the days of voice mail, cell phones, and the like. Back then if you wanted to leave a message, you gave it to a person and he or she would write it down. Some company made a fortune on the pink sheet "while you were out" forms. On this particular phone message was a note to call a particular man. He was well known in church staff circles and was the executive pastor of Germantown Baptist Church. They were looking for a minister of recreation and had received my name from one of my friends I had bombarded with résumés.

An interview was arranged, a visit made to the church, and the options of working together were explored. Their church was without a pastor, and the one I was serving was bringing a new one in. I already had an idea that the new pastor and I were not going to get along, so I felt more secure without a pastor at Germantown than I did with a new one in my home church. So I made the move to Tennessee.

The following January I made my trek to the annual workshop for recreation ministers called the Rec Lab. Upon my arrival a friend pulled me to the side and let me know that several in attendance might be upset with me because they felt they were more qualified to work in this particular church than I was. He said they might even approach me and ask, "How did you get that job?" My statement to him was the same as it would be to them: "Of course they're more qualified, but for some reason God put me there instead."

After leaving church work and bouncing around a few jobs, I discovered I had the same sense of judgment when other people would find fulfilling jobs. Despite the bad I had done that led me to my current circumstances, I would inquire as to how "someone like that" could get a given job, or how he or she could keep that job while obviously not qualified or performing to the same standards I would hold myself to.

Finally my situation changed for the better! I got the opportunity to work at the University of Mississippi as an instructor in recreation management. All the things I had tried to do in recreation leadership for churches I could now teach people how to actually do! A couple of years earlier I had applied for a similar position at the University of Memphis and didn't hear one word from them. I have always felt that if you apply for a job, the least you should hear from the potential employer is a kind letter of rejection, or even laughter and a statement that I'm the worst possible candidate. I'd rather hear no than wait. I'm still waiting to hear from some employers from 2003. I'm sure the rejection letters got lost in the mail.

I survived the interview, and despite not having a huge amount of experiences in academia, I was offered the position. I gladly accepted. I was so excited. I felt that this was God placing me back in a place of leadership I had left years ago because of sin that had overtaken my life. Taking on this new work gave me the feeling of going home, much as the Prodigal Son would have felt. I figured a party was in order! I wrote, e-mailed, and called numerous friends about the move and received wonderful words of encouragement and offers of prayer.

Then the one call came in. A "friend" acted with feigned excitement but finally could not contain himself. "How did you get *that* job?"

I shared that I saw the ad and sent an attempt at a curriculum vitae (academic résumé) to the search committee, and apparently no other remotely qualified people applied. Then he asked again, "But, with all you've done in your life, how did you get the job?"

Luckily, Ole Miss was not concerned with my past, but only my present and my potential for the future. As with my acceptance of the job at Germantown Baptist, God had, for some reason, opened this door for me. I wasn't going to question it; nor was I going to offer His blessing designed for me to someone else. Sometimes we have to figure God does know what He is doing.

Like my friend, I find myself asking the same type of question: How come that guy finds a girl to date? Why did that girl get the promotion over the other one? Why in the world would they choose that guy for that part in the play? The judgment that drives me craziest is the judgment I use on others.

The older brother in the story of the prodigal son was quite a character. Now, to look at him, most would say, "What a fine young man." He was polite, cordial, obedient, and compliant. He always cleaned his room and made his bed. He even took out the trash without being asked. I thought it was tough living up to my brothers' examples, with Allen's incredible intelligence in school and Mark's amazing singing talent, but this brother would have been even worse! Can you imagine being compared to someone that doesn't disobey or rebel at all?

His father never had to worry about him wasting money on wine, women, or song, as his younger son was doing. Deep inside this older brother was a root of pride that led him to foolishness. It's that "holier than thou" type of thinking. It's the spirit that drives a judgmental view on others. Unfortunately it's the spirit you'll find in many churches on any given Sunday morning. It's the same kind of thought process to lead a Pharisee to pray, "Thank God I'm not like that sinner." Unfortunately I am like this at times. I get very frustrated with judgmental people until I realize that my feelings about them have made me judgmental.

Upon the return of his younger brother, the older brother got bothered at the fuss the kid brother was getting. In other words, he was thinking "How did he get that job?" He watched a robe that should have been his being placed on the rebel. He viewed a ring being placed on his brother's finger that should have been on his finger. He saw the fatted calf that should have been his being slaughtered. He observed a banquet that should have been his being set up on the troublemaker's behalf.

So he pouted and refused to go to the party. His dad found him and encouraged him to join the festivities. Then the brother asked his dad, "How did he get that job? With all he did to you and to us, how can you reward him like this?"

The father gave the most wonderful answer for the worst of us prodigals and lost children: "My son, you are always with me, and everything I have is yours. But we had to celebrate and be glad, because this brother of yours was dead and is alive again; he was lost and is found."

In one sense, the older brother was dead to him as well. Like him, my pride compares me favorably to others and refuses to look inward at my own sin. In acting like this, the older brother and I can never see or accept true grace. Older brothers and I need to come back to the Father as well.

You have to love the way that God the Father waits upon us. This story was so good to point out this fact. You have to enjoy the way that sometimes God kills the fatted calf, puts rings and robes on us, has parties in our honor, and offers us jobs at Ole Miss.

So how did you get your job?

NAAMAN: IS THAT IT?
(2 KINGS 5:1–19)

I've always been one to enjoy the spectacular. If it can be done, why not do it with flair and fireworks?

I've had a few medical conditions in life that have kept me in prayer. The first one was a muscular disorder called Charcot-Marie-Tooth, or CMT. It's a condition that erodes away at ligaments and causes myriad symptoms and consequences. Included in these are deformities in the feet, lack of balance, and little toes that curl over the toes next to them. In the worse cases, you literally end up walking on the sides of your feet.

When I would read about Paul's thorn in the flesh, I would identify it with my affliction of CMT. I would pray, beg God, negotiate with God, and demand (the old nonbiblical name-it, claim-it types of prayers) of God to clear it up. I had this idea that I'd go to bed one night and be awakened by a bright light in the room. When I got up, a miracle such as those where Jesus told the man to grab his mat and get up and walk would take place. I'd go from a clumsy kid to a mobile man!

The only thing is, it never happened. A few years ago I was referred to an orthopedic physician who said he could fix it. He recommended a surgery that would not remove the CMT from my system, but it would repair the damage done in my left foot. The surgery was done and the miracle occurred–though not like I had imagined.

In 2001 I was preparing to go to the annual workshop for church recreation ministers. It was being held in Orlando, Florida. I was particularly excited because I had two on my staff that were attending,

I was presenting in two workshops, my senior pastor was scheduled to be the conference speaker, and my wife at the time was going with me. In our years of marriage, she rarely got to go with me on these trips because of her work with raising our sons and work outside the home.

About a week prior to the trip, I was starting to get my annual sinus infection. Often, being the man that I am, I would avoid going to the doctor and then suffer through a week at the conference wishing I'd taken care of the illness. Being smarter and wiser now, I went to my doctor, who ushered me immediately into the hospital. Apparently I had developed atrial fibrillation. In layman's terms it means one half of the heart is pumping and the other half is dancing and not fulfilling its duties according to the job description. My worship pastor asked for a description of a-fib. I asked him if he'd ever seen me trying to clap in rhythm during the worship service. He stated then he understood the problem.

I was told to go home and rest for one month. Not only was the trip cancelled for me, but I was not allowed to go to work or go anywhere else for that matter. I prayed for a miracle. I could see lightning coming down from heaven, through my living room window, and zapping me right on the couch. I figured that even if the lightning blew out the television, I would have another way of sharing with everyone about how God healed me.

Instead, after making sure my blood was thin and a clot was not a threat, I was put back in the hospital and went under a procedure called cardioversion. Basically I was shocked back into rhythm. So much for my lightning miracle I had hoped for. There was an electrical strike, but not the kind I was expecting. The spectacular was accomplished in a simple routine medical procedure.

In 2012 my friend atrial fibrillation performed a reunion tour in my heart. It had come back. Once again I hoped for a lightning-style miracle. Once again I was shocked back into rhythm. I discovered things were worse this time. The heart was very weak, to the point I had to wear a vest that had a defibrillator attached in the event I went into cardiac arrest. I was told to eat a particular diet, do light exercise, and take my medications. I decided to do this and finally understood that ordinary acts can become the foundation for spectacular miracles.

I did just that, as well as prayed and shared with others my prayer for a miracle of a strong heart. When I visited the cardiologist for my next visit, he was pleasantly surprised to see my heart restored to the level of a healthy man's. When asked how I did it I replied, "A little bit of diet, a little bit of exercise, and a whole lot of prayer.

In each case, God supplied the spectacular miracle healing in an ordinary fashion. In each case, it seemed simplistic rather than grand. Naaman had the same problem I did. Naaman was a commander in the army of the king of Aram, and it was discovered he had leprosy. His wife's servant told them of a prophet in Israel that could heal him. The king of Aram sent a note to the king of Israel with Naaman so that he could be cured of his leprosy. The king of Israel tore his robes and got nervous that he would not be able to heal him. He figured the king of Aram was trying to start a fight. The king of Aram, by the way, was not known for his faith in God. Elisha heard about his king's response and instructed the king to invite Naaman for a visit. Elisha knew this would be a moment that God could be glorified.

So Naaman went to see Elisha to inquire about how to be healed from this terrible disease. Prior to arriving at his house, Elisha chose not to meet Naaman but instead sent a servant out to him with the orders to bathe in the Jordan River. "Wash yourself seven times" was his order.

Naaman was ticked. It was as if Naaman were saying, "The rivers in his home are cleaner and more suited for healing than the Jordan. Also, why didn't Elisha come out and wave his hand or do something so everyone could see the miracle take place? Just who does he think he is? Does he not know who I am?" Naaman thought Elisha would come out and wave his hand or do a dance or something spiritual. A simple bath in a dirty river did not live up to the expectations of how Naaman thought the God of the Israelites would operate.

In the modern day, Naaman would have expected an altar call and a spectacular crowd watching as Elisha hit him in the head, making him fall over backward and immediately go into spasms. It would be broadcast on several religious television networks. Naaman was even prepared in the event there was a chance to give something in an offering for the healing. He brought all sorts of priceless items to pay for the miracle in the event it was needed.

Modern-day healing performers have nothing on Biblical healing. There were no special services. No special offerings were taken for the healer's expenses. Nothing spectacular was to happen. It would be just an ordinary bath in a dirty river. Naaman saw no reason to comply. I understand Naaman. If it isn't spectacular, how will I really know it's from God?

Thankfully, Naaman had a servant that spoke some sense into him. The servant made the point that if he had asked Naaman to do something huge, Naaman would have done it. Why not try the simplistic measure given and see what happens? So Naaman went to the Jordan River and followed the instructions and was immediately healed.

I think far too often I want God to do something in my life and I write out the script for Him of how it should happen. That way I'll know for sure and can control my life. Of course we all know that's not how it plays out. In reality, most miracles are performed in the ordinary things of life, such as a visit to a doctor, a phone call from a friend, or the appearance of someone special in our lives. So in our trust of God we not only have to rely on Him to work things out the way He sees them, but we also have to wait patiently while He works things out.

Pretty spectacular, wouldn't you agree?

GEHAZI: WHAT'S IN IT FOR ME? (2 KINGS 5:20–27)

I have discovered in my life that my motives are not always pure, noble, and altruistic. I never thought of myself as a mercenary, but I was one by definition. In my careers I have usually enjoyed what I do and have received adequate compensation for the work I gave. I have always held a false sense of importance in my altruistic ways of serving people. My dad once made the comment that people work for a living for the money. His point? Money makes the world go around. In my role in church work, I put up a strong argument about helping people that are unable to repay me. I sounded like the poster boy for "Altruism Weekly."

As I was driving the point home, my father looked at me and said, "What if they stop paying you?"

You would think I would have been used to him being right so often in life, but I never wanted to give up easily. Despite my claiming, again with a wonderful false sense of piety, that I would continue in my work and lean upon God to provide a way, dad knew I was blowing smoke. I had to get paid for what I did, because that's how I cared for a family. Take away the money and I wouldn't be able to do as much as I did. So in a sense, I would do what the church required of me as an employee. The salary answered that age-old question that I often ask in life: "What's in it for me?"

The question we seek when we ask, what is in it for me? is not just a monetary answer. I have decided whether to take on certain tasks based on how much attention I would receive. I would quickly agree to things that would put me in front of an audience. I liked the feeling these things gave to me. I would accept opportunities that would make me look important or needed. I have denied those that would not do the same. I've had relationships end because I felt like my friend wasn't putting as much into my life as I was into his or hers. In other words, what can he or she do for me?

If I could have this same conversation with my dad again, I would have to admit that while I do work for the money, I work as much for the praise, attention, and affection of people. Even to this day I find myself donating to the church in anticipation of what it's buying me. I volunteer for projects that will give me a good image boost. I attend so that people will see me and talk about how active I am and how good of a Christian I am. Remove my tax benefits of giving to the church and see how quick I am to lower the amount of my gift.

This is not an abnormal behavior in me. Never has been. It affects others, as we see in the story of Gehazi. Gehazi was a servant to the prophet Elisha. In Elisha's story we see Gehazi being the one that delivered the message to the Shunammite lady that was housing Elisha regarding the birth of a son. Gehazi was also the messenger to lay Elisha's staff on the child that had become deathly ill. Gehazi was unable to heal the boy, and Elisha ended up lying on the boy eye-to-eye, hand-to-hand, and mouth-to-mouth. It was then that warmth came back to the boy. Knowing the rest of the story, I wonder if Gehazi's impure motives and lack of faith might have been what kept him from healing the boy. Perhaps he was looking for the payoff or the "what's in it for me" question in his mind!

Once, a man named Naaman came and asked Elisha to heal him of his leprosy. Naaman was a commander in the armies of the king of Aram. Elisha heard of his coming and sent a messenger, probably Gehazi, out to deliver the message to him. Elisha told him what to do, and eventually Naaman followed the advice of Elisha to wash in the Jordan River, and with that he was healed. Naaman came back to Elisha and declared the God of Israel to be the only God. Then Naaman offered to pay him for his services, but Elisha wanted nothing to do with payment. He was not looking for what was in it for himself. Elisha just wanted God glorified in the matter and sent Naaman off with a blessing.

Gehazi couldn't stand this. Here was all this money and wealth and goodies, and they were going to let it go. So Gehazi got dressed and rode after Naaman. Gehazi was probably figuring in his mind how much he deserved this payment. After all, who worked harder for Elisha than this poor soul? Having served in positions in the church that weren't as high on the food chain, I often felt like Gehazi might be feeling at that moment. I work so hard and get so little in return. I start to reason that I deserve this extra benefit even if I don't. Rationalization is one of the best lies Satan uses on me. It apparently worked on Gehazi as well. He was chasing after Naaman with the thought, *What's in it for me?*

Upon catching up with Naaman, he asked for the offering Elisha was to have received. He lied to Naaman and reported that Elisha had changed his mind about the offering. Gehazi told Naaman that Elisha would like the goods for a couple of prophet friends that were visiting. Namaan was more than happy to oblige and had two of his servants carry some clothing and silver back with Gehazi. It is not abnormal to get pretty generous following the receipt of huge gifts like life and health. Naaman, with a new lease on life, was more than willing to give all he could simply out of gratitude for what God had done for him.

Gehazi, knowing that newfound wealth would be pretty obvious in a servant's bank account, diverted the delivery of the gifts to his house and hid them. Even in that day, the FedEx and UPS of Israel could alter directions of deliveries! Gehazi, after arriving home and hiding his bounty, wisely sent the servants away and then reported to Elisha.

I know what Gehazi was doing. I do the same thing. It's funny how I think if no one sees me committing the sin, then no one will know anything wrong has occurred. When I'm hiding my "payments," I tend to look over my shoulder or take a full-body turn to see if anyone is watching. I never seem to worry that God is watching. I just don't want anyone else to see me doing what I'm not supposed to be doing. If I were around back then, I could have hollered, "Gehazi! Don't do it! I've tried hiding my sin and it always pops out at inopportune times!"

When Gehazi did report back to Elisha, the prophet knew exactly what had happened. He asked Gehazi where he had gone, and he did exactly what I would do when the deeds were discovered. He lied about it. He told Elisha he had not gone anywhere. Elisha, of course, knew what had happened because, as he said, his spirit traveled with Gehazi. Elisha then gave Naaman's leprosy to Gehazi, and it was said his skin turned as white as snow.

I know, for myself, it is nearly impossible to have a pure motive. Even when I give something with no strings attached, I find myself thinking about what I might get in return. Maybe I need to reconsider my motivation on a lot of things. Maybe I can work on doing things for God's glory and not seek what's in it for me.

What are you doing for God? Why?

ESAU: SUPER SIZE ME! (GENESIS 25:29–34)

I am one of those guys that live to eat. This type of eating is done out of enjoyment and not for the endurance of life. I have a particular weakness for various foods, which often gets the best of me. A slab of slow-smoked ribs, nachos, fried chicken, dark chocolate, and donuts serve, in Superman terms, as my kryptonite.

When I served First Baptist in Springfield, Missouri, I volunteered at a local elementary school as a tutor. I would go to the school midmorning one day a week and give a student about thirty minutes and then head back to the office. One block away from the school was a Dunkin Donuts store. It became tradition to tutor and then, on the way back to the church, grab a couple of donuts. I was always careful to wipe away the sugar from my mouth before going back into the office. Of course I somehow always left a little bit of sugar on my mouth.

There was an unbelievable donut shop in Natchez. It was a mom-and-pop place, and to this day I believe those were the best donuts ever created. This place became a popular spot for me. I would take the boys by there some mornings for a breakfast treat on the way to drop them off at school. It was not abnormal to see a dozen appear in the recreation center at least once, maybe twice, a week. When I would carry them home, they never seemed to all make it. I would swear to the boys that the lady must have miscounted as she placed them in the box, but they weren't buying that. I thought I was being smart when I started ordering two additional donuts in a sack; I could eat those and then share the dozen when I got home. This worked for a few trips before James noticed the leftover pieces of glazed sugar all over my chin.

A couple of years later, I went back to Natchez to close on the house after a move to Springfield. I went for my "last visit" to the shop. When I got out of the car, the mom put her head out the window and screamed, "David Waddell, where have you been?"

My wife knew at that point that I was more of a frequent visitor than just the times I brought donuts home.

When I interviewed in Memphis, I carried ten dozen boxes of Krispy Kreme donuts back home. Springfield did not have a Krispy Kreme at the time. Going through the pre-TSA security, the two guards decided they should do a random check of my boxes and ate two of the donuts. I don't think, to this day, my sons or my teammates at the church believe that story.

When my middle son lived in Missouri and my youngest was in Arkansas, I would drive right by my favorite barbecue place in Memphis. I would stop in and get two slabs, one for the boys and one to devour on the way. I'd go sixty miles out of the way on trips to St. Louis to see my brother so I could pick up a slab of ribs from another favorite restaurant. I learned a special technique in steering with my left hand, and in my right I could hold the rib with my thumb and the pointer and middle finger. If held correctly, it would leave the ring finger and little finger and the bottom half of the hand to shift gears in my standard automobile. There's still a part of the steering wheel that is glossed over from pig fat!

Don't even get me started on fried chicken! Gus's in Memphis and Oxford, Stroud's in Kansas City, and any KFC or Popeye's franchise can keep me happy. "Hankering" is a word used to describe a desire for food. At certain times I'll share a hankering for fried chicken. I feel one coming on as I write these words!

While all of this sounds good and the Food Channel would want me to start my own show, I must point out it was my eating habits that led to some serious health issues in my life. I weighed more than I ever had before. I wasn't watching myself, and all of a sudden I found I had developed some heart problems. Forget the Food Channel; I was aiming for the Cardiology Channel on cable instead! My love of food almost snuffed out my love of life.

I'm not, however the first one to sacrifice life for food. One of Isaac's kids was named Esau. He was actually the first born of twins that fought in the womb and continued the battle of siblings as they grew up. When Esau was born, Jacob was literally hanging on to his heel.

One day after a long hunt, Esau returned to their home and was famished. He felt he was literally starving to death. I don't know that I've ever been that hungry, but I have felt like I was. Jacob had made some stew, and Esau asked him for some. In true brother form, Jacob made a deal. Esau's birthright was to be traded for Jacob's stew. Esau knew a birthright was no good if he was dead, so he made the trade with his brother and proved that he, too, lived to eat. Birthrights gave the firstborn male double the amount of property and riches upon the death of their father. The firstborn generally took the place of his father at his death. The firstborn was also seen as belonging to God (first fruits, so to speak). So Esau was literally giving up his future wealth and special connection with God for one bowl of stew. He could have at least held out for some nachos!

This incident only fueled a fire that stayed active between the two boys. Jacob turned even more evil when he stole Isaac's blessing from Esau, leaving Esau with nothing much to live on. He did this by creating a favorite meal for Dad by using well-prepared goat rather than venison. I've always heard you shouldn't go shopping when you are hungry. It sounds like you shouldn't give your blessing either! I've had goat and venison, and there is a difference, but I suppose it's like eating imitation crab. If you don't know it's not real, it tastes just the same. I tend to fail blindfolded sample tests anyway.

The tricks with food left Esau very angry and determined to kill his brother. I've shared that anger when my brothers or sons have eaten the last bit of something left over in the refrigerator. I remember one time my middle son was eating some ribs I had purchased for dinner, and I told him to put what he didn't eat back in the fridge. When I got home that night, there were no ribs. He pointed out that I had said to put what he didn't eat back in the fridge. He had eaten all of the ribs. I know how you feel, Esau!

Later in life the two brothers met again, and God performed a miracle of restoration as they shared hugs and kisses. At first, Jacob was a tad bit tentative about the reunion. Gee, I wonder why?

While I was in the hospital, I would watch one of the cooking networks on television and think about how good that food would be. Then, during my recovery from the heart situation, I wondered what the actual price of a good plate of nachos would be. How much does a good slab of ribs cost me? Is chicken the only thing getting fried here? Is it worth my life, my birthright? My mother told me that my father was about my age when he discovered some similar heart issues. He didn't change his habits and died fourteen years later. I wanted to make it longer than that, so I made changes.

So I continue the diet and exercise plan. Sorry, Esau, I'm just not willing to trade my life anymore for a bowl of stew, plate of nachos, or a slab of ribs.

Bon appétit!

LOT'S WIFE: ONE WRONG TURN (GENESIS 19:1–29)

The issue of right and wrong has never really had a lot of gray matter to it. It's usually black-and-white, so to speak. That knowledge, unfortunately, has never been enough to keep me out of trouble. The first problem with sin is my draw to it. Like many others, I put myself in an unsafe place where my sin lives and thrives. I know what triggers the process and hang out where the trigger can be pulled. Then I flirt with the sin, thinking I'm strong enough to stop when necessary. The flirtation is fun, exciting, and risky. Very exhilarating! Once the flirtation begins, reason takes over. I start rationalizing why I need it, deserve it, or have to have it. Then, all of a sudden, I'm knee-deep in sin.

A second problem I find with my sin is that it is momentarily pleasurable. You can name any sin or fill in the blank on your repetitive sin, and there will be some joy found. That's part of the draw. Adam and Eve didn't just eat the fruit out of rebellion. They took the fruit because it looked pleasing to the eye. The short-term part of sin is pleasurable, but it is the long-term effect that is painful and hurtful. It has been years since the period of darkness and sin consumed me, and despite knowing how painful and hurtful that sin was to me and those close to me, I find I still entertain thoughts of going back. Sometimes the road to "back there" seems easier than the road to "up there." I convince myself this time will be different. The known of yesterday, though wrong, seems like less conflict than the unknown of tomorrow.

A third problem with sin is the lie that is told in our hearts and minds. Here are some of the lies I fall for time after time:

- You'll never get caught.
- No one will find out.
- Everyone's doing it.
- You deserve it.
- It'll be good for you.
- It will make you a better servant for God.
- Nobody has to get hurt.

The lie will draw me in at a moment of weakness and sound logical. I try to load the skeletons of my past in the closet. Then I discovered I had to hire a construction company to renovate and add new closets to hold the new skeletons! I figure that if I hide them, then no one will know. Okay, I bought the lie!

It's similar to being around a campfire. At a distance it appears to be a light. Up closer one feels warmth. But if you get too close, you get burned. Some burns leave scars for life. Some of mine have, anyway.

What I have discovered is the old adage "If I cover my sins, God exposes them. If I expose my sins, God covers them." Sin is not something I can manage. When I try to do so, the emphasis remains on my sin rather than my Savior. Sin, I have come to discover, is dealt with only by having a relationship with God.

The flirtation with evil is not new to me. In fact, one of the characters in the Bible had an extremely difficult time with it. We read in Genesis that Abraham and his nephew Lot both had a lot of land and a lot of livestock. Rather than continue a family feud regarding land and livestock, Abraham gave Lot the choice of real estate. Lot looked toward Sodom and saw a land that was well watered, similar to the land of Egypt and the garden of the Lord. Lot chose the land known for good gardening even though it was close to a city known for its sin and wickedness. In other words, he placed himself and his family in an unsafe place where sin was their next-door neighbor and could be flirted with.

While living in the area near Sodom, Lot was once captured by the king of Sodom. After a thrilling rescue by Uncle Abraham, Lot chose to stay in the area where difficulty was brewing. Despite a local king having kidnapped him, He found living there pleasurable!

Later God had shared with Abraham what He was going to do to Sodom and Gomorrah. Abraham prayed and negotiated with God to save the place. He asked God if the righteous in the city would be wiped out with the evil. Abraham wondered if God would destroy the city if fifty righteous men could be found. When God said that for the sake of fifty he would not destroy the place, Abraham carefully negotiated the number down little by little. He knew his nephew lived in the area. In the final deal, God agreed not to destroy the city if ten righteous men could be found.

They couldn't find ten men. They all believed the lies.

Two angels visited Lot, and he invited them to his home. The citizens of Sodom wished to do some evil and perverted things to the two angels, and Lot tried to protect them. Lot offered his daughters, and that got the crowd angrier. They wondered who this "foreigner" was to come and tell them what they could do. When the men started trying to force their way into Lot's house, the angels pulled Lot back in, blinded the men, and told him to get his family together. He spoke with his daughters' fiancées about running away with him, and they thought he was joking. Remember, the fiancées did not protest against the girls being offered to the crowd. In other words, the future sons-in-law were buying the lies of Sodom! The angels told Lot, his wife, and the girls to run to the hills and not look back. In other words, they were to look to tomorrow rather than hold on to a sinful past or present.

Lot and the girls were on their way when all of a sudden Mrs. Lot decided to turn and see what must have been an amazing laser light show. More than likely she was looking back because she knew that life would never be the same and desired to be back home. I understand how you felt, Mrs. Lot. Sometimes the known of a difficult past and present is more desirable than the unknown of tomorrow. Whatever the reason, once she looked back, she turned into a pillar of salt. I remember telling this story in a day camp once, and a camper said,

"That's nothing; when my mom was driving once, she turned into a telephone pole."

Yogi Berra, a famous baseball player once stated, "When you come to a fork in the road, you should take it." We face a fork in the road. One path is the "been there, done that, got the scars" path. The other is a path of the unknown, other than that we know God is with us. We can proceed toward the protection of the hills, or we can look back to the flirtation with sin, the short-lived pleasure, and the pain of the consequences. If you turn back, watch out for those pillars of salt!

No U-turns allowed.

GEUEL AND THE GANG: I-SPY (NUMBERS 13)

I am generally optimistic and enthusiastic about life. I tell people I'm not "glass half full" but rather "glass half full and the server is coming with a drink on the house!" I've given the motivational speeches about eating an elephant one bite at a time and living each day as if it is your last. I've used all the clichés about "letting go and letting God" and "turning it over to Him." I am embarrassed to admit that I have heard people's pain and offered advice such as getting more involved in church or giving more money. It's easy to deal with if it's someone else's problem.

Then one of my own problems hits my life. I find no peace in the clichés and empty promises of an inspirational poster. When I ask for advice and someone offers the same routine answers and clichés, I find myself frustrated. Of course, my problems are different. Okay, maybe not so much.

Such a problem hit me a few years ago. Following a resignation from a twenty-year career in church recreation due to a period of sin and darkness, I found myself trying to find work in a secular world. I discovered that despite managing large staffs, large budgets, and large facilities, the world saw my church work as a soft career with no connection to the real world. I read all the clichés over again, and while they would give me a sense of inspiration, they didn't offer any real support to an employment situation. All I wanted was to be restored to a position of developing leaders.

During the next three years I held a total of six jobs before landing the instructor's position at the University of Mississippi. Despite asking a congregation for help, nothing seemed to be opening up for me. I felt as if I had leprosy or as if *The Scarlet Letter* were being revisited in the Memphis area. I took the first job offered to me, and it was with a church friend that builds fences. During this time I prayed for a restoration into my career path, only to see fences (literal and figurative) being built and difficulty growing. I even recruited and paid for a company that helps people transition into new careers. It was like going into a land that devours the people!

I took my next job in a nonprofit Christian fitness facility. I was the volunteer coordinator. While I was there, the director's position became open, and I thought that with my experience I'd be the perfect choice for the leadership position. It was offered to someone else in the organization. How in the world could I not be considered, with my qualifications? I felt the negativity growing inside me. I felt that perhaps the consequences of my sin would haunt me forever. The problem was making me feel like a grasshopper in the land of giants.

I had always been told I had the perfect personality for sales. That advice was wrong. My next position was in trying to recruit businessmen into leadership development courses offered by my company. Basically I had to cold-call a business, arrange a meeting with a CEO or president, and convince that leader that he or she stunk and that for $4,000 I could help. Needless to say, there wasn't a lot of dollars pouring through. I wondered if I would ever get back into recreation leadership. It seemed as though I were a grasshopper living in the land of giants.

The answer came soon. One month later, after continual crying out, I became the activities director of a retirement community. The answer was short-lived, as difficulties at home, brewing from my period of darkness, led me to move to another retirement community in town. When it was evident the marriage was over I even changed career paths one more time and took on a position with a company that helps people find new jobs and different career paths. It was the same company that had helped me a few years prior. Even still, I felt as though I were being devoured. It was like being a grasshopper in the land of giants!

While working with this company, I found an advertisement for a position at the University of Mississippi. I had earlier applied for a similar position at the University of Memphis and didn't even get any contact of any sort. By this time I figured, "What do I have to lose?" What happened next was the miracle in my heart. Instead of seeing the size of the problem of getting back to a career of developing leaders, I saw how big God was in the process.

Geuel is not a recognizable name in the Old Testament. He was one of the twelve spies sent into the land the Israelites were to possess. I could have easily picked on Shammua, Igal, Palti, Gaddi, or the remainder of the twelve spies. The spies were to scope things out and make a report back to Moses. Moses wanted an advance report on what the land was like, what the people inhabiting the land were like, whether they had strong fortresses set up, and whether they were weak or strong.

The report came back. "We went in to the land where you sent us; and it certainly does flow with milk and honey, and this is its fruit. Nevertheless, the people who live in the land are strong, and the cities are fortified and very large."

Caleb and Joshua became famous as a result of the exploratory trip because they saw how big God was. Caleb said, "We should by all means go up and take possession of it, for we will surely overcome it." He knew the other nations stood no chance against God. These two spies recognized this fact. Caleb and Joshua recalled how God had brought them out of Egypt. They remembered how God had destroyed the most powerful army of the time. They had faith that God wanted them to have the land and that nothing could stand in their way to obtain it.

Geuel and the others didn't become well known, because they saw how big the other nations were. They saw fortresses and people that made them look "like grasshoppers in our own sight." I couldn't have named any of the ten spies prior to this writing. I just knew them as the ten that saw the other nations as bigger and stronger, making them look like grasshoppers.

The people, in the fear these ten spies created, opted to not take the land. In fact, there was a movement to appoint a new leader and go back to Egypt. Their advice kept the Israelites from going into the Promised Land for another forty years. God was determined to keep the unbelieving generation out of the Promised Land. The ten spies that started the grumbling all died of a plague.

I believe the appropriate cliché here is "Quit telling God how big your problems are and start telling your problems how big your God is."

I was part of the ten. I saw the difficult road. I lacked the faith, despite seeing my own versions of parted seas and defeated armies in my life. Luckily God gave me the opportunity to be part of the two and possess the land.

What are you spying?

PHD PRAYERS: THE SHOW MUST GO ON! (MATTHEW 6:1–8)

Recreation ministers rarely get to preach in church. I don't know if it's because of the nature of our job trying to reach people by having fun or if there's a sense that this particular ministry field doesn't read the Bible. I heard the senior pastor outside my office door once, and to play a little prank, I held the Bible upside down and pretended to be reading from it when he came into my office. It got a laugh but probably reinforced the idea presented earlier.

I was not called on too often to fill in for the preacher. But it did happen occasionally. In twenty years of church work I probably filled in for the preacher around twenty-five times. Only once was it a Sunday-morning appointment. You may refer to the two reasons above for the lack of Sunday-morning opportunities.

With limited engagements to preach being booked, I did what a good number of nonpreaching staff members would do. I utilized the time I was given to lead in prayer as my sermon time. I came up with some very good sermon prayers throughout my ministry.

Prayer is one of those funny times in churches. I have read that the two main fears people hold are public speaking and death. Public speaking is number one. People would rather die than stand in front of a crowd and speak. Many church folk would move praying in public to the number-one spot! The churches I grew up in and those I served on staff had a habit of calling on someone from the crowd to voice the prayer. There are some great moments in churches when this happens. Some will start in on a bedtime prayer, while others mutter and mumble something, hoping the Lord understands even though no one else does.

When one of the ministers approaches the pulpit, watch the crowd for the experienced church members. They'll already be bowing their heads so the minister won't be able to make eye contact and call on them to pray. The minister will find some rookie or freshly-ordained deacon, and off we go. The newbie to public praying will white-knuckle the pew in front of him and start off with a cracking voice, as if puberty were visiting the church that day. The nervousness takes over some people to that point where they can't even talk legibly. I call one version of public prayer "prayer overLord." That prayer goes like this: "Lord, we thank you for this day, Lord. And Lord, please help the missionaries, Lord, because, Lord, they need your help, Lord. Lord, help us to stay awake. Lord, during the message, Lord, because you know, Lord, how the preacher is most days, Lord."

We also find a lot of "just" prayers being offered. For example: "Lord, we just want to thank you. Just be with us today, and just help us to hear you. We just want to please you so you can just be happy with us."

Knowing the nervousness of the amateurs, many large-staffed churches just rely on the other ministers to provide the prayers. You know, they keep it professional!

While I was in seminary, I was serving a church as their recreation minister. It of course goes without saying that I would not be getting any invitations in the pulpit. So one Sunday night I was told I'd be giving the offertory prayer. I immediately formulated a three-point prayer/sermon in my head and was ready. It came time for me to pray, and I confidently walked to the stage. With a loud, bold voice I said, "Let us pray."

I have to tell you, I was really getting into the message of the prayer. I was talking about all of us as Christians going out and finding people to love and invite to church. It was during this part of the prayer that I found myself so wound up I almost spoke as I would have in my college days. My prayer/sermon continued, "Lord, we're not doing what you wish. We're just sitting around and not going out for new people. We need to go find those that need you. Right now get us up off our big, fat ..."

I stopped just in time.

I was about to say something that rhymes with bass (the fish, not the musical part). I was in midsentence, hoping something would come to mind. At times like these, my rational mind tends to take a coffee break. While it was only seconds, it seemed like minutes as I scoped my brain, searching for something to say. I couldn't even come up with anything like "buttocks," "butt," "rear," "rump," "backside," or "derriere." I couldn't help myself, so I started peeking around the room. People with bowed heads were now looking up to see what would come next. A few people left one eye closed just in case I popped right back into prayer mode. I could feel the impending spirit of revival about to break out.

Finally, it hit me. The youth group I had been with in high school had a pet name for one of the girls in the group. While the pet name had nothing to do with that part of the anatomy, it was that nickname that came to mind.

I continued, "Binkies."

Now this quiet, conservative, and reserved congregation began losing it. A passerby would have assumed it was a charismatic Pentecostal church based on the hooting and hollering that was going on. Trying to salvage any part of the prayer, the sermon, the job, and my reputation, I closed the prayer with "And Lord, please forgive me for what I almost said."

Prayer is supposed to be communication with God. Unfortunately I have turned it into a production and a performance at times. Instead of speaking with God the way I would a friend, I practice and rehearse so that people will be incredibly impressed with my theological wherewithal. To state it in other words, and to rewrite the old song "Everything's Coming up Roses," "There's no prayer like a show prayer!"

There was a guy like this in the Bible. This guy wasn't given a name because Jesus knew it would describe a good number of us. I call him the PHD, for "praying hypocrite dude." Jesus described him during his Sermon on the Mount. The Dude stood in the church or on the street corner and made a dramatic performance about his prayer. His hope, like mine, was to gather attention to himself in a way of demonstrating his theological wherewithal! Jesus said prayers are better intended to be made in the quiet place of my room, away from any other eyes or ears I might try to impress. It's a little easier to cut out the "thous" and "thees" when I'm not trying to impress anyone. When I talk to God as a friend in private, I find that even the prayer overLord and use of the word "just" disappear.

Jesus gave a model for prayer rather than the performance-based creations I have created. And I will give it to you: "Our Father in heaven, hollowed be your name, your kingdom come, your will be done on earth as it is in heaven. Give us today our daily bread. Forgive us our debts as we forgive our debtors. And lead us not into temptation, but deliver us from the evil one."

There's no prayer that's show prayer, like no prayer at all ...

PETER: MR. FIXIT! (MATTHEW 14:22–33)

He was one of those old men that looked grizzly. No doubt life had been tough for him, and he took it out on those of us in his class. It was eighth-grade shop class. He would caution us to be careful, and he used his missing ring finger on his right hand as impetus to not sleep in his class. One of the projects I had to make was a footstool. *I've got this*, I thought. I bragged to the teacher. I carefully measured and cut the wood and screwed it together without any loss of blood or digits! I was so proud until the teacher came to inspect it and gave me a C-. Apparently being level is important in these things. Anyway, Mom liked it when I brought it home!

I have never been accused of being a handyman.

There's something about do-it-yourself (DIY) projects that just gets the best of me. While I was living in Natchez, my wife grew tired of reminding me about the leaky faucet in the kitchen. I wondered how many times she was going to have to remind me about it before it actually got fixed. One Saturday morning I decided to take on the task. I went in and first took off the faucet. I figured it just needed a replacement washer. I discovered that in some of the newer faucet mechanisms, there are no washers, as it's all sold as one whole set. I thought to myself, *I'm not falling for that marketing trick.* I did not want to purchase a whole new faucet set.

I looked underneath the sink and saw a drip coming off the connector tube. *Aha!* I thought to myself, *I've got it!*

So I twisted and contorted myself to fit under the sink and remove the tubing. I was then off to the store to get new copper tubing and fix the sink. I returned home with the materials and discovered that I had to slightly bend the copper tubing in order to make it fit. So I started the bend, and before I knew it, I'd gone too far and bent the tube in two. As I pulled it apart, I realized I'd put a hole in the tube. So back I went to the store to try this whole process again. I dealt with the next set a little more gingerly before accidentally bending it too far again. A third trip led to a third set of tubing being sacrificed.

So at the end of the day I had made four visits to the hardware store, bought three sets of copper tubing, cleaned up five water spills, and spoken numerous swear words under my breath. I finally, in an act of desperation, wrote a note to alert family to not use the sink. Then, the following Monday, I called a plumber, who fixed the problem in no time at all.

After moving to Oxford, I entered back into the world of home ownership, which means I now get to fix some stuff myself. Recently I've had two opportunities to improve my handyman reputation. One was in fixing a toilet, and the other was in patching part of the ceiling in the bathroom. The toilet had a small leak out of the thingy that goes into the intake place. Forgive me if I use "plumbing terminology." I recommend you utilize a dictionary to keep up. I purchased the materials to repair the leak and successfully had it stopped. That is, until the water was turned back on. Over the next few weeks I would tighten, retighten, and tighten once again to stop the leak. Finally I got it and began bragging to my friends about the great handyman I am.

Sensing that I was no longer taking a leak in the bathroom, I set my efforts on the ceiling repair. A leak from years before had rotted out a bit of the Sheetrock, so I cut out the old damaged piece and cut a piece of drywall to fit into the spot—that is, all but a big chunk on both sides. I got the mud stuff (again, you may want to refer to a construction guy dictionary) out and placed it into the openings and covered it with the paper stuff that goes over it.

I admit I was feeling pretty good. I told my friend about the work and that I was feeling rather masculine and was going to eat some meat. She suggested I should also drink a beer and scratch ... well, you get the idea.

Shortly after the brag fest, I ran back into the bathroom, for obvious reasons, and discovered the leak was back. All I could do now was wait for the ceiling to fall.

It seems that in my life, the fall has been greatest when I've been the loudest in my bragging. When I am most adamant about being right, I am the most wrong. One of my Biblical heroes, Peter, suffered from the same disease. It's not ironic that he makes more than one appearance in my writing, as I feel I'm more like him than any other character in the Bible.

Peter was the one disciple that was not afraid to speak up. He made the first confession that Jesus was the Christ. Shortly after that he tried to quiet Jesus about his impending death. He saw the glory of the transformation and then spoke (without knowing what he was saying) about staying there. When the tax collector came, it was Peter he approached and asked whether Jesus paid the temple tax. Peter said He did without knowing one way or the other. In fact, Jesus, in a story, explained to Peter that they were actually exempt but were to pay it anyway. Then he told Peter to fish and look in the first fish he caught. There in the mouth was enough for both Jesus' and Peter's taxes.

When Jesus was walking on the water, it was Peter who declared, "Lord, if it's you, tell me to come to you on the water." He walked a bit too until he let the wind frighten him. When Jesus talked about who could enter the kingdom of heaven, Peter boasted, "We have left everything to follow you! What, then, will there be for us?"

But his greatest handyman boast came during the last supper he would have with Jesus before his death. When told he would deny knowing Jesus, he boldly declared, "Even if all fall away on account of you, I never will. Even if I have to die with you, I will never disown you."

There you have it! The boast is out there! The bragging has begun! Then, a few hours later, the toilet and ceiling of his life began to leak and cave in. Peter did indeed deny he ever knew Jesus. Even after seeing the resurrected Jesus, Peter went back to fishing. He assumed Jesus was done with him, owing to the denial following the "go to death with you" claim. The cowardice haunted him until Jesus brought him back into their friendship by offering forgiveness and restoration—the same forgiveness and restoration he offers you and me. No matter how much bragging and boasting take place, the only real fix in our hearts and souls is in Jesus.

By the way, remember that C- footstool? It's still in operation forty-two years later with my Mother in San Mateo, California. She uses it to assist her in setting pots in the bottom of her kiln. So maybe I am the handyman after all! Uh oh, there goes the ceiling!

What are you bragging about?

ABRAHAM: HURRY UP AND WAIT (GENESIS 15–18, 21)

I fell in love with the comic strip *Kudzu*. It was about a preacher and the work he did for a congregation. He felt a calling to work with the well-to-do and instead got stuck with the same people in the pews.

In one of the cartoons, the preacher, in the first panel, prays for patience. In the next two panels, you see pictures of a man sitting there waiting on the answer. The final panel has the preacher looking at his watch and saying "Well?"

It's called the waiting game. Hurry up and wait! Nothing ever happens in a hurry.

When I was in high school, I couldn't wait to get to college. I was going to be a debate coach or go into some form of ministry leadership in church. I enjoyed my high school years, but tugging at my heart was the next step. When I dated girls, I grew impatient that we couldn't have a five-year-old relationship after only a couple of dates. It seemed that life was a huge hurry-up-and-wait proposition.

While I was in college, I couldn't wait to get to the seminary. I worked my freshman year as a youth minister at a church sixty miles out of town. I completed my college career working in the recreation center of my home church. Working part-time in what I wanted to do full-time was more than I could stand. While in college I got engaged and didn't actually get married for another nineteen months. Talk about hurry-up-and-wait!

While I was in the seminary, I couldn't wait to get into my first church to work. But the two years of school seemed to take forever.

I graduated in December, and as of the next March, nothing was happening and no one was talking to me about potential positions of service. Luckily I was working at a church during that span. I was quite fortunate as well to finally find a church that would take me, because the church I was serving part-time was trying to hire another new student to take my place before I was even gone.

I had been employed only a few months out of the seminary when I couldn't wait to figure out a way to get back to high school! I regretted being in such a hurry to get into the real world that I lamented I might have missed out on some of the fun. Great, one more thing to wait for!

While I was in church work, I couldn't wait to figure out a way to get to a bigger church and a better position. I never really appreciated what I had in the churches I served, for I was always looking for something bigger and better. I often tried to get ahead of God by sending résumés to churches I didn't really feel God wanted me to work with. The reason was only that it would provide me a better reputation with my peers.

When I left church work, the waiting got even more intense. *When will God restore me to church leadership?* I wondered. I even asked *if* God would restore me to church leadership. *When will this silly sales job be replaced with something better?* Why didn't the University of Memphis want me? I'm glad it wasn't the forty-year sentence the children of Israel got before entering the Promised Land, but the three years it took for God to open the door to Ole Miss seemed like forty to me.

I found at times that I looked to the future so much that presently I wasn't worth much to anyone. I was in a shopping mall and saw a cute sign at a jewelry store. The sign stated, "Ears Pierced While You Wait." *Really?* I was going to drop mine off and come back later. I've often considered putting up my own sign for God that states, "Character built while you wait!"

Abraham knew all about how to hurry up and wait. He waited for the promise of a son for twenty-five years. I heard all the stories of how Abraham is the father of our faith. I've heard all about how he is the patriarch to a nation that led to the coming of Jesus. I also did the math. The promise of a son came. The delivery of that promise (pun intended) took twenty-five years. That's also 300 months, or 9,131 days, or 219,150 hours, or 13,149,000 minutes. Now some might think that's facetious, but when you're waiting for something, the minutes drag on and on. When we read about the twenty-five years, it takes us a few moments. Let's remember that Abraham went to bed 9,131 times with regret the promise hadn't happened that day mixed with the hope that maybe tomorrow it would come. With that in mind, the hurry-up-and-wait sounds a little more difficult.

Somewhere in the middle of the hurry-up-and-wait game, Abraham and his wife figured out a way they could accomplish the promise on their own. Around the 6,837,480-minute mark they devised a plan for Abraham to have a baby with Sarah's handmaiden. They named him Ishmael. God honored some of His promise in making a nation from Ishmael but was quick to point out to Abraham and Sarah that Ishmael was not His promise being fulfilled. In other words, Abraham was having character built while he waited! God used the twenty-five years to prepare Abraham to be the father of a nation, just as He used three years to show me the true worth of the ministry I offer to family, friends, and this world.

You can imagine the joy when a one-hundred-year-old man and his ninety-year-old wife celebrate a pregnancy. You can imagine the look on the face of their gynecologist. How about the Medicare agent regarding maternity bills? The two named their son Isaac. This means "laughter." I can imagine that when these two old folks recognized the restoration and the fulfillment of the promise, there was a lot of laughter. I can also, from experience in raising boys, imagine there was a lot of laughter in the home.

The idea of waiting seems to be thematic throughout the Bible. Joseph hurried up and waited to get out of prison. Jacob hurried up and waited for the girl he loved. Moses hurried up and waited on his purpose. Joshua hurried up and waited on his chance. Caleb hurried up and waited on entry to the Promised Land. Gideon hurried up and waited for a sign. Ruth hurried up and waited for a husband. David hurried up and waited to be king. Esther hurried up and waited to speak to her husband, the king, about her people. Daniel hurried up and waited on the restoration of Israel.

Several centuries later it started all over as Judah hurried up and waited on the delivery of the promise of a messiah. During that span they ended up with skewered views of what the Messiah would be. Most of the nation wished for things to return to the way they used to be. In other words, they wanted to go back to high school. I understand their regret.

What are you waiting for patiently? Well?

MOSES: TEMPER, TEMPER (NUMBERS 20:1–13)

I've generally been easygoing all my life. I usually don't get rattled too easily. I have had relationships in which the other person would get madder than I would in a sticky situation because I don't express anger the way many people do. I get that from my father. I'd watch him trying to fix something, and he'd hit his thumb with a hammer. Where most folks would jump up and down, swearing up a storm, my dad would pull his hand back, calmly look at the throbbing thumb, and say, "Well, that's going to hurt."

I upset one person once in the heat of a fight because she said, "I want you to be mad about this!" I calmly stated, as dad would, without any emotion or fluctuation, "I am mad."

Before you submit my name for the Mother Teresa Patience Award, I must admit I do have a temper. He comes out every so often. When I was younger there were some kids around the neighborhood that liked to bully me. I'd usually take it or run home crying. One day, my mother tells me, I snapped and went chasing after one of the bullies and had him pinned to the ground, pummeling him with rights and lefts. He was the one crying that day! Mom said she was scared to approach me with that look on my face.

I once took the family on a vacation where we explored the sights and sounds of that area and that night decided to eat at a Mexican restaurant. One can never go wrong with the choice of a Mexican restaurant. I approached the maître d' and asked for a table of five. He explained it might be just a moment for us to be seated. I understood, as the world is discriminatory with families that are over the size of four people. Four people can be seated anytime they want, but once the fifth one comes into the family, you are relegated to a second class of citizenry. But we liked the youngest son enough to put up with the discrimination.

We'd been waiting about twenty minutes when a man approached the maître d' and asked for a table for eight. "Right this way," said the man, and he immediately seated them.

Now, don't get ahead of me. I hadn't lost it yet. I approached the young man serving as maître d' and politely inquired as to why a party of eight would be seated before a party of five. As you can tell from the reading of that statement, I was incredibly composed. The man told me it was easy. "For a table of eight you just put two tables of four together. For a party of five you have to wait for one of the corner tables."

I was beginning to brew. My debate partner in high school said he could always tell when my temper was about to go because the shade of crimson would start in the lower neck and start working its way up to my forehead. "You know," I said to the youngster, running the mathematical formulation in my head, "you can also push two tables of four together and seat a party of five."

When he said he couldn't do that, my blood started boiling. Then it got worse. The manager came by, and when the situation was explained to him, he looked me square in the eye and told me that the young man was accurate and that my family and I would simply have to wait for one of the corner tables.

My sons figured that people in the parking lot could have heard my rage being expressed at that moment. The old debater in me was creating arguments for being seated. The repressed temper was coming out. We were finally seated at a place created by pushing two tables of four together. I don't even want to think about what the cooks might have done to my enchilada!

My sons, watching an episode of *Everybody Loves Raymond,* saw a similar display from Raymond. From that day on, they referred to my temper as Raymond. If I'm driving or dealing with a situation that should cause anger, they will ask me if Raymond is coming to visit.

While I'm still fairly even tempered, I will admit that Raymond comes to see me occasionally.

Moses, of all people I found in the Bible, is a character with the same affliction. I'll admit I never saw this in Moses until I started thinking about how the different characters teach me about my own inadequacies. When Moses was still living in Egypt, he got mad one day at some Egyptians picking on and bullying another Hebrew. He went to work in the same "snapped" mind-set that I had adopted in the neighborhood. He looked around to see that no one was watching, and he killed the bully and buried him in the sand. My bully should be thankful, as he was able to go to school the next day.

Later, while Moses was coming down from the mountain with the tablets containing the Ten Commandments, he experienced another "Raymond" moment. While he was up the mountain conversing with God about the law, it seems Aaron and the other boys had made an idol and were worshiping it. So Raymond—rather, Moses—tossed the tablets to the people, breaking the tablets at their feet. On a side note, I find it difficult to read or talk about Moses anymore without seeing him pictured as Charlton Heston. Then Moses burned the golden calf down and crushed it into powder and scattered it on the water and made the Israelites drink it.

When Moses was taking the whiners and gripers of Israel around the desert, he got upset with the people requesting something to drink, and God told him to speak to the rock to get water. Instead of following God's direction, Moses, in a fit of frustration, struck the rock with his staff, causing water to come out. He used an instrument designed for God's glory in frustration and anger as a way to shut up the people. Because of his Raymond-like temper tantrum, God did not allow Moses to enter the Promised Land. That's a bit heavier of a punishment than unknown substances in Mexican food.

There always seems to be a consequence that follows one of my visits from Raymond. Sometimes it's just the knowledge that I let a situation get to me. I get tickled at how I think having Raymond screaming at someone in traffic is really going to help anything. I know that my outbursts or lack thereof have hurt relationships and caused people to wonder about my faith. There's got to be a better way. Now I try hard to catch him when he first shows up at the door and let him know, "I've got this, Ray. Thanks just the same."

What's a good name for your temper?

ANANIAS: YOU WANT ME TO DO WHAT? (ACTS 9:10–19)

During elementary school I had difficulty pronouncing the *R* sound. I sounded like a young Elmer Fudd. You can imagine the laughter in the church when I was a part of a musical where a child (me) had to constantly sing, "Please don't send me to Africa!" I suppose it was good that the people knew Afwica and Africa are located in the same continent.

The words to that song have played through my heart for all these years—not because of the *R* sound, but because they are so accurate. I have had a fear of doing what God wants for fear He'll make me do something I don't want to do. I read the words of Isaiah when he said, "Here am I Lord, send me." The fear of going to Afwica had me saying, "Here am I, Lord; send Tom."

This challenge of finding God's will for our lives is one that produces far more stress and pressure than it should. I remember people in church telling me that I needed to go into the ministry. So was God calling me or the people of First Baptist Church? I struggled with decisions as to classes, majors, and extracurricular activities, wanting to make sure I was right in line with God's desires. I tried setting a fleece of sorts out for God on several occasions. *It worked for Gideon,* I thought, *how come it's not happening for me?*

During the summer between my sophomore and junior years of high school, our church took a trip to a campsite in New Mexico. I had toyed with the idea of church work simply because I enjoyed doing some of the things we did in our youth group and things I was able to assist with in the recreation ministry, such as camp counseling and drama. While in this camp, called Glorieta, I observed a presentation during a worship service of kids struggling in the inner city. Photographs were shown on a screen while a choir sang. The photos depicted kids using drugs, meeting in inappropriate places, and obviously doing things that were wrong. I knew what I had to do. I made a decision to go into the ministry. The church called it a decision for "full-time Christian service." What I didn't realize then is that everyone that follows Christ follows a calling into a certain area of need in this world based on gifts, abilities, passion, and experiences. So, in a sense, we are all called into the ministry. Some people just get paid to do it. Some even do it in Afwica!

The path was set, and off I went to college, seminary, and five different churches to serve. The choice of each academic pursuit, as well as the churches served, were different struggles in seeking God's direction. It was always difficult to determine the correct direction. I set a pattern for myself in deciding that God's will was always the decision that took me upward on the ladder of success. Bigger churches and better positions and bountiful pay increases determined the path. The joke was always told among paid staff members that you could always doubt someone was following God's will in moving to different churches unless the person was moving to a smaller church, less money, or less prestige.

My sons grew very mission minded after our move to Memphis. All three contemplated career paths that would take them to remote places of the world. I had to come to the decision that my sons belonged to God and not to me. After all, I'd rather they be where God wanted them to be (in Indonesia) rather than where I wanted them (in Indiana)!

What is it that causes the fear of doing what God wants? Is Afwica that bad of a place? I think part of it may be the comfort I feel in my life playing it safe. I think another part is me staying in control of my life. Yeah, like that's really going to happen!

Ananias received even a stronger calling into danger than I did. God put it on his heart to go speak to Saul, the Christian killer. I was thinking Afwica didn't sound so scary after I learned of this. This call would be like telling me to admit to my dad that I drank the last bottle of his favorite soft drink. There are stories from a visit to Tombstone, Arizona, where a cowboy entered a saloon alone to confront someone and never came out. That would have been a safer situation than what God was directing for Ananias. I remember facing some tough personnel committees and pastors that could come close to Saul's tenacity, but I never really felt my life being threatened until *after* I began working in their church.

I imagine Ananias, at the time of his call from God, was remembering the famous heroes of the faith in receiving unimaginable directions with a chance of death. Abraham was told he was to go to an unknown land. Noah was instructed to build a huge boat when it wasn't looking like rain at all. David faced death threats from his kingly predecessor. Elijah took on the prophets of a false god and almost tasted death because of it. Numerous prophets were martyred for preaching God's message. While it sounds heroic now, each of those heroes faced the imminent possibility of death, with some actually being killed. After some discussion with the Lord, Ananias complied and went to see Saul. I might have actually run away like another hero, Jonah!

In the churches I served, there was always the responsibility of visiting the people that were in church the previous Sunday but were not regular members. Usually this would be on a particular night of the week. In most of my churches, it occurred on Monday so that the people that visited would still be fresh from their experience. The odd part of this is that none of the members remembered anything from the previous Sunday, but we figured an outsider would. Most of the folks that visited did not want you coming unannounced to their homes, but it was, after all, tradition, so off we would go. We'd find some people open to a visit, and some we'd find already in their bathrobes and pajamas, settling in for the night. The event was actually titled on the church calendar as "Monday Night Outreach." A meal would be served, an inspirational speech given with a spiritual "rah rah ree, kick them in the knee" motivation offered, and then we would be sent out into the community.

The night of visitation would generally, by reputation, be made known in the community, and suddenly you'd think the rapture had occurred and you'd been left. No one was ever home, or they weren't answering their doorbells and knocks. The real "type A" visitors would knock really loudly. There were some nights on which I'd make the effort, but generally I'd knock lightly on the door so the people couldn't hear it. Then I could write a note stating "Not at home" and could get on with my life. The scariest part was finding someone that actually enjoyed talking, because you could end up being there all night long.

I have no doubt that the first knock on the door from Ananias might have been like mine and was just a little light. Then he knocked again, knowing someone would answer the door and he could meet the Christian killer face-to-face. Ananias didn't know it at the moment, but he was part of the plan to restore Saul's sight and launch him into his called ministry. Because he followed God's calling, he was an instrumental part of God's plan being fulfilled. Maybe if Afwica is calling, I should reconsider the journey!

When I think of some of the decisions I made to go to school here and work in that church there, I can only hope I was an instrumental part of God playing out His plan in everyone's life. I have a feeling I have been.

So when God says "Go!" how should I respond? My recommendation is to pack up and head to Afwica!

ISAAC: LIKE FATHER LIKE SON (GENESIS 26:1–11)

I don't know why it was such a treat for my boys, but if they could snatch away one of my favorite foods, then the treat was all the more delicious. I might earmark the last piece of pie in the fridge, but if the boys knew it, then one of them would make it disappear.

I remember once telling the middle son to leave some leftover ribs in the refrigerator. Later that night I was looking for them and was told there were no leftover ribs. I played along with the game, occasionally telling them sugar-coated cereals were for dads only. I have no doubt that if I had done this with spinach and broccoli, then my sons would have been all the healthier.

The worst case of this took place one cold February in Springfield, Missouri.

I have always had a weakness for the Girl Scout Thin Mint cookie. The word of this addiction traveled fast among the Girl Scouts in the churches I served. When I moved to Oxford, I did not have the Girl Scout connections as I did before. I also learned it is best not to scope out complete strangers in town and ask, "Do you know any Girl Scouts? I need one desperately." Not only does one get weird looks, but people start talking about you and pointing at you. I had to find a different method of finding the treats I felt I was "mint" to have.

I was an easy target. Generally I would end up with two or three cases (not boxes) of the chocolate treats. The delicacy was not available at any time of the year; only once a year were the cookies available from this particular girls' organization. My favorite way to eat them was to stick an entire cookie in my mouth, chew it up just a bit, and then take a swig of ice-cold milk to soak into the cookie in my mouth. Before I would know it, the sleeve of cookies would be gone in one sitting and one large glass of milk. This was the reason I purchased so many. I'd store them in the freezer, hide them in closets, and would often take a few boxes to my office for safe keeping. This is not something you want left available for boys that enjoy eating dad's treats.

This particular year I had ordered the boxes and unfortunately had to be out of town when the shipment came in. The dutiful Girl Scout delivered them to my family with a sense of dedication to the task. God bless those Girl Scouts! I was at a conference at a camp in the mountains of New Mexico. When a call home was made to check on the gang, I was informed the cookies had arrived. I breathed in the thin New Mexican air and imagined the cool breeze I inhaled was similar to my reaction to the mint and the ice-cold milk. No more talk was given of the cookies, and I could only assume they'd be there for me when I returned.

I assumed incorrectly.

I did find out, with my in-depth investigation, that my name had come up for consideration before the boys opened the last sleeve of cookies. As the last cookie was taken from that sleeve, they did confess they should have left me some. I have this image of all three boys saying it together with chomped-up cookie bits in their mouths. I'd like to say I felt the love they were sharing, but somehow I just couldn't muster up the feelings. I told the boys it would have been easier to have dealt with a note upon my return that stated all of them were leaving me. I think my anguish at receiving no Thin Mint cookies made them more satisfying to the boys.

I later shared the story with my father. I started developing the habit of not telling Dad about stories regarding my fatherhood and raising his grandsons. He always enjoyed the stories way too much, claiming I was getting payback or something. I felt for the old man because he undoubtedly was confusing me with my brothers.

After sharing the story with dear old Dad, and after he finally stopped laughing, he reminded me of a time he carried home a case of a soft drink called Grapette. It was the best grape soda ever created. Unlike soft drinks today, this particular soda was not readily available. The chances of getting it were about as few as Thin Mint Girl Scout cookie sales. I didn't realize until later that it was one of my dad's favorites. If bottles of this stuff had been on the Tree of Knowledge of Good and Evil, then I would have understood better Adam and Eve's sin. It was one of those drinks you couldn't sip. You found yourself at the bottom of the glass before you knew it. Then you'd suck on the ice cubes, hoping for a smidgeon of flavor to come out.

Dad knew all of this about the Grapette and was quick to divide the bottles among the family. Since there were twenty-four bottles and five in the family, he surmised that we would each get four bottles to enjoy and he and Mom would split the remaining twelve. So we all enjoyed a couple on the weekend he brought them home. Then it was Monday. Mom and Dad both worked outside the home, leaving me and two brothers at home. I don't remember how it happened, and I'm sure I was innocent of any wrongdoing, but just prior to Dad's return home, we discovered the tray of Grapettes was full of empty bottles waiting to be returned for the deposit.

Like father like son.

I have ended up being my dad in so many ways—in my humor, my wit, and the way I conduct myself. Isaac went through the same aspect of life as well. He followed God with the same amount of dedication his own father possessed. He lived knowing he was the next step in the promise given to Abraham, the father of a nation. He also copied some of the less-than-desirable traits of his papa. During a famine, Isaac took his family to the king of the Philistines for help. The men in the area asked about his wife, seeing her incredible beauty. Isaac said, "She is my sister." Isaac tried hiding the Thin Mints and Grapettes rather than trusting God to take care of him and his family. Luckily God protected the poor woman from being taken by others and Isaac got in trouble for his lying. Later the king saw how he was caressing Rebekah and realized she was not his sister. He chastised Isaac for the trouble that may have come upon him and his people had someone tried to be intimate with his "sister."

I know where he learned the trick.

His own father, Abraham, tried the trick twice, sacrificing the possibility of losing Sarah to save his own neck. Isaac had probably heard the stories and seen how his dad avoided trouble by relying on his own abilities rather than trusting God. Unfortunately, Isaac did not learn the lesson of the consequences of such an action and nearly put his own wife in jeopardy.

Rodney Atkins has a great song titled "Watching You" that refers to what we can learn from our fathers. While I have copied some of the good in my father, I also, like Isaac from Abraham, have repeated some of the sins of my dad. I know some of the less-than-desirable traits in my father have exhibited themselves in my life. I am also proud of my sons for discovering this before it ruined them and declaring that the cycle of this sin pattern stops with them.

I pray for the boys as they move in this direction. Of course, I also look forward to the stories when their children eat their special treats. Some cycles should not stop!

JUDAH AND TAMAR: SHE'S GUILTY! OOPS, SO AM I! (GENESIS 38)

I have had the mixed emotions of having watched two impeachment discussions taken by Congress against the president in my lifetime. The first was with President Nixon, who resigned before the actual impeachment vote was taken. The other was President Clinton, who was actually impeached by the House but not convicted by the Senate. This was the second actual impeachment in our history, the first being that of Andrew Johnson during the Reconstruction era. The mixed emotions are not party line, but rather because of the respect I hold for the position.

President Clinton was accused of numerous things, but what was hurting him most was his inappropriate relationship with a White House intern. Despite his denial, his opponents and the media were determined to expose all of his sins. I was extremely outspoken myself about his errors, claiming we don't need that kind of leadership at the top of any organization. Several representatives and senators joined in the witch hunt in asking for his resignation because of his infidelity. I was fully in agreement with them.

Then the reports started to fly in. It seemed as though any official that was outspoken about the president's sin was discovered to be guilty of the same sin. One by one those that spoke out about the president's lack of morality were found to be guilty of the same charge. It was as though a feeding frenzy, such as those that occur at a fish hatchery, was taking place as woman after woman came out in the news with the names of their congressional and senatorial liaisons.

That's when I decided to back away from my attacks on the president. I knew I was as guilty as he and the others. I didn't want my skeletons to make it to the church newsletter, let alone the Memphis newspaper. My skeletons did, however, make an appearance a few years later and had to be dealt with. As was the case with those accusers of the president, my shame felt heavier because I had been so judgmental and hard on those guilty of my own sin. It's not that odd that those who speak loudest against certain crimes and sins have a few skeletons of the same bone structure locked away in their closets. Unfortunately I had large walk-in closets.

Judah must have been thinking the same way as the president and me. Being one of the sons in history's most dysfunctional family, Judah had moved away after selling his brother Joseph into slavery and married a girl from another tribe of people. His firstborn son, Er, married a girl named Tamar. He was corrupt, however, and God punished him with death, leaving Tamar as a widow. In that day, widows had no rights and no protection, so the law claimed that if one brother died with no heirs, the second brother had to impregnate the widow, with the child carrying on the deceased's name. So the second-born son, Onan, was told to fulfill his duty to Er.

Onan did not comply, out of his selfishness to not be a part of Er's legacy, and therefore God killed him too. Judah's third son, Shelah, was quite young, so he hid him away, claiming that when he was of age he would give him to Tamar. In the meantime she was to move back in with her father as a widow.

As the third-born got old enough to fulfill his duties, Judah backed away from his promise to Tamar. This left Tamar in a very undesirable place in this particular culture. Not having the third son provide offspring for Er left her in a place of desperation. She had literally no rights and no way to provide for herself.

Judah, now a widower himself, was to travel to visit a friend. Tamar found out about the trip and dressed up like a prostitute. She met him at the roadside with a veil-covered face. This led to an inappropriate visit with Judah. To pay her, Judah promised a young goat and left with her his signet and cord, as well as his staff, as a form of collateral until the goat could be delivered. When he tried to pay her off with the goat, she was no longer in the area. Even people in the area claimed they had never had a shrine prostitute there. Judah decided it was best to let her keep the other items to avoid any shame upon his own name. In the sinner's world, that's what we call damage control. It is an effort to cover up or minimize sin and avoid the consequences.

Three months later it was discovered that Tamar was pregnant and had no husband. Judah demanded her to be put to death by burning. In the same way as people brought a woman caught in adultery to Jesus without her partner, Tamar was facing judgment alone. As she was being brought out to death, she told them the father of the baby was the owner of the seal, cord, and staff Judah had left behind. I know how this must have hit Judah. My skeletons were revealed through e-mails that reappeared after having been deleted. The immediate confrontation with our own sin has a terrible sinking feeling to it. In fact, it was not until she delivered his pieces of identification back to him that Judah faced his own faults.

Realizing the jig was up, he then confessed his sin being greater than hers. He admitted he should have given his third son to her and did not sleep with her again. Please note that the death-by-burning-consequence-of-sin discussion ended at that point. Those of us that are caught like mercy more than judgment at such a point. Judah finally came clean, regarding his keeping his son Shelah from fulfilling his duty to Tamar. From that pregnancy Tamar gave birth to twins that created the next step of Jesus' lineage.

Judah discovered mercy that day for his sins. He portrayed the same kind of mercy later when trying to protect his younger brother Benjamin. What Judah also discovered, along with President Clinton and me, was that if we cover our sin, God exposes it. The hope lies in the fact that if we expose our own sin, God covers it. A few years ago, when Tiger Woods was going through his turn with all of this kind of sin, my heart was more forgiving, as well as desiring his ultimate restoration with God. I just didn't have it in my heart to sit in judgment of him while knowing I had not only committed the same sins but still faced the same temptation.

Which sins are you must judgmental about? Shall we look in your closet?

JOHN THE BAPTIST: CREATING THE LESSEN PLAN (JOHN 3:30, LUKE 7:20)

I've often said a good father wants his children to bypass him in accomplishments. My three sons pretty much met that goal by the time they were twelve. I attempted to connect with each of my sons according to his own likes and dislikes. My youngest son loves a good argument, as do I. You may disagree, but I do. Yes, I do. We would argue over the most minute of items until his mother would tell us all to be quiet. My middle son took on a passion for movies, theater, and creative stories. He and I would spin yarns about portable bathrooms (porta-potties) at construction sites becoming superheroes. The tales were of the Green Toilet and his sidekick, Potty!

My oldest son took to sporting events. To this day he and I share a love for the same professional teams in basketball, baseball, and football. He also took to playing the games as well. I put a basketball goal out in our front yard, off the side of the driveway, when he was around twelve years of age so that he and I could play. At that time he was a little shorter than I was and a whole lot lighter. Even at that age he had loads more natural talent than I did. In my basketball career my claim to fame on defense was that when my opponent would try to drive past me for a basket, my first step was quick enough to pivot in time to watch him make the shot! Because of his size at this young age, I was able to dribble in, back him down, and turn to make easy short shots.

While I am fairly competitive, I find no joy in trouncing opponents. I got fairly decent for a while in table tennis, and when I would play an inferior opponent, I might play left-handed or try new shots. I would try to win, but I didn't need to do so in a way that crushed one's spirit. So in playing my son in driveway basketball, I might win four or five games in a row and then try new shots or only shoot from the outside. I didn't wish to destroy his spirit. After several losses, he would pull out a victory, and it kept him motivated to keep playing. They were great moments, as were the arguments and theater in building up the father–son relationship.

Then the day came when he shot past me by several inches. I also discovered at this point that when I tried to back him in under the basket, he somehow found a brick wall in his chest for me to try to back down. It quickly became a case where he was taller and stronger. But at least I was still slower! All of a sudden the games became more of a struggle for me. Shots that used to go in the basket were now being blocked back into my face. Rebounds that used to be muscled out easily were now going to him.

Now, whereas I did not wish to destroy his spirit, my beloved son did not share the same version of sports mercy. The kid was trouncing me as often as possible. I worked with a man that had three very athletic sons and asked him, "What do you do when the sons start winning?" His comment was, "You teach them how to lose gracefully."

That was something I could do. I'd been learning how to lose most of my life. So I tried to hold in my temper. I tried to not let the advancing years become a frustration in our games. I tried to teach sportsmanship on both sides of the victory-and-loss equation.

On one particular mission trip, my oldest son had the opportunity to speak. He introduced himself as "James Waddell, the son of David Waddell." I've worn many titles in my life, but none made me prouder than that one. Seeing what my sons can do and what they had become as young men, I realized it was time to let them take the forefront and for me to take a backseat. I'm proud of the men they've become. In most cases I now introduce myself as their father. I like that introduction.

I've seen a similar situation with those that followed me in positions of leadership in the churches I've served. I used every aspect of my personality and leadership while I held the positions in those churches, but after I left I tried to lessen the impact of my influence. Some people like to hold on to the past, and church staff members have to be careful not to allow the ego trip of being "needed" past the time we serve that particular church. I was blessed by following some very talented and able leaders in each of the places I've served. I was equally as blessed that they "lessened" themselves after they moved away. It's hard enough to work your own way into people's hearts. It's easier if the predecessor has moved on gracefully.

John the Baptist, while not being Jesus' dad or predecessor, faced a situation similar to the one I did. John, being older, began his ministry before Jesus went public with his. The baptizer was gaining accolades all over the countryside. He went toe-to-toe with the Pharisees and the religious leaders of the day. He called upon them to repent and be baptized. This is a group of people that believed they had no sin in their lives and therefore had no need to repent. John, on the other hand, didn't fit into their definition of a prophet, based on his camel-hair outfit and diet of wild locusts and honey.

John even took on King Herod, calling out his immoral lifestyle. One day when John was baptizing people, Jesus walked out to be baptized as well. John stated later, "He must increase, but I must decrease."

It was all a part of John's "lessen" plan.

John had learned the lesson on how to lose gracefully. Just as a teacher develops a lesson plan to keep students on a learning path, John had a lessen plan. He would slowly disappear from the limelight and allow Jesus to get the attention. John understood and accepted the fact that someone better was on the way. He recognized his calling as the messenger and allowed his ego to convince him he was bigger than the story. He also knew he was to bow out for the message to be understood without competition or complication. He even declared that someone greater than him was coming and that He would baptize people in the Holy Spirit.

What makes John a character and makes him like me is that he later had to check one more time to make sure Jesus was who He stated himself to be. Despite hearing the voice from heaven himself when he baptized Jesus, some doubts rose in his head. He needed one more affirmation that Jesus was the one. Like John, I occasionally want to check on my boys and make sure they are still way ahead of me in being men of God.

I'm reminded of the line in the fourth episode of the Star Wars series where Luke's aunt comments about Luke having too much of his dad in him. Uncle Owen admitted that scared him. I have the same fear for my boys as well. There's too much of me in them to remove all doubt. So John the Baptist, it looks like we have that "double check" in common!

I will talk with people in former churches to follow up on my successors as well. Somehow I want to know that these men are doing well rather than trusting God to play out His will in their lives. Like John, despite the good I hear, I wonder if they'll hold up to the rigors of working in that particular place.

It takes a great deal of security in a person to back away from the crowd and perform his or her part in this world behind the scenes. It takes a good swallow of pride and ego to let the next person or group advance you. John the Baptist ended up being great at just that. I think I'll try to do it some more as well.

What lessen plan are you on?

ABIMELECH: I HEARD EXACTLY WHAT I WANTED TO HEAR (GENESIS 20, 26)

When I first moved to the Memphis area in the late 1990s, the University of Memphis still played their basketball games in a venue called the Pyramid. It was named as such because of the history of the city of Memphis in ancient Egypt. The structure was built in such a way that it literally looks like a glass pyramid in downtown Memphis.

I had the joy of attending several games in the Pyramid. Most of them were university games, but my family and I also enjoyed a couple of National Basketball Association exhibition games held there. Later, when the city adopted the Grizzlies, we watched some of those games as well.

One particular evening, my oldest son and I had two tickets for a University of Memphis game. We parked and started the trek toward the Pyramid. As we drew near, a man approached us carrying a stack of booklets. He asked if we would like to purchase a program outside the stadium for five dollars. He pointed out they cost more in the arena and further explained that a group was doing this in order to help those that lived in the downtown area. The implication was they were selling the programs for the needy.

I heard exactly what I wanted to hear. This tugged at my heartstrings. I saw this as a perfect opportunity not only to benefit the unfortunate but also to teach my son about generosity and giving. "Sure," I said, "let us have two of them." My sense of pride in myself grew for this opportunity to teach the young lad a lesson that would be sure to stay with him for a long time. I gave the man a ten-dollar bill, and my son and I proceeded to the arena with our programs in hand.

We made our way through security and the entrance with no problems. We got our drinks and snacks and found our way to our seats. I ate my hot dog, still beaming at the wonderful life lesson I was able to teach my son. I thought to myself about how lucky my sons were to have me as a kind, loving, and generous father. If they would have handed out nice-guy awards at that particular game, I would have won hands down.

Then it happened.

James opened up his program and discovered it wasn't a program. Not only was it not a program for that particular game; it was, in fact, *Downtowner* magazine, which could be picked up for free at any restaurant, retail store, or hotel in the downtown area. I had been taken in one of the best con jobs ever.

This was not what I wanted to hear.

I could quickly see the Father of the Year Award slipping through my fingers. I did, in fact, teach my son a lesson that night. It was not about giving and generosity, however, but was about not believing everything you hear. There are apparently people in this world that see suckers like me and do all they can to separate me from my money. In one sense, the man was not lying. The money, I'm sure, did benefit those living downtown—just not necessarily the way I had imagined.

A king that ruled Gerar in the days of Abraham and Isaac had to learn this same principle. Abraham was traveling through this particular area and had settled in with his knockout wife. Seeing her, the king of the area, Abimelech, inquired about her. Abraham told him it was a game program. In other words, he lied and told the king she was his sister. This is the actual truth in some realm of technicality, as she was Abraham's half sister. I love it when sins are attempted to be justified that way! I try it all the time, but with the same level of success as Abraham. The sale of the *Downtowner* did actually help those living downtown.

The king heard exactly what he wanted to hear. Seeing as how it was a "sister," King Abimelech took her to his place. God gave the king a dream and told him the lady was actually Abraham's wife. In the dream Abimelech was told he was as "good as dead" because the woman he had taken was a married woman." Luckily all this happened before anyone could take advantage of Sarah. All ended well in the story, with a covenant being made between the two men.

Later Abraham's son Isaac was traveling through the same area. Some of the men in the area inquired about his wife. Fearing death, Isaac claimed the same lie about Rebekah being his sister. Hearing this, Abimelech observed the couple. Once he saw Isaac caressing Rebekah, he knew that she was not his sister. That *Downtowner* magazine salesman back then must have been quite the manipulator! Abimelech once again had to confront someone selling something that wasn't truthful.

Once again the king heard exactly what he wanted to hear. Both father and son found their way into Gerar in their travels. The king, performing his kingly rights, could take the unmarried women of their entourage to be part of his own harem. Both times the men told the king the girls were their sisters. Both times the king heard what he wanted to hear. Both times the king believed what he heard. Both times the king barely escaped with his life from God's judgment. Both times the king ended up with a *Downtowner* magazine!

Discerning the truth can be difficult at times. When I took over the job as recreation pastor at Germantown Baptist Church, we revised the rules of the recreation center to include people from the community. We faced a little bit of difficulty with some that desired the building to serve the members only, but we were able to accomplish the policy revision with some help.

One morning, shortly after the center had opened, a couple of long-time members walked into the secretary's office. I happened to be standing there. They pointed out that some people from another church in town (our main "competitor") were talking to some people in the fitness weight training room about Jesus. I commented on how great that was and how the building was doing what it was designed to do.

After they left, my secretary pointed out that I had heard what I wanted to hear in their statement. They had not been pointing the experience out to me to affirm my policy decision. They were truly afraid someone would choose to follow Jesus and go to the "other" church instead. I suppose they thought we had some sort of "squatter's rights" to anyone in our fitness room that trusted Jesus.

Jesus said, "Look, I am sending you out as sheep among wolves. So be as shrewd as snakes and harmless as doves." (Matthew 10:16) In other words, "Practice some discernment." All that glitters is not gold. Don't hear what you want to hear, and don't believe everything you hear. Help whomever you can, but beware of men selling *Downtowner* magazines!

Whom will you listen to today?

THE DISCIPLES: IDENTITY THEFT? (MATTHEW 16:13–20)

I always seem to be mixed up with someone else. When I was growing up, I always had to correct people at church that would call me Mark, the name of my younger brother. I suppose I understand the mix-up, as we were both incredibly handsome! Well, something mixed them up just the same.

I would get compliments for the great way Mark sang in church. Even people that should have been close to one of us or the other would call each of us by the other's name. I believe I was called "Mark" more in that church than I was my own name. It got to be very frustrating.

While I was on staff at Germantown Baptist Church, I met another David Waddell who was employed by FedEx and used the fitness facilities I was responsible for in the church. I had heard of other David Waddells but had never met one. I assured him that if he ever overheard people in the church claiming David Waddell stunk, they were not referring to him. Later that same year I met a person with the name Waddell David. No kidding, the name was completely reversed! I felt as if I were in Superman's Bizarro World.

When I joined the faculty at the University of Mississippi, another person with the name Waddell joined at the same time. I was in recreation management, and he was in exercise science. Both programs were housed in the same department. His name was Dwight, while mine is David. We've figured we're related somewhere closer than back to Adam and Eve's generation. Dwight had an earned doctorate, and mine was an "ornery" (not honorary) degree. His name is plastered on numerous publications and presentation posters, while my name was placed on dry erase boards with funny pictures.

Despite the differences, the identity confusion continues and worsens.

Since both of us are potentially "dwaddell" in Ole Miss e-mail protocol, I took that option and Dwight opted for one slightly different. This fact alone drives students, faculty, and administration nuts. It's amazing how many e-mails we get sent that are actually meant for the other. I warned Dwight early on that if he got an irate e-mail from a girl claiming he was stupid, uncaring, and insensitive that it was for me. Especially since he was married and I was not. We've had misdirected e-mail from our personal friends outside the university. I recall that one e-mail came in one summer from one of my former students to Dwight. He replied with questions as to whether he was writing the correct Waddell, to which the former student replied, "The one I want used to be in church work and walks with a brace on his leg." I lost the brace with some restorative surgery later, but I was so glad this was the impact I had made on him.

I had a student halfway through one semester tell me he would miss my test on Friday. I told him I wasn't having a test on Friday, yet he was certain I was. I asked him which class it might be in which I was having a test, and of course he mentioned Dwight's class. You did catch that this mistaken identity occurred halfway through the semester! Where my brother and I share family traits, Dwight and I don't look anything alike. Dwight actually looks more like our basketball coach, Andy Kennedy. Coach Kennedy ironically started at the same time Dwight and I did.

Now, to make matters even worse, our offices are right next to each other. It's fun to see students that don't know either of us needing one of us and getting the deer-in-headlights look on their faces as they approach two Waddell offices standing side by side. When I'm approached with a question that is actually for Dwight, I'll point out that he is the intelligent one. For some reason I don't get any arguments on that response. One lady who came by looking for Dr. Waddell stopped by my office first and asked if I was Dr. Waddell. I stated, "Oh no, he's the good-looking one," to which she replied, "Oh yes, that's right."

I don't offer that differentiating option anymore.

The disciples and other people that followed Jesus had some similar difficulties. There seemed to be confusion in the land as to who Jesus was. A lot of people were looking for a military leader to beat up the bully from Rome. Rome had conquered the area and were not known for being nice people. They could require a Jew to carry their heavy pack for a mile without question or complaint. There are, no doubt, untold stories of abuse, rape, and murder taking place at the hands of the Romans. Of all the oppressors in Jewish history, the Romans would have been considered the worst up to this point. Nazi Germany probably took over first place in that category in the twentieth century.

Others in the land were looking for a political leader to reestablish the kingdom of David. In that God promised there would always be an heir of David to sit on the throne of Judah, it made sense that Jesus, an heir of David, could be the one. History lessons come to life in the hearts and minds of the Jews as they imagine life with a strong king to rule the world.

A few were actually seeking a Prince of Peace as testified by the prophets. The messianic age of peace, in which lions and lambs would lie together, was the dream of some of the Jews. It was to be an age of peace without oppression or war.

When any of these groups looked at Jesus, they would mistakenly see who they wanted Jesus to be rather than who Jesus really was. I still have that tendency today. I try to make him my pain reliever, problem solver, and positivity provider. I was originally made in His image; now I'm trying to form Him into my image.

Jesus asked the guys once who everyone thought he was. Apparently the people got Jesus confused with others just like people in my life. The answer was that the world thought he might be Jeremiah, or Elijah, one of the prophets, or his cousin John the Baptist. For me it was a brother; for Jesus it was his cousin!

Jesus asked them who they thought He was, and Peter jumped out with the claim of Jesus being the Messiah, the Son of the living God.

Despite that solid answer of confession as to Jesus' claim to being the Christ, the disciples still struggled with the identity of Jesus. Even after His death and miraculous resurrection, the disciples still thought He was someone else and asked if He was going to restore the kingdom to Israel. They specifically asked this at the time Jesus rose into heaven. It wasn't until the Holy Spirit guided their thoughts that they understood the true meaning of the kingdom.

Whom are you confusing Jesus with?

PETER: JUST HOW FAR CAN I TAKE THIS? (MATTHEW 18:21–22)

My driving record is far from perfect. I have a problem with speed. I like to go faster than I'm supposed to. I find that when I drive, my mind wanders. A wandering mind doesn't pay attention to speedometers, and therefore the foot gets heavy and off I go. I drive an automobile without cruise control so my speed is dependent on my concentration.

I was stopped once coming home for lunch in Springfield. I was told I was traveling 35 in a 15 mph zone. I don't know what overcame me, but I laughingly told the officer, "That's because I was able to slow down some before your radar gun was triggered." He appreciated my honesty and recommended I approach the judge with the option of defensive driving classes. I still got the ticket.

The street I lived on in Collierville was in a 20 mph zone. There was a slight hill at the top of the street, and then it leveled out toward my house. I used to make the turn onto my street and get a little speed going before letting up off the gas and seeing if I could coast the rest of the way home. I got to where I knew that if I could push it up to a certain speed I would be able to coast all the way into my garage.

One Sunday afternoon I was taking one of the boys to choir practice at church when I was pulled over. The officer explained there had been a lot of speeding happening on our little road and they had been requested to monitor the street. He asked me where I worked, and I embarrassingly confessed I was employed by the church. The officer let me out of a ticket because of my being a minister. I explained

I wasn't on any ministry work and was just taking my child to choir practice. He still let me off the hook.

I've lived with the thought that one could always go about ten miles an hour over the limit. When on the open road I'll watch the speedometer so that it stays around nine miles per hour over the limit. I suppose the same concentration could be used to actually comply with the limit too, but that thought usually doesn't cross my mind. One summer I was doing some consulting work with Kirby Pines Retirement Community in Memphis and was going to visit a friend for supper. I was ticketed for going 72 in a 65 mph zone. I explained how I thought they always gave you ten more than the limit, to which the officer explained, "That wouldn't quite be the definition of a limit, now would it?"

I find that I don't limit my boundary push just to speeding. I practice it in other areas of life as well. If I tell a little lie then it gets me out of big trouble. If I think certain impure thoughts, then I rationalize that it's better than actually acting them out. I argue with myself that the pushing of the limits actually keeps me out of greater sin. I don't necessarily need correct facts to make an argument with myself.

What is it with me that I want to find the minimum or the limit and push it as close as I can to the edge? I always want to know what the actual requirement is or how far I can go without it being sin. *If I stop at this point, is it sin yet? If I don't do that, am I still okay?* I had a favorite youth pastor that always said, "If you are asking about whether the limit is sin or not means you already know the answer but just don't want to hear it."

There were some people that asked Jesus about what was the greatest commandment. I feel the people wanted to know so that they could decide which ones to keep and which ones could be pushed to the boundaries or ignored completely. My younger brother, when joining a different denomination of believers, told me they don't have ten commandments, but rather four commandments and six suggestions! I am good at trying to determine what it means to respect parents or what actually constitutes adultery. I push the limits to determine how far I can go without being wrong, or "sinful."

Where can we go a little faster than the limit and not get caught? When Jesus spoke to the crowd on a mountain, he gave new limits to us. Whereas we had heard it was wrong to kill, Jesus added that it was equally as wrong to hate. Whereas we had heard the act of adultery was wrong, Jesus told us that thinking about such things put us in the same penalty. The people at that time wanted to interpret divorce laws to suit their own purposes. Jesus established the limit for all of that as well.

Peter once posed a question to Jesus about how many times we should forgive our brother for an offense. I believe Peter wanted to know this so he could push right up to the limit and keep from sinning. In other words, he wanted to know at what point he could not forgive a person. He was asking how many times he could hold a grudge without being wrong.

Peter thought he was being generous in offering seven times. Imagine his shock when Jesus raised the limit to an astronomical number of seventy times seven. With the seven times seventy, I realize that if I start keeping count then I haven't really forgiven the person. I think I just made Jesus' point all over again.

When Jesus was facing death, he warned the disciples about what was going to happen. He told how they would all run away. Peter had to push the limit, of course, and boldly exclaimed he would not run even though all the others would. Peter was warned that he would not only deny knowing Jesus but that he would also do it three times. Peter later received the forgiveness of Jesus for the denial. Three times Peter denied knowing Jesus, and three times Jesus commanded Peter to feed His sheep. Jesus wanted to make sure Peter knew he was receiving grace and mercy. I also like how Peter is never referred to as the denier after Jesus' return from the dead. That's a good example of the seven times seventy.

So instead of pushing the boundaries, perhaps we should settle into the place God has us in today and enjoy where God is taking us within His speed limits.

What limits are you pushing?

JAMES AND JOHN: WE GOT THIS ONE, GOD (LUKE 9:51–56)

It wasn't too long after my brothers and I had finished college and moved out that the terrible news came to my father. After a long career in the steel industry and the last ten years at one particular company, he was being let go. Downsized. Fired. Just at the time he and Mom could start enjoying themselves, the fun of being empty-nesters was dashed with the prospect of finding work while being fifty years old. It made me want to hurt someone.

His company, looking to expand, asked Dad to train another staff member to do some of what he did in anticipation of the business growth. Once the other person was trained, they informed him that he was going to be let go as part of a company downsizing plan. It was the classic story of Hollywood: Boy gets job, boy is loyal to employer, employer turns out to be a corporate faceless demon, employer lets boy go. I wanted to add a new ending to the Hollywood story, that being "Son hurts someone."

For the next fourteen years of his life, I had to watch and listen as job after job rejected him. For those 168 months, Dad worked at various odd jobs but never really what is considered a career position. He lost any possibility of really enjoying his retirement due to the loss of savings over those years. When he passed away, there wasn't a lot to be left to Mom because of the financial situation caused by termination and age discrimination.

I really wanted to hurt someone.

To this day I forgive them, forget about it, and then remember all over again. Then I want to hurt them again. It is funny how others can step all over me, take advantage of me, and even hurt me and I can forgive much easier than when they do the same to a loved family member or friend.

I can't begin to count how many of my friends in ministry lost their jobs because their new pastor just simply didn't want to work with them. Untold men and women have lost their positions in churches because they were pawns in the ungodly competition for power in the church. Just a couple of years ago, a man with whom I worked and remain good friends was dismissed from his staff position in a closed-door, secretive personnel team meeting. Sounds like the "double secret probation" claim from *Animal House* to me. Despite promises of letting him work a couple more years till retirement, the pastor decided he wanted a change that day, and out he went. I had a new mantra for people entering the ministry: "God loves you, and the pastor has a wonderful plan for your life." I still want to hurt someone.

I remember times in school when punishments were doled out with no thought of fairness or justice. Teachers that gave preferential treatment to other students treated the rest of us as if we were second-class citizens. I had one teacher that allowed many in class to call him by his first name but told me specifically to call him by his last name. He commented that only his friends called him by his first name. I, apparently, was not his friend. Have I mentioned I wanted to hurt someone?

While my oldest son was in seminary, a church that had committed to support him financially backed out of the deal. This left my son and his family scrambling to make up the missing money. Now I really wanted to hurt someone.

Noticeably absent from this writing is the number of people I have wronged. I know that several of them would have loved to have the assignment of the C&P committee. In academia, that's the shortened version of "curriculum and policies committee." In dealing with hurt, it should be "consequences and punishments committee."

The idea of taking on God's judgment and doling out our own punishments is not new. The two brothers James and John had to deal with a similar temptation. Jesus once sent messengers to a Samaritan village in order to get things ready for His visit. Jews and Samaritans got along about as well as die-hard avid college football rivals. The people of Samaria didn't want Jesus there because He was heading for Jerusalem. James and John saw this and wanted to pray down fire from heaven to destroy them. These two got the idea from some of their Old Testament Scripture study, in which they found that God did smite some people with fire from heaven. They really thought they were being spiritual by offering the complete removal by fire of the Samaritan race. Jesus rebuked them and redirected His visit to another location.

I am so John and James on this one. Even though God said vengeance belongs to Him, I hope He'll sublet it out to me from time to time. I don't want to kill these people, just make them hurt as much as they hurt my family, friends, or me. If I had fire-from-heaven abilities, I know I'd take advantage of the power. No one in the city of Oxford would be safe in the traffic circle roundabouts if I had access to fire from heaven. Short-tempered fast-food personnel would also be in danger. I don't even want to think about what I'd do with ill-tempered receptionists on call center lines.

What a joy that would be to walk into my dad's former place of employment, introduce myself as Wes's boy, and then smite them right up in flames. I did mention that I wanted to hurt someone, right?

James and John had to learn, as I constantly do, that the punishments and consequences of certain actions are not up to us. God is the only one remotely qualified to perform that task in the complete light of grace. That's what fire-from-heaven prayers tend to neglect—grace.

How did the lack of fire from heaven turn out for me? Well, Dad's termination gave me some experiences to help countless other people in similar situations. Amazingly there are war stories of hundreds of people that were downsized by a faceless corporation.

The friends that lost staff positions found new places to serve, and God used them in amazing ways. The time in between situations taught them a dependence on God they would have never experienced if they had moved from one paycheck to the next.

The teacher that was not my friend gave me the motivation to succeed, which would not have arisen in me otherwise. I learned from him that life is not fair and that I had to figure it out one way or the other.

My own son, in my fit of rage over how he had been unfairly treated, reminded me that God's grace covers their decision just like it covers my sin. In the moment he shared this with me, I thought about a Darth Vader–and–Obi-Wan Kenobi moment. I realize that James is now the master.

Whom do you want to hit with fire from heaven?

BLINDED PARENTS: THROW HIM UNDER THE BUS (JOHN 9)

In most situations, my brothers and I would stand up for each other in difficult or trying situations. We would try to rip each other apart, but if someone else threatened us, then it went from "every man for himself" to the "all for one and one for all" cry.

Occasionally, however, we were not that good to each other. In some situations we let the others fend for themselves. I always felt it odd how some memories stick with us while others depart. When I was only six or seven, we were all playing at a local playground. I thought it would be funny to spit on the slide so that the next person would slide right into it. I know it sounds gross and disgusting, but that's what drives the spirit of a young lad from time to time. I didn't realize that the next person on the slide was my younger brother. When he went through the saliva, he had a look of disgust and then hurt in his eyes. I remember to this day that feeling of "throwing him under the bus."

As I grew older, I leaned more and more on what my peers thought about me than on my family. Getting the approval of my friends and peers was more important than protecting my family. I wouldn't always be the quickest to my brother's defense if I thought it would hinder me being part of "the group." Popularity drove my decisions, behaviors, and actions.

Our family moved from the Missouri cities of Kansas City to Springfield during my seventh-grade year. The following summer, we moved into another new house in a new school district. Beginning eighth grade as a four foot ten, ninety-five-pound skinny and scrawny young man did not help my desires to be a part of the "in crowd."

Then I got my opportunity.

The crowd of other eighth graders waited at the bus stop earlier than my older brother, who rode the bus to the high school. Allen would always have to walk by us to get to his stop. The guys at the stop started making fun of him. It was that typical insecurity of a person that tries to be more than he is by making fun of someone else that is more than he is. This was the process of knocking another down as a way to elevate oneself. As I remember, they were cruel and unusually mean in their comments.

Then I joined in. I look back on it with great regret and pain. The look on Allen's face that morning still haunts me, as does spitting on the slide. The guilt drove me to apologize that very night. Allen has long forgiven and maybe even forgotten about it. One of his greatest attributes that I continue to learn from him was his ability to not allow others' thoughts about him determine how he felt about himself.

What is it about making someone else happy that causes me to throw my own flesh and blood under the bus at the bus stop? Why was it so important to have others' approval and their pleasure? I found it wasn't original with me, however. There was a set of parents that did the same thing to their son in the story John tells us.

Their son had been born blind. When Jesus approached the young man, his disciples asked if it was his sin or his parents' sin that caused the blindness. They needed to know which party to throw under the bus. Part of our human nature is to discover the fault or guilt in someone else's problem. If it is his own sin, then our legalism pays off with the feeling that he deserves what he's got. If the sin is his parents', then our legalism can confirm that the next generation pays for the sins of their forefathers.

It tickles me how our minds have to know who is at fault, as well as any gory details we can hear. I find myself not just sharing that someone is going through a divorce but also gossiping about who did what in the situation. We often disguise this conversation as "the sharing of prayer requests." The disciples were, in a way, trying to discover the same thing.

Jesus answered that it was neither person's sin but instead that the blindness was so everyone could see God's work displayed in his life. I know the disciples were not expecting that answer. There's no way for my legalism to get a grip on that statement! Jesus made a couple of mud pies and placed them on the man's eyes and told him to wash them off in a local pool of water. When he did, he was able to see.

The community started to see this guy walking around without the benefit of a cane or others. They questioned whether this person was really their blind friend. It was an unbelievable miracle, except for one thing: Jesus performed it on the Sabbath, and that was a no-no to the man-made interpretation of the fourth commandment, regarding rest on the Sabbath.

The religious leaders questioned the man blessed with vision for the first time in his life. They just couldn't believe a religious person would do a healing on the Sabbath. Finally the formerly blind man claimed Jesus was a prophet.

Doubts started to arise as to whether he had really ever been blind. So his mom and dad were brought in, who immediately admitted he was their son. They admitted he had been blind at birth. They admitted he could now see. But then, when pressed about who Jesus was, the folks stuttered and stammered and didn't want to give the truthful answer. They knew the "popular crowd" wanted to toss insults and teases at Jesus. Mom and Dad, instead of coming to the defense and representation of their son, threw him under the bus of the religious leaders rather than take them on themselves. They spit on the slide and hurled taunts, so to speak.

In denial, the parents were able to keep their place in the synagogue, but they lost their place with their son. In refusal of the truth, the parents verified the miracle but vilified their son. The parents could now sacrifice kids (baby goats) at the altar because they sacrificed their kid (child) with the authorities. They had a chance to support the savior, but instead they chose to protect their own place in society. I had the chance to right my wrong. I can only hope his Mom and Dad at some point realized they were throwing their son under the bus and sought forgiveness as well.

The man known as the formerly blind guy placed his belief in Christ that day and worshiped Him. He really bothered the leaders when he asked them if they would like to be disciples of Jesus as well. They claimed to be disciples of Moses because they didn't know who Jesus came from. The man then really let them have a dose of indignation when he argued that Jesus came from God.

The religious leaders reminded him of what he must have heard all of his life—that he was steeped in sin at birth. Despite his being able to see, all they wanted to remember was what they thought was his reason for blindness. They were not going to be lectured by a man they believed to have been born in sin.

The religious leaders were told that while this man could now see, they would remain blind because they could not see the truth. The fear of losing face with these blind leaders cost the parents in their relationship with their son.

I can't think of much worse than losing a relationship with family to impress others. I know this because of my own stupidity, saliva, and sarcasm. Thank God the same Son of Man that cured this blind guy has helped me to see through His eyes as well.

Watch out for the bus!

PETER'S FRIENDS: SURPRISE, SURPRISE, SURPRISE (ACTS 12:6–19)

I have been able to witness some amazing miracles in my life. I have had the joy of seeing some marriages restored, people healed, and lives turned around. One in particular was a young lady in one of the churches I served. When she was about to become a teenager, it was determined she had leukemia. The church gathered together to begin praying for her. Together we confessed sins, anointed with oil, and asked a big, bold prayer for healing.

During the next few weeks, things turned to the worse for this lovely young lady. The doctors did all they could, but it looked pretty hopeless. The family was finally told to gather together and say their good-byes to their daughter. Some in the church felt defeat as they reasoned God had not answered their prayers. Other skeptics stated that they felt miraculous healings were rampant during Bible days, but not so much anymore. Still many others refused to listen to the pessimism of the report and continued to pray. I hate to admit I was mainly in the pessimist camp throughout the process. I prayed believing, but I had what I like to call "healthy doubt." With healthy doubt, I'm not very disappointed if God chooses another path. The problem is, it is still doubt.

The girl's mother, on the other hand, refused to gather the family, saying that her little girl would one day stand before crowds of people to tell them about this amazing miracle.

God did it! He performed the miracle! The little girl was healed. It remains one of the most amazing feats of spiritual healing I've ever seen. The young lady was literally brought back from the dead. The doctors, of course, were shocked, and yet they knew this one was out of their hands. Some of the physicians, I'm sure, were people of faith. Still other doctors that don't believe in God must be in awe of all that happens without scientific backing.

You can imagine the buzz that was going around the hallways on the following Sunday. Then I overheard a couple of different conversations with the same response: "I was praying for a complete healing, but I never really expected it to happen." How can you honestly pray for something without really believing it will happen? In fact, why am I surprised sometimes when prayers are answered? Gomer Pyle was a country character on the 1960s sitcom *The Andy Griffith Show* and was later spun into a show bearing his own name. When something unexpected would happen, he'd burst into a smile and say, "Surprise, surprise, surprise!" I felt like Gomer Pyle at the announcement of the healing.

When I went through my second bout of atrial fibrillation, the doctors told me to stay strictly to my diet and to start some light exercise. I became quite the legalist in maintaining my diet. My exercise regime started slowly but began to pick up as I regained some strength. I told the cardiologist and others that I was not only sticking to the diet and exercise but also that I was praying for a miraculously strong heart and the three-month checkup.

I know that when King David was praying for a new heart, he was referring to renewal from sins he had created. I know this because David and I share more than just a name. I've prayed his prayer numerous times. In this case, however, I was praying for a new heart, in the physical sense. I knew God was capable of taking a nearly dead muscle and bringing new life to it. I had a nurse friend that was keeping up with my ejection fraction. It apparently has something to do with heart output. I thought she was getting rather personal when she first asked the question!

Two nights before my checkup, I was talking on the phone with a friend. He asked what my best-case scenario was for the checkup. I told him I'd been praying for the stronger, new version, model 2.0 heart. He asked me what my backup plan was in the event the doctors didn't tell me what I wanted to hear. I pointed out that if you pray for a miracle, then it's not real faith if you create a plan B. I knew I was in God's hands one way or the other, which is where He wants me all along!

Chalk up another miracle! The doctors at the three-month checkup told me I had the heart of a healthy man. He asked how it happened, and I pointed out, "Some diet, some exercise, and a whole lot of prayer."

"Well, it worked!" The doctor said.

Praise God for that. I feel like saying "Surprise, surprise, surprise!" after prayers for miracles are answered with a miracle.

Why do I sometimes ask God for miracles and then find them hard to believe when they happen? Well, my friend Peter (a constant character in these writings) was actually on the other side of the coin for this story. He had been placed in jail by Herod, who was arresting Christians to make the Jews happy. Herod had already killed James, the brother of John, with a sword. The church started praying for Peter's release. I have a feeling that if this group was anything like my groups, some people in the crowd wondered if God could actually spring Peter from jail.

That night an angel came to visit Peter, and the chains popped off his arms as if the angel were as wise in the ways of the Force as Luke Skywalker. The angel then escorted Peter right past the prison guards and dropped him off at the house of the prayer meeting.

Peter knocked to get in, but fearful that it might be Herod, the fellow believers remained locked up. If this group is like me, they would find a knock on the door in the middle of the night to be extremely alarming. They probably got very quiet so that whoever was at the door would think they were already asleep and go away. A servant girl named Rhoda went to listen at the door and recognized Peter's voice on the other side. She went to tell the congregation that he was outside.

I love this next part. When she told them Peter, the man they'd been praying to be released, was outside, they told her she was crazy and that it must be his angel. The prayer was made for a miracle; they just didn't think it would actually happen.

There was a story I heard once about a community where a local group of believers were praying for the removal of a business in town that was teaching atheism and the idea that God does not exist. The news of the prayer meeting was broadcast over the entire community so as to draw a great crowd. On the night of the meeting, several of the community's pastors and civic leaders prayed that God would remove this business.

Later that night, the building that housed the business was struck by lightning and burned to the ground. Gomer Pyle would be saying, "Surprise! Surprise! Surprise!" No people were harmed, but the building itself was beyond repair. The owners of the business brought suit against the church, claiming they had caused the business to be destroyed. The church denied the charges. The judge summed it up by saying he had a group of atheistic businesspeople believing in the power of prayer and a church that did not.

Oh, what powerful prayers we can pray, especially when we believe they can come true. I wonder just how many times I've prayed for someone's healing or someone's salvation with a voice in my head saying, "This will never happen." Oh God, grant us the faith of the servant girl that prayed for Peter's release and then was not surprised to hear his voice.

"Surprise, surprise, surprise!"

THE ANGEL'S ANGLE: "FEAR NOT" IS GOING TO WORK WITH GIDEON (JUDGES 6–8)

I've never been a big fan of the horror flick. Getting scared and wetting my pants along with suffering a lifetime of nightmares is not my idea of a fun night. Despite my lack of desire for horror in movies, I have been a fan of scaring people all my life.

I was but a young lad when I found the section of the store that sold the little rubber snakes. I thought it would be a great gag to put one in Mom's pillow. The trouble was that I went to bed early, so even if it did startle her, I would never know it. Also, because she lived with four boys (three sons and one husband), not much ever really startled her.

During my freshman year of college, I went to a recreation conference that was held near Disney World in Florida. Following the conference, the group I traveled with went to the amusement park. I purchased one of those scary masks that are made of flexible rubber and cover the entire head. When I arrived home, I noticed through the living room window that Dad was still up. I sneaked into the house and quietly tiptoed up beside him. I put the mask on my head and jumped in front of him, screaming like a wild man. Dad calmly looked up and said, "Hello."

Realizing the gag hadn't worked, I took off the mask to show Dad it was me. At this point Dad had a fearful look on his face and screamed, "Aaahhh! Put the mask back on! Put the mask back on!"

In my years of church work, there were two men that held this same love for scaring others. Like me, both of them would wet their pants if they were the one being scared. We would hide behind doors, wait for each other in hallways, and jump in front of each other just to get a scare out of the other person.

Jesse had survived years of abuse from ministers long before me. One of the classic scares he received came from our pastor, who had placed a life-size cardboard cutout of some denominational worker with an Uncle Sam–style pointing finger, saying, "I want you in Sunday School." The pastor placed the cutout in Jesse's closet and waited for the reaction. While it scared Jesse in a huge way, the greatest scare came that night when a report was called into the police about a possible break-in at the church and the pastor had to open all the doors of the church as a part of the safety check. The poor cutout almost bit the bullet, so to speak!

The greatest scare I ever gave was to my friend I worked with in Natchez. He was vacuuming the sanctuary, and I sneaked in the front, crawled underneath the pews, and then laid down on one row and folded my hands as though I were a dead body. He was pulling the vacuum as he walked backward down the aisle. When he passed me and saw me, he was unable to speak and just groaned. He almost took my place on the pew as the dead body! I don't believe I've ever seen a man's eyes bug out as much as his did that day.

Now, don't feel sorry for these men. They pulled great scares on me and the rest of the staff as well. I was scared particularly well in Natchez one day as I was in an old organ chamber of the former auditorium-turned-gymnasium that had become a storage closet. My friend heard me in the room, sneaked up to the outside wall that was mostly acoustical mesh, and pounded on the wooden frame, screaming at the top of his lungs. Later he helped me clean up the mess I created on the storage room floor.

There seems to be a great rush during "near-death experiences" like this. I know in the Bible several people got to feel the rush of being near death as they met an angel from heaven. Rarely is an angel greeted with a joyful hello. The Scriptures, in several places, refer to observers being scared out of their wits! I don't recall ever coming face-to-face with an angel, but if I did, I have no doubt I would have the same reaction as when my friends hit me with surprise attacks. In reality, the most popular reaction to meeting angels in the Bible is fear. That's why angels learned early on to say "Fear not."

Samson's parents had to deal with "fearing not." An angel came to tell them about their son and the way they were to raise him in order to serve the Lord. They prepared a meal as an offering, and not only did it burst into flames, but the angel also ascended into heaven on the flame. In their best days, Siegfried and Roy could not have duplicated such a show! Samson's dad, Manoah, was sure they would now die, but his wife reassured him otherwise. After all, why would God give instructions on how to raise a son and then kill you before the son was born?

Mary and Joseph dealt with angels firsthand, as did the shepherds around the arrival and the announcement of Christ's birth. In each case, the plea to "fear not" came out of the mouths of the angels.

Gideon, however, played the greatest scaredy cat of the entire Bible. When he first met an angel, he went to all kinds of trouble to prepare a meal for him. The angel told Gideon to place it on a rock, and when he did, the angel touched it with his staff. In the same way as it is for covered-dish dinners at church, when the staff touched the food, it instantly disappeared! The angel disappeared, and Gideon thought he was a dead man. The Lord assured him he was not going to die and proceeded to give him a plan to redeem His people.

Gideon lived in a constant state of fear. It was as if he never knew when Jesse or David would bang on the organ chamber wall or be hiding in a closet. The first job God gave Gideon was to destroy the temples of false gods that had found their way into Israeli villages. Gideon, afraid to vacuum backward, now did the job at night for fear of being caught. He was afraid of his own family in this act! So Gideon, let me get this straight. The Creator of the Universe tells you to do something, and you're afraid of people? Unfortunately I understand all too well!

I really love the next battle Gideon faces. God tells Gideon how to go about destroying the enemy. God understands Gideon all to well. The story even reads with God saying to Gideon, "If you are afraid to attack, go down to the camp ... and listen to what they are saying."

Gideon heard the dream about a loaf of bread attacking their camp and destroying them. With that, he knew he must roll on with the battle plans! He resisted the temptation to look around every corner or slowly open closet doors and stood up to his fear and defeated the enemy.

What is it about the appearance of something holy that scares us to death? For me it's usually because I'm trying to hide or conceal something sinful. It's our system of judging ourselves, and the comparison to the holy is scary. When we compare ourselves to a heavenly creature, we tend to pale in the comparison. Our sin makes us fear death, and the holiness of the angel reminds us of where we have fallen short.

Despite our lacking in measurements, the angels are always quick to comfort and reassure us. "Fear not." These two words have the ability to put our past at peace. The same two words provide faith for our future. It is in these two words that the angels remind us that our hope is in heaven.

What scares you?

ANANIAS AND SAPPHIRA: I THOUGHT I GOT AWAY WITH IT (ACTS 5:1–11)

I was born ornery. Some claim it was in the birth order. I'm a middle child, born in between two brothers. One is fourteen months older, and the other is twenty months younger. Three boys were born to my poor mother in the span of thirty-four months. This explains the crying and the cursing, but we can't figure out why she never took up drinking.

Being in the middle meant I often had to attract my own attention. I turned this into an art form that carried me throughout my youth and often carried me to the *P* offices—those of the pastor or principal, depending on my location.

My orneriness grew and developed into seeking fun with or without the attention of others. If I could do something sneaky and get away with it, I found that was just as much fun as everyone discovering my ways and commenting on them. I found that entertaining myself and not being found out was just as much fun.

All of this takes us to the mission trip of 1974. Our youth group went to Nevada to operate a children's camp and present a musical to different groups and churches. One of the young men that accompanied us was one of my main targets for teasing. It wasn't that I didn't like him; he was actually one of my good friends. It was just that he was so easy to tease!

The men got the joy of sleeping on the wood floor of the American Legion building in this particular town. Sleeping bags were laid side by side, up and down the entire floor in two rows. An aisle was creating at the feet of the bags for those late-night "devotionals" caused by drinking too many soft drinks before bedtime. One of our sponsors, known as Papa John long before the pizza guy made the name famous, would bed us down and attempt to quiet a group of high school boys.

One night, feeling my oats, I decide to start bothering my friend. I know his tolerance level to me is low, which only drives my evil. We'd just received the "serious" warning about getting quiet and going to sleep. I made eye contact with my friend in the neighboring sleeping bag and reached up and scratched the bag right next to his ear. It hardly made any noise at all, and if ignored, I would have rolled over and gone to sleep.

I knew my friend could not ignore it.

So I'd scratch at his bag and he'd whisper for me to stop. I'd wait a moment and then scratch again. He'd whisper a little louder for me to quit. This continued until he got loud enough for one of our sponsors to tell us to get quiet.

"You guys hush!" Papa John screamed out.

I'd give it a few seconds. I'd let him relax and then scratch by his ear once more. Each round would start off with whispers to stop, and each attempt would be greeted by a louder request until Papa John warned us again. It was on the third round that Papa John got up and walked over and asked him what the problem was. When he explained what I was doing, Papa John tried to get my attention. "Dave! Dave! What are you doing?"

"Huh, what?" I replied in a feigned sleepy stupor. I expressed my innocence with a look of misunderstanding aimed at Papa John. I claimed I had no idea what he or anyone was talking about.

Papa John warned my friend to settle down, which for us teasers is a win-win. He got in trouble, and I got away with it. Papa John returned to his sleeping bag.

Basking in my glory, I looked over at my friend, smiled really big to show off my victory, and scratched his bag one more time.

At this point he jumped out of his bag and started screaming and waking up the entire group. He was pointing at me and accusing me in front of everyone. The rest of the group knew the game, but then

Papa John was screaming for everyone to get quiet and go to sleep. I decided it might be a good time to quit.

The next morning at breakfast, as I was feeling rather confident after my successes of the night before, Papa John was waiting for me. He saw me and said, "Come in the kitchen, Dave."

Upon entering the kitchen, I was greeted with the knowledge that Papa John had known all along what was going on. He said to enjoy my short-term victory because if I kept him awake the next evening, something would be scratching me. I felt it best to quit while I was behind. It makes me wonder how much of my shenanigans I actually got away with and how much just wasn't worth addressing.

The early church had a couple of sleeping bag scratchers too. In an attempt to meet the needs of the poor and hungry among the new believers, people were selling houses and land and were donating the proceeds of the sales at the apostles' feet for distribution to those that needed assistance. Even a man named Joseph did this. It was noted that the apostles called him Barnabas, which means "son of encouragement." It was also noted that the people were all in one heart and one mind and believed that possessions were not personal anymore and shared with all.

One couple named Ananias and Sapphira sold a plot of land, but instead of giving the entire amount to the church, they sneaked some into the cookie jar and reported the amount of the sale as being that which they donated.

Peter, being well trained in the psychology of Papa John, asked Ananias about the missing funds. Peter pointed out that the property was his and the money was at his disposal. Then Peter asked him why he'd do such a thing and then said, "You have not lied to men but to God."

Ananias, being well trained in the orneriness of David Waddell, never had the chance for damage control or confession. Upon hearing Peter's declaration, he suddenly died. I'm glad I dealt with Papa John and not Peter! Some men took Ananias's body and immediately buried him.

Three hours later, Peter brought in Sapphira to question her. She was unaware of the previous interrogation and internment. When asked if the donation amount was the amount they had made on the sale, she tried selling the same lie, which resulted in the same outcome. The same men that had buried her husband were waiting on her as well. The church had one of their first funerals that afternoon.

One of the lies we often buy when we sin is that we can get away with it. Oddly enough, skeletons don't like living in the closet and will often come out at the most inopportune times. The Papa Johns of this world are waiting for us at breakfast. Peter will ask the questions that demand honest answers.

What is it you think you're getting away with?

AARON: I TOSSED IN THE GOLD AND OUT CAME THIS CALF! (EXODUS 32:1–24)

There should have been some kind of medal. At the very least, a certificate printed out on paper. Survivors of Royal Ambassador cookouts should start their own support group and Facebook page.

The Royal Ambassadors was an organization for boys in the Southern Baptist Church. I often called it Boy Scouts Baptized. The term, to make it easier to say, was shortened to RAs. It offered the same badges, pledges, and wedgies as the Boy Scouts did, along with the introduction of some sort of mission study.

The best part of being in this organization was going on the campouts. Badges could be earned as a part of these campouts. We would hike, practice knife crafts, go on snipe hunts, and use hand axes, along with all sorts of camping fun.

As in any camping experience, the food had to be top-notch. These were not any old camping experiences. The Friday night hot dogs were cooked on a stick, followed by roasting marshmallows. Lunch the next day generally was bologna or peanut butter and jelly sandwiches. The meal, however, that took the cake was breakfast and the special hotcakes cooked and served on those Royal Ambassador campouts.

Somehow the adult leaders hadn't read how to actually cook a pancake. They'd throw some water in the Bisquick mix and stir it up and pour it onto a pan that was way too hot. So in order to cook the pancake all the way through, the chef had to pretty much let it burn on the outside. My father would try to coach them in the proper way to prepare a pancake. Dad had a Barney Fife style of teaching, saying words progressively louder and slower. Unfortunately Dad had no influence on the pancake chefs. Excuses would fly about it not being their normal skillet, the fire on the camp stove being unevenly distributed, and how they'd be better if mixed with milk instead of water. One of the leaders, in explaining the blackened pancakes, stated, "You have to mix the stuff up and just throw it onto the pan. They just always seem to come out this way"

One year Dad got hold of the pan before it was too hot. He carefully mixed his batter and threw it on the skillet. This father of three boys watched it closely, tending to it as if it were his only baby daughter. When he flipped it, the pancake became one of the most beautiful sights ever seen on one of these journeys. It was a golden-brown pancake.

News traveled quickly across the campsite that a golden-brown pancake had actually been created. It literally became an idol as experienced RA campers began worshiping the thing. You would have thought it was in the shape of Elvis Presley or something with all the oohs and aahs it received. Dad was so proud of himself. He turned to get a paper plate and the syrup for his masterpiece, and while he was turned, my older brother stole it and scarfed down half of it before Dad got back to the griddle.

Dad was careful not to cuss on a church campout. But he did call my brother a dirty rotten scoundrel, a slob knocker (this was one of Dad's favorite names), and a pancake thief. While Dad was lamenting the loss of his pancake, one of the other cooks prepared a really nice blackened pancake to help him drown the loss of the golden-brown one. Alas, it was too late. The golden-brown idol was gone, as was my dad's appetite.

This cooking philosophy of throwing something in the pot was not new to the camping leaders of my youth. No, the method had been long before tested. While Moses was up on the mountain conversing with God and collecting commandments, Aaron was in the camp, trying to keep things calm. Rebellion began to rule, and they demanded of Aaron to create a god they could see. After all, what had the God of the mountain done for the people of Israel other than release them from slavery and bondage, defeat the mightiest army known to man at the time, and care for them in both physical and safety needs?

Aaron, giving in to the pressure, took up a collection of jewelry, watches, and class rings. He tossed them into a pot and melted them down. He formed it all into a golden calf idol. The people pointed to the golden calf and said, "These are your gods, O Israel, who brought you up out of Egypt."

I guess sometimes people cannot believe without seeing.

Aaron announced the next morning that they would set up a feast for the Lord. The people got up early and gave burnt and fellowship offerings, ate, drank, and indulged in revelry.

Meanwhile, the Lord told Moses about all that was going on at the bottom of the mountain. God was ready to start all over with Moses, but Moses turned down the offer and begged God to turn from His anger. When Moses returned from his time with God, he questioned Aaron as to what happened. Aaron was quick to blame the people. Then Aaron had the most amazing answer for what had happened. He said, "We threw the gold in the pot and this golden calf came out!"

You would think he was cooking campout pancakes.

Now, being in the education business, I have heard some unbelievable excuses as to why projects and papers are not submitted on time. It used to be only that dogs had eaten the assignments, but now there's a whole new group of technology-related excuses; printers that go bad from campus-wide viruses, flash drives that won't open, and hard drives that crash just after saving the A-grade paper are the top excuses shared among colleagues. I have to admit, however, that Aaron's excuse is the best—that they threw in the gold and this intricately sculpted, decorated calf came out.

Before I give Aaron too hard of a time about this, I should remember some of my burnt pancakes in life. Far too often I turned up the heat and got in a hurry with things in life that are supposed to take time. Relationships that didn't form as quickly as desired were traded for more superficial ones that gave more immediate gratification. I took shortcuts in jobs in order to get my way back into a career path I felt I deserved. I have the greatest sense of impatience while waiting on God to do something or anything in my life in certain areas. I often throw good stuff in the pot and form worthless stuff out of it instead of waiting for Moses to return on his own.

Truth be told, I just can't toss in a bunch of priceless aspects of life and watch a golden calf come out. The real treat is in gaining the same right to speak to the Creator as Moses was given. To get that, however, means taking my time and making sure the pancake comes out just right.

What are you tossing into the fire? What's coming out?

THE DISCIPLES: I AM THE GREATEST (LUKE 9)

I never served in the largest church of any community. The ones I worked in were always the second largest or smaller. That fact did not stop us at trying to become the best church in town. It became like a personal drive. If we weren't going to be the largest, we'd at least be the most loving or the one that offered more programs. The drive was held deep inside me to become the pace-setter church. I wanted to be a part of a church that was viewed as the greatest church of all time. Competition for converts would become huge to us. While new converts are always great, I'd get more excited over someone changing churches to mine than I would for a sinner to become a saint! Especially if the newly found saint didn't want to join my church!

Monday mornings in many communities of faith include an evaluation of the previous day's services. Pastors get together at their weekly meetings with other community pastors to hash out the day and compare notes. Now, the evaluation usually focused not on how to communicate the gospel in a clearer manner, but rather on how many people we had in church compared to the bigger boys. We somehow felt better if they had an "off" Sunday in attendance.

You would think an auction was taking place because of all the conversations going on. One would offer, "We had forty-five in Bible Study!" Another would toss in, "Well, that's nothing; we had forty-six in worship." And on and on the contest went. It seemed as though the first liar didn't stand a chance in the game, as some church always topped what was stated last. If it wasn't more in attendance, we'd claim a much richer worship experience. It was easy to determine the losers, because they'd be the ones actually talking about the worship experience rather than how many bodies were present. Of course, we all know that in church attendance it is possible to be present in the body and absent in the spirit!

It wasn't any different for those of us in church recreation. We'd gather at our annual conferences and talk about how many players we had in our sports program and how many teams and how many leagues filled the gyms or the baseball fields. The first liar, again, didn't stand a chance, as the number seemed to grow with each story. Like pastors, if we didn't have the largest numbers, we'd claim the more quality program or better-trained leaders. We had to have something to put us into the "greatest-ever" discussion.

One church I served decided to open the doors of their recreation center to the community. One morning a couple came into my office and told the secretaries and me that someone from one of our "competitor" churches was telling other people in the exercise room about Jesus. I thanked them for sharing the story and talked about how wonderful our mission was to be open for everyone. It wasn't until after they left that my secretary, much more powerful in discernment than I, pointed out the couple had not shared the information with me as a good thing. They would rather the "competitors" not come around. That was more crucial to them than telling someone about Jesus. For goodness' sake, we don't want him to become a follower of Jesus and go to some other church and make that other church the greatest!

The search for attention and greatness has always consumed my heart. I desired it in athletics but ended up playing right field. For those that may not know, playing right field in Little League generally means you are the least talented person on the team. I desired to be the greatest on my speech and debate squad, but there were always several that could talk circles around me. I desired to work in the largest church and be recognized as the best church recreation director, but there was always a larger church and always many leaders more talented than me.

Ever have that feeling? Do you want to be the greatest in what you do? The disciples of Jesus had that very same feeling. They even expressed it in a conversation or a debate over which one of them would be the greatest in Jesus' kingdom. I can imagine some of the arguments. Peter is making himself the spokesman. John is reminding everyone that he's the disciple Jesus loves. Judas is equating trust with the money bag as being the top dog. Andrew is thinking about how most of the disciples wouldn't be there if not for him. I wish I knew Bartholomew better. He probably had his own argument.

The funny part of this story, according to Luke, is that just prior to the discussion of who was the greatest, there was a situation where a man took his child to the disciples in order to heal him. The disciples were unable to heal a boy with an evil spirit. So they went from failure in fashioning a faith-based miracle to a discussion on the disciple that was most desirable.

Jesus overheard the conversation and had a little child stand next to Him. He explained that it is the welcoming of a child that determines greatness. When you welcome a child, you welcome Jesus. When you welcome Jesus, you are actually welcoming God. It's one of those dichotomies of the Scriptures; when you become the least, you are then the greatest.

The disciples, not quite catching on, had John confess that they had met someone that had enough faith to drive out demons but was stopped by the disciples because he "wasn't one of them." Jesus of course rebuked him not to stop anyone that was "for" them.

The discussion apparently never had closure to it, because later in the story Jesus, at the last supper with his disciples, tells them of the impending suffering and death. Jesus proceeds to declare that one of his closest will betray him. As they're discussing who it might be, the topic quickly moves once again to who is "the greatest."

Jesus constantly reminds us that being the greatest has nothing to do with numbers of people, programs, and places. If we are to be the greatest, we should become the least. This is a hard lesson for me, because my ego wants me to be the greatest in human terms. It's far more difficult to be the greatest by being the least. That means helping those that can't pay me back or, even worse, that may have no influence or contact to make sure my being least gets headline coverage.

In mathematics, the following signs are used: “>” is used to indicate something being greater than the other. “<” signifies something being less than the other. So in order to be > we must learn how to be <.

So we find the person that needs his or her feet washed. We search out the person that is alone and needs a friend. We smile at the cashier even though she just let someone go through the twenty-item line with twenty-two items. The gospel is spread by being the least. So in a twist of words, in order to become great, we must be least, but not last!

“Be <.”

DAVID: SOMETIMES YOU CAN OVERPLAN THESE THINGS (2 SAMUEL 24:1–17)

My sons and I loved to watch movies together. The youngest would sometimes watch the same movie consecutively up to three or four times before getting another one to watch. One of our favorites was *¡Three Amigos!*.

My boys were also great at remembering particular lines out of the movies. Once, their mom was entertaining a very dignified and cultured guest. She also happened to sell Mary Kay cosmetics. The middle son approached her and quoted a line from the movie, saying, "Can I have your watch when you are dead?"

One of my favorite scenes is when the Three Amigos break into the bad guys' fortress to rescue the fair maiden. They create a plan to get inside, and two of the three are caught. The one that makes it finds the damsel in distress. He explains the plan of how they are going to get inside. She explains that they have done this and asks what is next. His statement is classic: "We didn't really expect the first part to work, so we didn't plan the next step. Sometimes you can overplan these things."

That last line became very important to me.

When I graduated seminary, I went to work for a church in a Texas town called Port Neches. It was a great place to live, and I have fond memories of my time there. My first two sons were born in that area. I worked at the First Baptist Church.

Ego can sometimes get the best of a person. While working at this church, we were honored with the privilege of picking up the famous evangelist James Robison for a one-day crusade in the Golden Triangle. Doing well for a man like this could really make us look good and would do wonders for bringing new people into the church. If we could impress his team, then we'd be recognized above and beyond all other churches and staffs.

The four of us on staff plotted and planned as to which cars and vans we would use to get sound systems, equipment, and the evangelist to the meeting in Port Arthur. Finally it was determined that the senior pastor, Brother Tony, and his wife would take James Robison to the hotel for a luncheon that would launch the crusade. The luncheon was to be videotaped in order to run as a public service announcement on Port Arthur television. The other two staff members, Ed and Troy, would take their vehicles to escort the other personnel attending with Reverend Robison. I would bring the church van to pick up all the video and sound equipment. Our Custodian, Jesse, pulled the seats out of the van to prepare me for my responsibilities.

Again, let me remind you that sometimes you can overplan these things!

As the time came for their flight to arrive, we all synchronized our watches and hit the road to put the plan into effect. The senior pastor took off with his wife. I ran by the associate pastor's office and told him I was getting the keys to the van. He told me the pastor had changed the plan and that I was to ride with him and Jesse would be bringing the van. I questioned the statement but was told emphatically that the change had been made.

We arrived at the airport, and the entourage came pouring out of the gate. Quickly the pastor escorted Reverend Robison and his wife toward the exit. The rest of the crew was discussing with our other two staff about the logistics of getting the team and the equipment from the airport to the hotel. I waited for the tech crew while keeping an eye out for Jesse with the church van. Sometimes you can overplan these things, you know. As Brother Tony was headed away from everyone, Ed called out to him, "Brother Tony, Jesse is bringing the van, right?"

Brother Tony pointed right at me and said, "No, David brought it."

Sometimes you can overplan these things.

We waited for Brother Tony and his crew to take off before going into full panic. In that this was before the age of cell phones, I rushed to the phone to call the church and request Jesse that get there as quickly as possible. Ed put one person in his car, which seated five, and took off for the hotel. Troy and I were stuck with three additional men and a vanload of equipment, sitting on the runway, awaiting a van.

Finally we decided to scrap the videotaping of the session, so we put the minimal amount of sound equipment necessary into Troy's Chevy Chevette. The compact Chevette was Chevrolet's answer to the late 1970s gas crisis. The equipment took up a good portion of the car, leaving enough room to carry one additional team member. Although he fit, he did have to sit sideways, sharing the seat with two speakers and an amplifier.

I was left standing with two remaining Robison Evangelistic Team members and the remaining equipment. I'm usually good at striking up conversations out of nothing, but that day I was blank. I had nothing! I kept a watch for our white van with purple lettering to come around the corner. One of the team sarcastically commented on the efficiency of our plan. I told him it is possible to overplan these things.

Jesse arrived with the van and parked it directly next to the equipment. He got out of the van, took one look at me, and shook his head while saying, "Four college-educated men. Four college-educated men."

Jesse unfortunately found out that sometimes you can overplan these things. Another Jesse was the father of a man that overplanned an event as well. His son was King David. King David got the idea of taking a census of the people of Israel despite it not being in God's heart to do so.

David, in a desire to bolster his own pride, wanted to find out how many people were under his rule. Out of this he would also determine the size and strength of *his* army. He forgot his might came from the hand of the Lord. Joab, one of his leaders in the army, tried to convince him not to take these steps, but David insisted. He wanted to overplan this thing.

The writer of the story in 1 Chronicles tells us that prior to the census, numerous battles were being won around the countryside. The battle plans drawn up were being blessed by God, and amazing praise was being given to David for his many victories. Working on David's pride, Satan, at a prime moment, mentioned the census. Sometimes you can overplan these things.

"Why not show everyone how powerful you are" may have been the way Satan let the thought enter David's mind. "You've won all these battles [emphasis on "you"], so why not let the world know how powerful you are by counting all the people. The number should be so astronomical that no one would ever want to fight you." Sounds like a great overplanned plan to me.

So, instead of going with the original plan God laid out, David decided at the last minute that someone else was bringing the van. God was not pleased and offered David the choice of three consequences: three years of famine, three months of death by enemies, or three days of an extreme plague. David opted for the three days. God stopped the angel of death just prior to it destroying Jerusalem.

David learned the lesson of going with God's original plan. He wanted to commemorate the moment by building an altar. The land belonged to someone else who was willing just to give it to David. David's response was "No, I insist on buying it for the full price. I will not take what is yours and give it to the Lord. I will not present burnt offerings that have cost me nothing!"

Learning from David, I have built a mental altar of my own. Whenever I think of the Beaumont, Texas, airport I laugh all over again and am reminded that God's plan is the best plan. He really does know what He's doing! Maybe I should ride it out and see that His plan works rather than reinventing the ideas toward my own plans. Perhaps pride will someday die and we'll get to the airport with the van in tow, ready to launch life's plan of action.

Who's getting your van?

BARN BUILDER: PUNKED! (LUKE 12:16–21)

I was freshly out of seminary and serving in my first church. For some reason I had imagined the daily routine of church work as all the staff hanging around the copy machine, singing hymns and talking about the deacons in the church. Oddly enough, we rarely sang hymns.

One of the joys I discovered early in working on a church staff was the coffee break. This particular church had members that would bring by homemade blueberry muffins, assorted sweet breads, and occasionally some donuts. It made the first break of the day quite interesting, as we would share something fairly unhealthy and talk about things that had nothing to do with the work of the church.

One particular day, I walked into the office, and sitting on the pastor's secretary's desk was a brown paper sack that appeared to be full of some kind of fruit. It looked like apples of sorts, but having grown up in the city, I had never seen anything like this.

I asked the secretary if they were for coffee break. She said they were. I asked what they were, admitting I'd never seen them before. She said, "They're called persimmons."

I further admitted I'd never heard of them either. She commented, "They're a little green, but even still it's one of the juiciest, sweetest fruits you'll ever put in your mouth."

I could hardly concentrate on my work that morning. While some people eat to live, I have always found myself living to eat. The clock finally struck 10:00 a.m., and off I was, running down the hallway to experience this beautifully sweet and juicy fruit.

As I got into the kitchen, a couple of the staff members were washing off their persimmons in the sink. The pastor then came in and screamed at the top of his lungs, "All right! Persimmons! I hope they're green enough!"

I was buying the lie.

I took one in my hand and washed it off. Looking at the situation in hindsight, I realize a couple of things. First, no one else had actually bitten into a persimmon. Second, they were all watching me as if it were Christmas morning and they were dying to see what was in the package I was holding. Third, the pastor was talking about how good they were, and in cases like this he was never to be trusted. He was notorious at setting others up to be punked.

So I looked at the fruit and thought to myself, *If it's that good, why waste time with a little bitty bite?* So I took a huge chunk out of the green persimmon.

That's when the reaction began.

Everyone was now grinning as I felt the skin on my cheeks slowly pull in between my teeth and toward my tongue. My eyes began to cross, and my bottom lip started to quiver. The sourness of this "juiciest, sweetest fruit" was about to kill me.

Now, a sensible man would have turned around and disposed of the bite by spitting it out. He would look straight at his pranksters and say, "Ha ha, very funny." I, however, am not a sensible man. I kept chewing.

Often in the lifespan of men, we are stricken by the appearance of our male ego. The male ego is that gene our gender carries with us that gets us into trouble by making us do things we are too old or physically unable to do. My male ego said, "Swallow it."

With each chew I could feel the moisture in my body being sucked into that bite of persimmon. It seemed to grow larger and larger in my mouth. *If I can just swallow it then the punking won't have the same impact,* I thought. Yet in my heart I knew I'd been had! They had played a joke on the jokester, pulled a prank the prankster, and punked the punkster. It was more fun for all of them because the one that usually was on the other end of the prank was now standing there with a mouth full of green persimmon. I finally gave up, spat it out, and enjoyed the laughter of those I work with.

Getting punked is something that happens often enough that television shows have been created to demonstrate how it occurs. A good punking, or prank, involves the believability of a lie. There is an element of truth in the lie, which makes it believable and therefore makes the punking achievable. Another example of someone that fell for the lie of a "juicy green fruit" is with the punking that occurred to the barn builder in Luke's gospel.

The barn builder was the character in a story told by Jesus. He was a farmer and apparently ended up with a stellar crop. With no place to store what he had gained, he reasoned he would tear down the old barns and build new ones to hold all his wealth. The Bible doesn't say what the crop was, but I'm guessing it was persimmons!

You see, the barn builder had bought into the sweet and juicy lie that he would live a long time. He was set for life financially. He reckoned he might as well enjoy some of the wealth. His motto became "Take life easy, eat, drink, and be merry." I know that lie has punked me numerous times.

But God called him a fool and took his life from him that night. All he had worked for was gone. The lie about security through material items did him in. All of his wealth could not prevent death by green persimmons. His punking had a bad taste similar to mine, the difference being that his punking resulted in his death. Someone else would enjoy all his work and riches.

There is a tendency to think we can wait for tomorrow. It's one of the best lies we encounter in setting up life punking scenes. I can apologize tomorrow. I can restore relationships tomorrow. I can make that change in my life tomorrow. I can build bigger barns to store my green persimmons tomorrow.

In our own strength, we think we can handle the persimmon if we only keep chewing. We fall for the punking because we depend upon ourselves. We fall for the punking because we want to believe we can do it on our own. We fall for the punking because we rely on our own strength.

Anyone care for a sweet and juicy green persimmon?

HOPHNI AND PHINEHAS: MEMBERSHIP HAS ITS PRIVILEGES (1 SAMUEL 2:12–17)

We would sit right next to the window. In the summer it was more comfortable because the church air conditioning didn't always work. Plus the view was incredible from the window. You could see the corner and the parking lot where the deacons hung out. In fact, if you worked it just right, you could make it appear that you were pondering what the teacher was saying while watching the activities that were going on in the parking lot.

The Bible tells us it's a good thing to aspire to be a leader in the church. I would look at these deacons in the parking lot, and even as a young boy I aspired to be in their positions of leadership at some time in my life. Please know it wasn't because of their servant spirit, although I'm sure they possessed such. It wasn't their grasp of theological truth or their knowledge of the Bible. I aspired to be like them because they got to skip Sunday school and stand on the street corner smoking cigarettes.

These were the men that went to the business meetings in the church and made the pastor look uncomfortable. They seemed to be in control of the finances, the rules, and pretty much the church. Those that didn't sing in the choir took up the offering each week. Did I mention they didn't have to go to Sunday school?

Despite my aspirations, I never took up smoking cigarettes; nor did I become a deacon. I did, however, become one of the ministers in the church. While I never felt as powerful as I remember those guys from childhood being, I can still say membership has its privileges. As one of the ministers, I didn't have to go to Sunday school!

As I got into the work, I also realized there are a few other perks to the position. I was driving one of my sons to church one Sunday afternoon for youth choir practice. The stretch of road our house was on had a slight incline, and the speed limit was fifteen miles per hour. To be honest, I always viewed that as more of a guideline that a set rule. When I was going toward the house, I used to build up speed at the top of the incline and see how far I could coast with the car in neutral. The game was to see if I could get the car all the way into the garage without putting the car back into gear. I would build up a good bit of speed in order to win this game.

This particular day, however, I was driving up the incline at a rate of speed higher than the posted guideline. One of our local city policemen put on his lights and pulled me over. He asked for my license and proof of insurance and asked me where I was going. I told him I was taking my son to church. He asked what I did for a living. I was embarrassed at being the recreation minister at this church and having to admit I was breaking the law. But I told him that I was employed by the church. He excused himself and walked back to his car.

In a few moments he approached me once again. He handed me my license and said he did not wish to give me a ticket, as I was a minister on my way to church. I must have lost my mind or found my conscience, but I argued with him for my son's sake. I insisted that I was not on my way to church for any ministry opportunity but was just a father doing his duty of transporting his child. The officer refused to budge and allowed the warning to stick. He reiterated his belief that he did not want to ticket a man of God.

Wow! Membership has its privileges.

On a few other occasions, I tried this same excuse when pulled over for speeding. Go with what works for you, right? I was enjoying this benefit of this membership of ministry. Finally the word must have been released that the white blur of a Chevy Cavalier was not on its way to emergency ministerial duties. I received a ticket and decided it might be better to slow down than to wear out an excuse.

During the early days of Samuel, there was a priest by the name of Eli. His two sons were also priests, and they set up a few guidelines of their own. These may have been some of the first to take advantage of the "membership has its privileges" club. The story goes they would steal the best part of the food from the burnt offerings set aside for the Lord, have their way with women servants of the church, and refused to heed their father's warnings about their behavior.

Hophni and Phinehas were playing the system beautifully. The law did allow them to stick a fork into the burnt offering for their portion, but they would twist the fork so that it would pull out more meat than normal. They were eating some of the finest foods. Each of the boys was enjoying the manipulated company of the servant girls. They ran the temple, called the shots, and maintained a holy image. They didn't even have to go to Sunday school! They definitely knew how to play the system to their benefit. I imagine you might have even seen them outside the synagogue, lighting one up! They knew how to claim ministerial service to the ticketing officer for their own benefit.

Eventually the "privileges" caught up with Hophni and Phinehas, as happened to me. The wrath of God was upon them, and they both suffered death because of their lack of listening to their father and failure to repent of their sins. It's not odd that you don't see many, if any, people name their sons Hophni and Phinehas.

I often wonder how much giving I would do if I lost the privilege of deducting it from my taxes. Would I be a cheerful giver if the only benefit of membership was in the giving? How many of us would join certain groups of believers if it didn't benefit us for business or for our social standing? What if those benefits were removed and we had to face the ticketing of our speedy pride?

What privileges will you give up?

THE EARLY SHIFT: WHAT'S MY SHARE? (MARK 20:1–16)

I have never been the top dog or head honcho of a company or organization. I have always been at the lower part of the totem pole of leadership. This also has led me to be on the bottom rung of the salary ladder as well. I might add that I have done my fair share of complaining about this matter.

One place I worked always gave percentage increases to their staff. It had nothing to do with merit or the cost of living. Usually it was just what the financial people in the church decided they could do for us in the next fiscal year. Each year I'd see the gap between those salaries above mine growing larger and larger. It's simple math that 5 percent of a thousand is more than 5 percent of six hundred. I might add that I have done my fair share of complaining about this matter.

I asked that pastor about setting it up so that every other year we do a dollar increase rather than a percentage increase to maintain balance in the personnel budget. His claim was how unfair that would be because I'd be getting a higher percentage raise than everyone else. I tried explaining the concept again but couldn't get past the inequity of giving me a higher percentage increase. I might add that I have done my fair share of complaining about this matter.

Another church I served didn't offer me a raise in pay after my first year of service, because during the year prior to my arrival my predecessor had received a large increase. I reminded them that my predecessor was not paying my bills or feeding my family, but it was to no avail. I might add that I have done my fair share of complaining about this matter.

It's difficult to keep morale up and running when you see yourself doing the same amount of work or more than those being paid more. It becomes an easy way of getting yourself into trouble. I like to call them "whine and jeez" parties. I whine about my low salary and long hours. I think about the injustices and say, "Jeez!" I've always understood "jeez" to be a combined form of the phrase "gee whiz!" There are other derivations for the word, but I'll go with mine.

The worst of these situations was where one of my coworkers received a salary increase to the same level as mine despite not having nearly as many responsibilities or years of service. The reason given to me was that this man was the same age I was and therefore we should be paid the same.

I lost my temper and professionalism with this situation more than any of the others. I went to the pastor and complained vehemently about it. After a long discussion, I was told there was nothing that could be done. This was the decision of the responsible committee, and therefore it would become the law! In the book of Daniel, an unalterable law was called the law of the Medes and Persians. Personnel decisions must fall under the law of the Medes and Persians.

I might add that I have done my fair share of complaining about this matter. To this day this will pop into my head and I will go through the whole process all over again.

Jesus told a story about some workers that went through a similar situation. A landowner was bringing in his crops and hired some people early in the day to help him. As the day went on, he realized there were not enough workers to adequately bring in the harvest. He hired more at noon. He then hired more in the middle of the afternoon and even made some hires with about an hour of sunshine left. Finally, by the end of the day, the task was completed and the harvest was brought in.

When the employer starting handing out the day's pay, the early shift noticed that the one-hour employees were making the same wage they'd been offered when they started. They got excited and assumed this meant they would be getting paid more. *If the crew that worked one hour gets our wage, then the employer must be raising our wages more,* they thought. Well, not so much. The employer paid them the amount they had agreed upon when they began.

I might add that the early shift probably did their fair share of complaining about this matter. You can imagine the "whine and jeez" party that ensued. After all, they worked all day, and others worked only half the day or even only an hour.

His argument was that as employer he could pay people whatever he wanted. Since they had agreed to work the day for a certain wage, they got that wage. Viewing the matter this way kind of leaves my "whine and jeez" parties without a reason for attending.

My time and efforts would have been so much more effective had I not been worrying about the "late shift" and had just done my early shift work. My complaining not only dragged me down but was also a constant morale killer with other staff members.

Jesus, in the parable, was teaching us to not worry about when the other workers come aboard. He was conveying that many that are "children of Abraham" will see the kingdom of heaven, as will a lot of last-minute Gentiles. Instead of "whine and jeez," we should celebrate with rhyme and glees! Let's sing and celebrate the late shift's arrival into the kingdom.

I should simply do what I know to do, even if I work longer for less pay. After all, this is what I signed up for!

JEPTHAH: THINK BEFORE YOU SPEAK (JUDGES 11)

I have a knack for being loud. You don't want to talk to me discreetly if there's anyone remotely close. Projection of my voice is not a problem. On the other hand, failure to keep it at a quieter volume is a problem. I've had sound technicians in the churches I've served claim I didn't need a microphone, but rather a sock in my mouth!

I left seminary and began working at my first church. The music minister was a fun-loving sort of guy. We hit it off quick. I knew I would like him right off when I saw he drove a 'Vette, just like I did. Of course ours was a Chevette rather than a Corvette.

I also discovered that he was a Pink Panther junky. I love Inspector Clouseau (that's Chief Inspector) as played by Peter Sellers. Many of the quotes on my Facebook page are statements made by the famous French detective. I immediately nicknamed the music guy "Cato" after Inspector Clouseau's manservant. He would call me Chief Inspector. Others could often hear us in the church hallways, talking about one of the scenes and laughing like crazy.

In the movies, the inspector has Cato trained to attack at any time. So the music guy and I would do this with surprises and scares around corners or in dark hallways, or by sneaking undetected into each other's offices. Clouseau pronounced words uniquely, and I was careful to mimic him. "Cato" was actually pronounced "Ket-O." It was not rare to hear me walking toward the music office saying, "Cato, are you hiding there in the dark?"

Quite often in my life, I speak before thinking. This gets me in various degrees of trouble. This one particular day I had just come to work and checked in at the main office to check messages and pick up mail. I cautiously approached the first corner to the main hallway. I looked down the hall and saw the lights on in the church library and further down the hall in the music minister's office. Two beams of light partially lit the hallway from these two rooms. I loudly whispered, "Cato? Cato, are you hiding there in the dark?"

There was no response from his office, so I knew he must have been busy or on the phone. So I said it a little louder. "Cato? Where are you hiding, my little yellow friend?" (This was a phrase the inspector used to describe Cato.) I was hoping for either an interruption or for laughter to burst out while he was trying to take care of church business on the phone.

So I started calling out for him loud enough that he was bound to hear it. I was pulling every Clouseau/Cato line I could think of, saying them with momentary breaks for his response or laughter. After several attempts, I heard some rustling in the library. I took a few steps to see what was going on. There, around the big circular table in the library, sat all the leaders from the church's women's organization. Of course, they had been trying to pray, and every time they had started, I interrupted with one of the Pink Panther lines in the hallway. Apparently they were not fans of the Pink Panther movies.

Speaking before thinking is not a good habit to create. Just recently I accepted an opportunity to teach first aid to a group of outgoing student teachers. After accepting, I realized I had just booked the Friday afternoon of Labor Day weekend. No early flights or early travel for me. Often I accept assignments without thinking of what may lay ahead in my life. I speak and then think, which usually gets me in trouble.

Speaking before thinking got another guy in trouble once. Jephthah was the son of Gilead by a prostitute. Because of his background, his own people drove him out of town. Later, when he was needed to lead an attack against the Ammonites, he was welcomed back with the promise of being the leader. The Spirit of the Lord came upon Jephthah, and he advanced against the Ammonites.

Then he spoke without thinking. He made a vow that if God handed the Ammonites over to him, he would offer the first thing that came out of his house to greet him upon his return as a burnt offering. Vows back in that day were pretty serious. If you broke one, you would get stoned. And that isn't in the modern-day meaning of getting stoned. You would literally get rocked to sleep. Well, you get the idea.

God gave Jephthah the victory! Unfortunately, upon his return his one and only child, a daughter, came running out to greet him. As sick and sad as it sounds, he kept his vow and sacrificed his daughter.

I have to wonder, since the Spirit of the Lord was upon him, whether the vow was really necessary. Perhaps a little more trust in the Spirit that had come upon him would have done the trick. I understand the Jephthah dilemma though. It's easy to talk quickly and commit yourself to something without thinking through all of the consequences. Perhaps I should think a little and pray a lot before hastily deciding things that impact the direction a life will take, especially if the off-the-cuff promise involves and impacts other people.

Wait! Don't say it just yet ...

SHECHEM: I MISREAD THAT ONE (GENESIS 34)

Pranks seem to keep certain staffs going. I am not sure why I was always a target in particular prank planning, but there seemed to be a deep sense of glee if I could be had. One such prankster was a man I worked with while I was in seminary. After seminary I moved to the Beaumont, Texas, area, and not too much later Ray was working in a church in that area as well. When I moved to the Memphis area, Ray was already at a church in Memphis. We seem to be inseparable.

I served on staff at Polytechnic Baptist Church in Fort Worth, Texas, as their recreation minister during my years at seminary. They were involved in a new trend in church growth that created a second location. It was one church that met in two different buildings on Sunday morning. My office was in the new location, which also housed a "gymnatorium." This was a design that made the space a gym during the week and a worship center on Sundays. The main church office was in the old location, near Texas Wesleyan University.

The normal run for me would be to drop by the main office to get any messages or memos and then drive out to the new location to operate the recreation center for the afternoon. Part of my duties as the recreation minister was maintaining supplies in the new location, such as Styrofoam cups and plates for different social functions. Of course, being a young seminary student, I was avid in my desire to impress the powers of the church.

One particular day I stopped by the office and saw a pink slip noting a missed call and a request to return the call. This was prior to the invention of voice mail. Businesses used these pink sheets that were titled "While you were out." There was space to write a number and check whether to return the call or just read the message. The name listed on the pink slip was Ruby, and a phone number was included as well. The message line read, "Please contact, has a great deal on cups."

I immediately went into daydream stage and saw myself saving the church hundreds of dollars which would, of course, be diverted to world missions. Thousands of African children would someday sing my praises in heaven for the ripples of my cup decision.

I could see it was in Ray's handwriting, so I stopped by his office to see if he had any more information on the call. He simply said the lady could make me a great deal on some cups if we were interested. I went immediately to a phone in the office and dialed the number.

The call was answered with some sort of mumbling or muttering. I didn't really catch what the person on the other end said. I proceeded to ask whether Ruby was there. The person got her on the phone. I introduced myself as being from the church and asked her about the deal on cups. I told her the church always likes to get their hands on a good deal. She said, "Excuse me?"

I repeated my name and my request, to which she inquired whether I was serious or this was some sort of prank. I assured her it was a serious request and that the church went through several cups a week.

That's when she said, "You know this is Ruby's Brassiere Shop, right?"

I knew I had been taken. I had completely misread that one and fell right into the trap. I was the one then mumbling and muttering. I apologized for having the wrong number and hung up. A good prank has to have an element of truth in it to work. Ray had picked a perfect one for me, using my responsibilities and a classic play on the word "cup."

Shechem once made a similar error with far greater consequences. Shechem was the son of Hamar, the leader of the Hivites. Jacob purchased some land from him in Canaan in order to pitch his tents. Shechem was attracted to Dinah, Jacob's only daughter, and ended up raping her. Jacob heard about the violation but kept quiet about it until his sons returned from the fields.

Shechem's dad offered to pay whatever price Jacob saw fit in order to get Dinah as his wife. Jacob's sons pointed out they could not offer Dinah without the men of the city becoming like them in circumcision. They argued that this would make this city of men just like them. The men of Shechem would be, in a sense, a cut above, just like Jacob and his sons. There was an element of truth in this. Since the days of his grandfather Abraham, circumcision was making them the same. They didn't bother to explain the fact that circumcision was the way God designed to set His people apart from others.

So the men of the city thought through the possibilities. No doubt their thinking was that this meant they would get a cut of the share of Jacob's wealth by marrying the two. Being family would mean a great deal of wealth would be theirs as well. They probably went into daydream mode and saw their cups running over with sweet wine. So they agreed to the cut (circumcision), and all of the men of the city went through the surgical procedure. I can tell you, they completely misread this one.

Three days later, while the men were still in recovery from surgery, Simeon and Levi, two of Jacob's sons, attacked the city and killed all the men and took all their possessions as plunder. Jacob was a good bit upset by the situation and was fearful of what other Canaanites might do to him. The two boys felt it was a just punishment for what had been done to their sister.

My dad used to always say, "If it's too good to be true, then it's probably not true." Yet I find myself falling for half-truths and out-and-out lies that sound remotely spiritual. Sometimes I'm an easy mark because I don't practice my discernment skills. The desire of my pride to succeed overcomes the wisdom God has given me. Perhaps I should think things through more thoroughly. In this I allow God to fill my cup with whatever blessings He wishes to send my way.

When it comes to discernment, let's read it correctly so that our cups can run over!

JOHN: "FUR US OR AGIN' US" (LUKE 9)

I feel sometimes as though I need to join a twelve-step program to overcome some of my church background in my life. The support group meeting might go like this: "Hello, my name is David, and I'm a recovering Southern Baptist."

The crowd would call back, "Hello, David!"

It's a story that many have experienced. Not only fellow Southern Baptists, but people of all different denominations and Christian-based churches have exhibited the sense of arrogance that we have all the correct answers. We have assumed that our positions on certain items were biblically correct and the others were missing the boat. We knew that at the return of Christ somehow we'd be right and the others would be left.

I recently had a discussion with someone that was convinced Catholics had the corner on guilt. I argued for the Southern Baptists, but in reality I believe he is correct. I did win the argument that Southern Baptists are far more manipulative. Of course, anyone that loves Jesus will agree with me.

I grew up admiring two football teams, the Kansas City Chiefs and whoever was playing the Oakland Raiders. The same principle applied in baseball. I loved the Kansas City Royals and whoever was playing the New York Yankees. There was such a loved rivalry between these teams! My maternal grandfather had such a hatred for the Yankees as well. In fact, he used to refer to them using the name of the Broadway musical about the certain type of Yankees. One time I went to visit

Grandpa for a Saturday afternoon. When I returned home, Mom asked what we had done. I told her we watched a baseball game. She asked who had played, and I told her the Baltimore Orioles and [Grandpa's term] Yankees. She was, of course, shocked to hear such words out of my mouth. I told her that's what Grandpa called them. She quickly informed me I was not to say words like that, even if Grandpa did.

It was then I learned they were actually the New York Yankees and not the other name.

When I got into church work, I sensed the same kind of rivalry going on. You could almost sense the choir being the cheerleaders, doing the "Rah rah ree, kick them in the knee" bit. I got to the point where I loved two churches a person could join, the first being my Southern Baptist church and the other being anything other than the Methodist church. Thankfully I always referred to them as the United Methodist rather than copying the Yankees' previously mentioned title.

The arrogance got even worse. In the midst of our culture was a very good leadership development program for boys called the Boy Scouts of America. Thinking we could top that, we stole all their good ideas and "baptized" it into a church program. We started making our churches the one-stop shops for anything and everything the family needed. Sports programs, children's programs, music programs, and even classes in how to change your oil were offered. Of course, it had to be Southern Baptist or else it just didn't count.

When I attended civic meetings, I always felt this sense of arrogance about me. After all, I was from the flagship church in the community. Everyone wanted to be like us, with our great facilities, great program, and great staff members. I emphasized the great staff members, of course.

We got so good at this that we even started competing with other Southern Baptist churches. I interviewed at one church and met with people that had an interest in the recreation and sports program. One of the items they were using to influence me to work there was the fact that in the previous year they had a winning record against the largest Baptist church in the community. After we opened the recreation center, a couple came in to share that a couple from this larger church was telling someone in the workout room about Jesus. I thought it was great until the couple let me know they weren't sharing it as a good thing. They didn't want someone to believe in Christ if it meant going to "that other church!"

We had created a culture in which we were right and had the corner on truth. It didn't matter to us that we were slightly off because of our attitudes. Even if another church became successful in reaching people, we would offer excuses and rationalizations that left a feeling that everything must not be above board.

John, the disciple that Jesus loved, had a similar problem. There was so much to love about John, but he also had his "character" moments. In this case he told Jesus that he stopped someone from healing people in Jesus' name because the man wasn't "one of them." Apparently there was some rogue believer claiming the name of Jesus and healing people. Because that believer wasn't in John's circle, the belief was that he must be stopped. They couldn't afford to have someone other than Jesus' special twelve doing the work, right?

Jesus conveyed a wonderful truth to John and the others. "Do not stop him," Jesus said, "for whoever is not against you is for you." In my native Missouri hillbilly language, this would read, "If they ain't agin' ya, then they be fur ya."

This is the great truth for all to hear! Recently a friend shared with me that her pastor and her church prayed for my pastor and my church in their worship service. She said he picks a different Bible-believing church in town or Christian-based university ministry to pray for each week. I was amazed at the "kingdom of Christ" mind-set exhibited by this young pastor. So many leaders in my day would have never prayed for other churches privately, let alone in public. In fact, I remember several speaking "agin' 'em" for daring to believe differently in some of the less important aspects of our faith.

The realization that whoever is not against us if for us gives us freedom to rejoice at the growth of other churches regardless of what name they carry. Instead of becoming bitter when the bigger becomes bigger, we can rejoice that someone else is "fur us rather than agin' us." As Jesus states in the story of the lost lamb, we can be happy that the one lost lamb was found by another shepherd while the ninety-nine, of which many are in our individual churches, were set aside for the search.

The greatest irony in this story is that a few verses before this discussion with John, a man brought his son to Jesus because the disciples couldn't heal him. So not only was this other person healing people in Jesus' name, but the very ones that had been taught to do so were failing in their attempts. This is so ____________ (fill in the appropriate denomination here) of John!

So whose side are you on?

ORPAH: LET'S TRY THAT ONE MORE TIME (RUTH 1)

People make fun of me because of this. When I make nachos, I lay out the chips individually on the plate. I like to have them barely overlap so that none of the shredded cheese can escape through the chips down to the plate. I meticulously lay them side by side until the plate is covered. Then I take the shredded cheese and try to set an equal amount on each chip. Then I take one or a combination of bacon, tomatoes, bacon, refried beans, bacon, pulled pork, bacon, avocadoes, or bacon and toss it equally on each chip. Then the jalapeños go on top of all that, followed by another heavy covering of cheese.

I can look at the plate and feel my arteries hardening. I don't consider it a good plate of nachos unless the cheese forms a long, thin string as you try to remove one chip from the rest. I have a system of nacho preparation, and it works for me. It's orderly and organized.

One of my daughters-in-law was making nachos for me once and just grabbed a bunch of chips and tossed them on the plate. Then she just tossed some shredded cheese on top of all that. She was a little concerned when she turned and saw me in the corner in a fetal position, sucking my thumb. This method seemed so haphazard!

I'll admit it; I think I have developed a disorder. It's known as OCD. Yes, I suffer from an obsessive cheese disorder.

I love cheese on just about anything: nachos, grilled cheese sandwiches, cheeseburgers, and so on. The list is just about unlimited. I even get into pun wars with my brothers, students, and friends about cheese. Cheese puns? Some of the better ones I've been hit with are

"Ricotta Brie curding me!" and "Some might dis a Brie, but they're Gouda puns!"

The disorder started early in life with the introduction of a cheeseburger. It was from a place in Independence, Missouri, that still serves them. Dad took us there quite often. Since that time, I have never ordered a plain hamburger. It has to have the melted cheese on it. I even go to a couple of places in Memphis that serve great cheeseburgers. One of the places knows me as Mississippi Dave. I've earned a reputation from this great mom-and-pop-type shop.

When I was growing up in Springfield, Missouri, we would take trips back up to Kansas City to visit family. Dad found a cheese shop on the way, and it became one of our normal stops. We would go in and sample every kind of cheese possible before making a purchase. I carried on the tradition with my sons when we lived in that area. One of the things we all loved was the little sticks called string cheese. You could tear off part of the side and it would rip off as if it were a bunch of strings held together.

Please understand I'm not blaming my cheese addiction on my parents. They may have introduced me to the dairy product, but it was my own decision to consume as much as I have.

While in the seminary in Fort Worth, I ate at a particular restaurant that served nachos. I don't recall ever hearing about those before. I ordered a plate, and when they set it in front of me, it was love at first sight. Each round chip had its own bit of melted cheese and jalapeño on it. I was hooked!

Following my second round dealing with atrial fibrillation, I was placed on a special low-sodium diet. One of my first questions was about the sodium content of cheese. I didn't like the answer I discovered. It's high. I searched and found a low-sodium cheddar cheese, but it had to be delivered overnight, as the company would not guarantee the freshness of cheese delivered on a normal timeline during the heat of the summer. The overnight price was astronomically high. I was tempted.

After a miracle from God using prayer, medication, and exercise, the doctor told me my heart was getting stronger. When he asked me what I'd like to see happen from here, the first thing out of my mouth was "I'd like to enjoy an occasional plate of nachos!"

Part of my disorder is the way cheese makes me feel. I often use it to make myself feel better about life or circumstances. This is not good. If something goes wrong, I fix a plate of nachos. If a relationship goes bad, I order cheese enchiladas. I convince myself I deserve a greasy cheeseburger as a reward for something. It's a good thing that life is great for me; otherwise, I might weigh three hundred pounds with cheese.

Why do I have a tendency to return to such things for comfort? Why do food, alcohol, bad relationships, and gossip have such a return rate in my life? I think it is part of who I am as a human. As humans we experience the truth yet want to believe the lie. Of course, I'm certainly not the first to do so. The entire nation of Israel wished to go back to slavery in order to get away from the discomforts of the desert.

One of the greatest examples of a return is Ruth's sister-in-law Orpah. After their father-in-law and husbands passed away, Naomi offered them the chance to go back home or to go with her. Both chose to stay, but Naomi once again insisted they return to their own people, basically to go back to what had been working for them. Ruth opted to go with Naomi, while Orpah opted to stay. Despite seeing and hearing about the God of Israel at work in the men in her life, Orpah chose to stay with the Moabite gods. Ruth opted to see how God might work through the pain in life, but Orpah was more comfortable staying with gods that couldn't work than in seeking the truth of the God that is always at work. Perhaps she was also driven by a lack of trust in a God she believed killed her husband, brother-in-law, and father-in-law.

Ruth's story finished with an incredible ending. She was accepted by a man named Boaz and ended up marrying him. In the new family line she joined, she ended up being the great-grandmother to King David.

I once heard that rabbinic history indicates that, after Orpah's departure, an alliance was made by her marrying a Philistine king. Their offspring included one really tall child named Goliath. Now isn't that an interesting twist to the story?

I think it may be best to seek comfort in the Creator of cheese rather than in the cheese itself. Any other choice will string me out or shred me completely!

How are you going to slice it?

MARTHA: AN ORDER DISORDER (LUKE 10:38–42)

I had a couple of habits that would always drive my sons crazy. One dealt with light switches in the house. Certain rooms would have a light switch at two different places for the same overhead light. On this same panel would be another switch to work another light in the room or a hallway that was attached to this particular room. I worked hard to make sure that any switches that were double were always in the same position. If one of the boys turned the light on at one place and turned it off at the other, it left the double switches with one pointed up and one pointed down. I couldn't handle the thought of the switches being out of order and would turn the lights on and off at the appropriate places in order to ensure both switches on the double plate were either up or down together. I could be in the middle of a serious conversation that required great concentration, and I would lose all consciousness until the light switches were back in the same position.

The other habit was placing things back where they belong. I don't know how many times I got frustrated looking for a pair of scissors or a set of fingernail clippers. "Just put them back where they belong when you are through with them!" I would scream out into the house as I searched for particular items. I would continue with my rant, saying, "If you put them back where they belong, then you always know where they'll be the next time you need them!"

Some things are just supposed to be in order. There are consequences otherwise. I think I may have what could be called an order disorder.

My ex-wife had a habit of not putting jar lids back on tightly. She didn't want the lid to be so tight she couldn't open it next time it was needed. I had the habit of picking up jars by their lids. Despite smashed toes, bruised feet, and broken jars, I never could convince her to do otherwise. Of course, I didn't make any effort to pick up jars from the side either. There's an order to things that just aren't to be messed with.

I do the same thing when replacing a roll of toilet paper. I place the roll on so that when the toilet paper rolls around, it is removed with the remainder resting on top of the roll. It has an order to it. How about toothpaste? It should be squeezed from the end, not in the middle of the tube. Once again, there has to be an order.

I dated a girl once that informed me plates went in the dishwasher facing a certain direction. I argued that the water swirls and circulates and will hit every part of the plate. This was, of course, my way of facing the plates in the correct direction. To this she emphatically pointed out that I was to do it correctly. I think she meant "her way" by the use of the word "correct." I would set the plates in the direction she requested, but I hoped deep down in my soul for the plates to come out with food scraps and dirt still on them. There definitely has to be an order to these things.

One Sunday my pastor was making a reference to the creation of the world by using Scrabble letters as an example. Things working out by chance in the creation of the world is similar to being able to randomly drop Scrabble letters and spell out an extensive sentence. While he was making the point, one Scrabble letter fell onto the floor in front of the platform. It took all my energy to not get up and put it back in the box. I don't even recall what he said after that happened! At that point my world was out of order.

The winner of the silliness of my order disorder has to be my work in being organized and using a task list to get things done. I live by the to-do items on my list. If I think of something that needs to be done, I add it to the list. I used to keep a handwritten copy and would have to make a new list each day. The electronic versions are much better, because now I just have to change the due date when I procrastinate on the completion of a task.

The worst part of my order disorder in task lists is that if I perform a task to completion that is not on the list, I will take the time to type it into the list and then add a check mark to indicate that I've done the task I already completed before adding it to the list. I tell you, there must be an order to these things!

Martha, a friend of Jesus, had this same difficulty. She apparently liked things in order. When her brother died, she told Jesus that had He been there, the death wouldn't have happened. Some things are just supposed to be in order.

One of the times Jesus went to visit Martha and her family, she was in overdrive, getting everything to be just right. She was slaving away in the kitchen when all of a sudden she saw her sister, Mary, sitting at the feet of Jesus, listening to His story. Now, along with an order disorder, Martha also had a case of righteous indignation. "How dare she just sit in there and listen to the Son of God when there are dishes to be put in the right direction in the dishwasher!"

You must understand that in these times women did not usually sit at the feet of a teacher and listen. Their jobs were to get things prepared and ready for the men folk to feast or relax when the teacher was through teaching. Martha was doing what was usual. After all, there must be an order to these things. Mary got all caught up in the amazing truth that Jesus was talking about, and she forgot to put things back where they were supposed to be.

Martha did exactly what I would have done under the same circumstances. She tattled on her sister! She went to Jesus and complained that she had to do all the work. I know this complaint well! I always had to do more work than my brothers did. (Unless you were to ask them or my mom or dad.) I always did more work than anyone else on church staff too. Well, you can see where I am going with this complaint. Martha was begging for Jesus to put things back in order. Martha was asking Jesus to put both light switches in the same direction so that Mary could help me get things ready.

Jesus gave her the classic answer for people with an order disorder. "Martha, Martha," the Lord answered, "you are worried and upset about many things, but only one thing is needed. Mary has chosen what is better, and it will not be taken away from her."

Jesus, in a polite manner, instructed all of us that there are a few things more important than the order we think must take place in life. Jesus was not worried about where things were placed or whether they were in order. Jesus wanted to teach people about love and the kingdom of Heaven. He knew his teaching would change people. After all, people matter more than lids and dish direction and toilet-paper-roll installment. People even matter more than light switches being in the same direction. People are our first order!

Now the problem with my order disorder is that I desire for all the people to get in order. Oh, Jesus, here we go again.

Order up!

THE RELUCTANT FOLLOWERS: THAR SHE PLOWS! (LUKE 9:57–62)

Every semester, our faculty and staff advise students to ensure they are taking the correct classes toward their career path. Sometimes the conversation in these meetings leads to how I ended up teaching. What's fun is that as I think about the things I've done and the jobs I've held, I realize they all taught me a bit about what I'm doing right now. God certainly knew what He was doing, even though I had my doubts for many years. Sometimes I still have those doubts.

I've been a busboy, janitor, shoe salesman, recreation assistant, intern, youth minister, recreation minister, fence builder, volunteer recruiter, leadership development training module salesman, activities director, career advisor, and instructor. The five positions between ministry and teaching all occurred in a three-year span.

In all of that, I learned how to accidentally shoot someone with a nail gun, proper professional phone etiquette (no "yo" allowed), how to repair the pin-changing mechanism for a Brunswick bowling lane, and that I'm not a good salesman. I was taught the proper way to roll a burrito, how to refinish a gym floor, how to make a cold call in business, and how to determine someone's shoe size. I also learned that when the shoe-size indicator shows a woman wears a size nine and she says it's a size six, you go with the six and set the box down in such a way that her friends can't see the actual size posted on the box.

In all of those many-faceted careers, one of the things that gave me the most trouble was determining a straight line. Whether it was straightening shoes on a rack or setting a fence row, straight lines have always been a difficulty for me. I tend to want to see what I've done and determine if it's straight, which in turn sets the line on some wayward path. Some of this in walking is attributed to my poor sense of balance in my legs. Many that know me would blame it on some other sort of imbalance.

My career has, however, given me great insight to teach future recreation leaders about leadership, programming, and facility management. I'm presently in a class that deals with recreation facilities and fields. We look at how to design them and how to maintain them. A few weeks ago the topic was baseball and softball fields. I remember my days at the First Baptist Church of Natchez, Mississippi, where we had two softball fields on church property. I generally do well to avoid actual work in my jobs. My philosophy of leadership has always been to not do anything that I could find someone else to do for me. It worked well with employees, volunteers, and sometimes with family. Unfortunately my brothers and sons are all smarter than I am and figured out my system fairly early.

In this particular case, I had a crackerjack team of volunteers that groomed the field, set the bases in place, and laid the chalk foul lines. One particular weekend, during a fundraising tournament, I had to get to the fields and line the baselines myself. I wasn't worried, as I had watched numerous people do it before. How hard could it be? I mean, really?

I set the frame on home plate and chalked the open areas to create the two batter's boxes. Then I filled the chalk dispenser and went from the corner of home plate toward first base. About a third of the way up the baseline I turned to make sure I was laying the chalk straight. The problem was, I kept going as I turned to look. There's a bit of physics involved in this, and I never really understood physics, but I did understand that if I turn my head to the back, my body follows toward that same side. I often make that same mistake in driving an automobile.

Not a problem, I thought to myself. No one else was there, so I kicked dirt around the angled part of the line and set the chalk dispenser back where I first turned. Off I went again. This time I was smart enough to stop walking as I turned to view my work. Now I realized there was a break in the line, with the new line starting about a half inch outside the original line. More dirt was kicked, and the line began once again from the beginning point. I'd worked on the process long enough that I now had an audience. Early arrivals for the tournament were sitting on the bleachers, enjoying my varied attempts to chalk a straight line.

Finally, after several attempts, one of my talented friends took over. He claimed it was so I could be free to deal with the administration of the tournament and minister to the people attending. That may be, but I also know he wanted a straight line between home plate and first base.

Some other people had difficulties with straight lines as well. While Jesus was walking at one time, a man said he wanted to follow Jesus wherever he would go. Jesus let him know He had no place to lay His head. Jesus then offered a couple of invitations to follow Him. One person answered that he wanted to wait for his father's funeral. I don't get the idea it was happening soon, or else Jesus wouldn't have told him to let the dead bury the dead.

Another man was invited, but he wanted to wait in order to say good-bye to family. Jesus pointed out that one who looks back while plowing is not fit for the kingdom of God. Looking back always causes the head to turn in the wrong direction, thus making a straight path much more difficult.

Our main point of concern cannot be where we've been, but instead where we are going. I think God would want us to recall, remember, and recite how He has worked in our lives. I don't think remembrance is what Jesus is referring to in this case. I believe Jesus is trying to keep us grounded in the circumstances of the day and to look at where God is taking us tomorrow.

Chef Gusteau, in *Ratatouille*, said, "If you focus on what you left behind you will never be able to see what lies ahead." What is it in life that keeps us looking back instead of looking at where we are presently or where we will be in the future? I think I often look back to relish in my past sin. My memory takes me back to the good old days. The Enemy is good at twisting all sorts of pain from the past and reminding me only of the fun I had in a particular season. It's difficult to keep a straight line in life if the memory distorts the truth of where you've been.

Other times I look back to remember the praise I received and live through the glory of past accomplishments. While the good, the bad, and the ugly of life brought me to this point in life, they don't necessarily have to determine the direction of my straight line from this point.

I feel as though I have a little bit of control when I look back. I can remove things I don't want to think about by ignoring them and thinking of other things. I can remember things being better or worse than they really were. When I look back, I remember the events the way I choose to remember them. The difficulty with this viewpoint is that it creates lies about the past, which removes glory from God in getting you through the past.

When I work the plow properly, I can be concerned only with my next step. I can't look too far ahead, or I diverge from the straight line. I must concentrate only on what is immediately in front of me.

So where are you, and what are you looking forward to?

MOTHER OF JAMES AND JOHN: POWER AND GLORY (MARK 10:35–45, MATTHEW 20:20–28)

I observed during my college and seminary years that certain people had more prominence in gatherings of ministers than did others. The church recreation leadership team of what is now known as Lifeway Christian Resources worked to involve local church ministers in the conducting of national programs and conferences. People aspired to be part of the planning. Some desired the position for the ego, and some for the opportunity to get away from working with local church people.

It was like being asked to join the best fraternity or sorority. It was being asked to the prom by the most idolized guy in high school, or having the most beautiful girl agree to go with you. I never played any of those roles. Those in church work in the Southern Baptist Convention wanted to be recruited by the staff at Lifeway to be involved in a variety of leadership capacities. It was part of the ego and drive I maintain for my own personal sense of greatness.

While in college I worked for a man that was in this inner circle. He taught in several conferences and submitted articles for the organization's quarterly periodical. I had hoped that the connection with him would grease the wheels for my acceptance, but it had not. My mother, who worked as an administrative assistant in the recreation ministry, was one of the go-to people in regard to using arts and crafts as ministry. I jokingly told people that while some follow their father in ministry, I followed Mom! Even though Mom was in that inner circle, it did not gain me any additional favor in being invited to join.

Patience would indicate that you wait to be noticed, thereby giving the request more meaning, but I'm not a patient person. So I manipulated the process by networking with the right people and making sure they knew I was available. I sought them out rather than waiting for them to seek me.

Three years following my graduation from seminary, I was at one of the workshops for church recreation leaders. I overheard the director of the department talking with a friend of mine from another church local to my area. They were discussing a project in Alaska where certain ministers would go and train volunteers on how to create sports leagues, craft classes, senior adult events and other similar recreation programs. I jumped into the conversation and literally invited myself to join. Later that week, the invitation was made formal, my church voted to send me, and I was off to Alaska.

Despite my work with Lifeway on the Alaskan project, it still took another five years before I became a regular contributor to the workshops. Most of that work was in auditioning for the talent show and performing church-oriented stand-up comedy. A few years later I started teaching and writing for Lifeway and felt I had arrived at the mecca of church recreation. I felt as though I had achieved respect from my peers. I felt as though I had great influence, power, and glory due to my position of leadership that I had obtained. All of that is due to my one act of manipulation in 1983.

James and John had a similar situation. Despite Jesus' teaching about the kingdom of God, the boys had it in their minds that Jesus would sit on a throne like David did and that they would be part of the ruling class. They weren't alone. The other disciples had delusions of grandeur but weren't as loud about it. In fact, James and John were rather manipulative themselves in trying to advance in their idea of an earthly kingdom. This behavior was demonstrated in one story where a Samaritan village was not receptive to having Jesus pass through and the brothers asked Jesus if He wanted them to call unto heaven for fire to destroy the people and the village.

Another time John rebuked a person that was healing people in Jesus' name because the man wasn't "one of them." Ironically he did this shortly after he and the other disciples were unable to heal someone.

In Mark's account of the story, James and John go to Jesus and ask if they might sit at the right hand and left hand of Jesus when He becomes King. Jesus paints an ugly picture of what that might look like. So when all other attempts on their own fail, Mom does what the boys desire and asks Jesus to let her boys sit at the right-hand and left-hand seats of the King. Matthew's account has Mom asking Jesus for the favor.

Jesus asked if they were willing to drink from the same cup He was going to have to swallow the contents of. They claimed they could. Jesus agreed they would drink from that cup, but the occupants of right and left seats were to be determined by the Father.

The other disciples, the ones that probably wished to be at Jesus' right and left hands as well, got livid with the J brothers about their request. It's funny how Peter is remembered for His denial more than James and John are for their ego trip.

Jesus offered the advice of a simple mathematical equation: "If you want to be greater then become lesser." If your real desire is to be first, then you have to be a slave. If your desire is greatness then you become a servant. This is great news for the kingdom's sake but bad news for my ego!

So I've learned, as James and John did, that certain positions have already been reserved for those God chooses. My role is to do what God has called me to do today. There's no need to politic, bargain, or negotiate for a higher place in the kingdom. Jesus even instructed people to avoid taking the seat of honor until invited to take the seat. Jesus knew humility was needed to be a fully competent servant of the gospel.

What are you willing to serve or slave for?

PETER: WHAT ABOUT HIM? (JOHN 21:15–22)

I went through the normal nervousness anyone would experience while standing on a stage and speaking in front of people. I remember that the first time I ever preached to our youth group, the podium was removed from the church for dancing!

It was early in my stage life that I discovered the knack of making people laugh. It was the best thing I had as far as talent goes. When I was a little child, I was given one line in a play. I didn't even know what the line meant, but it made people laugh like crazy. The line, as best as I remember, was "Mom is thirty-five? Thirty-five is too old for gray hair!"

I'm positive most of the laughter occurred because my mom was around that age at that time. The feeling of creating laughter in front of a crowd was birthed in me that day. I haven't stopped since. Some even reason that I teach so I can have a captive audience for my humor.

In high school, having made the decision to go into some sort of ministry work, I decided to take speech class. I took the introductory class and was hooked enough to take the advanced class the next two years and serve on the speech and debate squad. I knew the speaking experience would help me in that career path.

I was one of twelve debaters that formed six teams that competed on a regular basis in the speech tournaments. Two teams each would take part in different levels of competition. Many of us competed in other speech events as well, but our expertise was the debate.

As is the case in many team competition situations, the debate coach had some favorites in the class. Many teachers attempt to hide such favoritism; in my opinion, this man did not. Some of that opinion may come out of a bitter attitude, as I was not one of his favorites. I look back at it now with some teaching experience under my belt and have more understanding and sympathy for the man. With my sarcastic tendencies, I wouldn't have liked me very much either. In reality, with me being one of twelve, I might have been serving the role of Judas to this poor teacher!

Respect for teachers was something that was demanded at my high school. In most classes the teacher was Ms. Someone or the occasional Mr. Someone. The speech and debate coach let things go a little less formal, and those on the team called him by his first name. This was actually good, as his last name, when the first letter was exchanged for another letter, made for an inappropriate word at the beginning of his name. Not that I would ever do that, but I learned that if I said it really quickly, I could get away with it.

One particular day, I must have really been under his skin. I referred to him by his first name, and he informed me that from that point on I was to call him by his last name preceded with the title of Mister. He stated that his friends called him by his first name, inferring that I was not his friend. My reaction was to call him by the inappropriate name. When questioned about it, I did what I normally would do in such cases and lied to protect myself.

I saw one of his favorites sitting close by, doing some preparation for our next tournament, and asked the teacher, "What about him? Is he to call you by your last name?"

"What's that to you?" he replied. That was the last I heard of that, although after the tournament season was over and graduation was coming, I started calling him by his first name again with no argument. I suppose I finally wore him down, or he could count the days until I would no longer be under his watch.

I don't really like criticism and correction. I was never a fan of time-outs and spankings. In the process of learning how to deal with life, I picked up a defense mechanism called defer and deflect. If I could somehow get someone concerned with someone else's problems, then mine would not seem so bad. I developed this into an art form. If Dad got on me, I would ask about my brothers. If a teacher got on me, I would defer and deflect him or her to another student's misbehavior. It normally wouldn't work, but I never gave up trying.

I found it extremely helpful when discussing sin in my life. I may gossip a bit, but what about those that murder? I have difficulties with lust, but look, I'm not one of those rapists. I found it easier to deal with my own sin by pointing out someone else's "bigger sin."

This particular habit occurred regularly during the time I was working toward restoration from some hidden sin in my life and trying to repair damage done to my marriage. I remember feeling good when the topic was diverted to someone else's ugliness. It gave me a break from being the target of the topic at hand. I found myself storing up stories and issues that could divert or deflect the conversation toward another path.

My hero in the Bible, Simon Peter, was excellent at the defer-and-deflect technique. When Jesus told of his impending death, Peter cautioned Him not to talk like that. When Jesus talked about how to redeem a brother that has sinned against you, Peter wanted to know just how many times he had to forgive him. He was good at diverting the topic in other directions.

The best job of defer and deflect came when Peter learned about his own death. Hearing that he would have his hands stretched out and not be in control of his life, he looked at John and said, "Lord, what about him?"

Jesus, in a real teacher style, told Peter it was basically none of his concern. Jesus told him, "If I want him to remain alive until I return, what is that to you?"

Peter reminds me to pay attention to my heart and not to defer and deflect to another's. The lesson learned is that I am to live my own life and not worry about whether or not someone else is caught or criticized. I need to be content with what I need to do rather than concerned about what needs to be done with others.

Of course that's what I ought to do. Or I could always say, "What about my brothers?"

PETER: I GOT THIS! (MATTHEW 14:22–31)

It was my home church in my hometown. I had been offered the job as the minister of recreation at the place where I once served as a recreation assistant during my college years. I had a feeling I knew what to do, but at the same time I had no idea what to do.

When I had worked during my college years, the recreation center had strict use policies. You simply had to be a member of the church to use the center. If you weren't a member, you could use the center if a member came with you and stayed for the duration of your visit. When I arrived as the leader, I sensed something else might be needed.

The church was located in the downtown area of Springfield, Missouri. The neighborhood surrounding the church, as in many urban areas, had gone down in value. This particular neighborhood was voted the worst one in Springfield in which to raise children. Yet as one drove through the neighborhoods, all one would see were children.

The church staff and I prayed about it and felt that the policy needed to be changed. We wanted to open our doors to any and all that wished to play. We knew that if we shared our toys with them, they might give us a little more credibility when we told them that we and Jesus loved them.

The reactions, as with any change, were mixed. We were asked what we would do if a neighborhood child painted graffiti on the wall. The pastor said, "We'll paint over it." Another question was, what if they break one of the toilets in the bathroom? The pastor said, “We’ll fix it.” We determined, following much prayer, that God wanted us to do this and that minor things like paint and toilets would not get in the way. We took a leap of faith, hoping God would honor this new path.

With this new mind-set of operations, we felt another need prior to the summer of 1995. The kids in the neighborhood had come on a daily basis to the recreation center the previous summer, so we felt that if we had an organized program, we could convey our message of hope and salvation through Jesus a little better. The entire church jumped behind the idea. Different age groups were providing snacks, finances, and leadership. We charged a whopping five dollars per child per week, and through a miracle God provided the rest through the people in the church. Both single-parent and dual-working-parent families benefited from the miracle we saw each summer.

That first summer was so successful that during the following spring we started looking at an after-school program with the same mind-set. We contacted various schools and transportation systems, and following the second summer program, the after-school program was launched.

I’d like to believe I’m a gifted leader and a programmer to have carried this off. But the truth is, we were smack in the middle of a miracle. In my years growing up and as a leader in that church, I never saw the entire group of people pull together for something like they did the neighborhood programs.

A couple of years later, I had made the move to the Memphis area to start working at Germantown Baptist Church. During my fourth year of leadership, I thought it would be a good idea to start an after-school program. I looked back over the action plan I had followed in Springfield and figured, “I got this!” I began to believe I was that gifted of a leader and programmer at this point.

I don’t recall praying about it much. Even the prayers I recall were more of an attempt to get God to sign off on what I was going to do anyway. I seem to be good at that type of prayer.

I ran into obstacle after obstacle, but with a dogged determination I was persistent in working the plan as I had in Springfield. Despite my efforts, I kept running into brick walls. Insurance issues popped up so often that it seemed I was playing a game of Whac-A-Mole. Transportation issues got me in trouble to the point that the bus company I had asked about helping us sued the church. I gained support from my immediate supervisor and the senior pastor, but few people in the church knew what was being planned.

The idea finally died.

I look back at the two situations and recognize exactly what happened. The first time was initiated by God and carried out by the people of the church. The second time, I carried it out individually and hoped for the miracle to happen based solely on my leadership. It was as if I were taking a walk and telling God to stay behind because I "had this." The same thing happened to Simon Peter once.

Peter was a professional fisherman. He knew the sea like a cabdriver knows his town. After Jesus fed over five thousand people with a boy's small lunch, He sent the disciples on ahead of Him in a boat while He went to pray. Night came while the boat was still out on the sea. Jesus walked toward them on top of the water and warned them to not be afraid. Peter insisted that if it was Jesus, they would receive an invitation to join him on the sea. Jesus offered such an invitation.

Peter started off believing but soon fell back into his own knowledge and perceived strength and began to sink. When Peter operated on faith and trust, he walked. When he depended on his own strength and understanding, he sank. I hate to admit it, but it sounds all too familiar to me.

The leaning on my own understanding has at its root my prideful ego. Doing things in my own strength glorifies me. What I have to remember is that God-sized miracles don't happen in my own strength. People can't walk on water, blow trumpets and knock down thick walls, or part large seas on their own strength. I had the faith and trust to start a program with nothing and maintain it with even less. We started with no resources and discovered that somehow all we needed was provided. The second time, when I had the resources without God's help, I found myself sinking quickly. Instead of "I got this" I needed to be saying, "God has this!"

I find it funny that when Jesus had been resurrected and was waiting on shore for the disciples to bring in their boat, Peter jumped in and swam to the shore. Even at that point he forgot he had received water-walking lessons. I cut Peter some slack because when the going gets tough I tend to go back to my own strength as well.

Part of the trust in God comes not only in depending on God's guidance but also in the results. I cannot fashion a miracle in and of my own abilities. I can pray, but the result is still in God's hands. I think that, like Peter, I'll learn to lean a little more on faith and a lot less on my own power.

Let's take a walk!

JOHN THE BAPTIST: IS THIS IT? (MATTHEW 11:1–24)

I have had the joy of traveling all over this country and in several other countries as a part of the jobs I have held in my life. While I worked for churches, I often had charge of the senior adult group, which took several trips. Some of the journeys were for ten days to two weeks, while others would last just a couple of days. I found some great success putting together Christmas trips on which we would go to areas where Christmas events were featured. Natchitoches, Louisiana, had a Christmas light display and featured some unbelievably delicious fried meat pies. Galveston, Texas, had Dickens on the Strand. Branson, Missouri, always put together a nice package of Christmas shows.

One particular year I took the group from Natchez, Mississippi, to Houston, Texas. We enjoyed one day in Galveston and then had some spots to go to in Houston. We observed the Christmas program of one of the larger churches on our first night in Houston. Then there was a theater that featured a Christian based play about Christmas that we watched on the second night in town. One of my church recreation friends told me about this great restaurant that would be halfway between the hotel where we stayed and the theater.

After an afternoon of shopping and rest, we loaded the bus and started toward the restaurant. I had timed it so that we'd have enough time to spare in the event the restaurant took longer than normal to serve a busload of seniors.

The bus driver took us down the street, but we could not find the restaurant anywhere. There were some restaurants, but none by the name we were searching for and none large enough to handle the number or people we had. As we continued down the street, I began to have some doubts as to the location and whether I had heard my friend correctly. With this being prior to having cell phones, I knew I would not be able to locate my friend for further instructions. I told the bus driver to just drive, thinking we could surely locate a cafeteria or similar place where a busload of people could be served.

I tried to be coy, but I think the folks on the bus were suspecting something was wrong when we didn't immediately pull into a place. I'm not the best at hiding doubt or frustration on my face. Here we were, in a forty-seven-passenger bus, touring the streets of Houston, Texas, during rush-hour traffic. Finally, after nearly an hour on the road, we came to the time when we would have to eat at the next place we came to or miss the play. Since tickets for the play had already been purchased and were nonrefundable, I opted for the next restaurant. Finally into our vision came a place we knew could handle a busload of senior adults quickly.

It was a McDonald's.

One of the jokes I would often tell on the bus rides was that our next meal was going to be at a McDonald's. The people learned that nicer places were usually already lined up, so they knew the McDonald's line was just that—a line. As we pulled in I could sense a bit of murmuring on the bus, as if they thought I was carrying out the joke a step further. When the bus stopped and the driver killed the engine, the folks knew the joke was on me. I made an announcement about the mishap with the assigned restaurant over the bus's speaker and explained that time wise it was McDonald's or nothing. Most of the people recognized the trouble we were in and made the best of it. One dear lady did not hear the announcement because she had hearing difficulties. She slowly stepped off the bus and turned immediately to me and engaged me in conversation, blocking others from getting off the bus.

"Do you mean to tell me we drove over an hour to get to a McDonald's?" she asked. Her eyes poked me about as hard as her walking cane would have had she chosen to use it for a weapon.

Recognizing that humor can often turn away frustration, I replied, "Ma'am, you may not be aware of it, but this location was one of the first McDonald's they put in this neighborhood. People drive from all over Texas just to get to this McDonald's."

She took one look at the building and the golden arches and turned back to me, and with a spirit of excitement she said, "Oh goody. Let's go!" She was looking for something special and ended up realizing that even McDonald's can serve that purpose with the right spin or attitude.

It's not all that rare in this life to be looking for one thing and discover something else entirely different. Often our expectations and attitude determine whether we look at such a situation positively or negatively.

John the Baptist had a similar situation. He had preached fervently about the coming of the Messiah. He had even baptized Jesus and proclaimed Him to be the Christ. He declared that Jesus must become greater and he must become less. John would have continued to hear reports of all the work Jesus was doing.

After King Herod had John arrested, the news John received about Jesus coming around was probably a little more limited than before. He probably heard a little from the Pharisees and other religious leaders as well. These people probably painted Jesus as some sort of clown, which can also be found at a McDonald's. Instead of a focus on miracles and lives being changed, the conversation was probably more about his defiance of the Pharisaical authority.

All this talk may have been what it took to put a little doubt in John's heart about Jesus. John's heart was taking a figurative drive around the city of Houston and was not seeing what he had been hoping for.

So John sent his disciples to inquire of Jesus as to whether or not He was the Messiah. John was sent to prepare the way for the Messiah. He figured that if Jesus was not "the one," God would somehow get him out of prison and out from under Herod's judgment. If Jesus was the one, then John would know his work was done.

Jesus sent back a simple answer as He instructed John's disciples to go back and report on what they heard and saw. Jesus even gave a bit of encouragement when he told John's disciples, "Blessed is the man that does not fall away on account of me." In other words, "Hang in there, John! The kingdom, which people have traveled from all over to enter, is here!"

Happy Meal, anyone?

DAVID: IT JUST HAPPENED (2 SAMUEL 11–12)

We were the champion creators of games. My younger brother and I, following Mary Poppins' advice of making a task into a game, were able to come up with numerous games in our shared bedroom. One was to take a sock and form it into a ball and play basketball with it. We would open the curtains up just a bit so that if the sock went over the curtain rod in the area where there was no curtain, it would count as a basket.

Rolled-up socks also served for a variety of games in which we would throw them at each other. In one we would sit on our beds, which were lined up on opposite walls, and play a form of dodgeball with them. If you were hit by the sock, you had to freeze in the position you were in upon impact. If frozen, you were allowed to pick up the sock, get back into the frozen position, and throw the sock using only the movement of the arm from the elbow. You would remain frozen until the other person missed you with the sock on a subsequent throw. Mom could never figure out how we lost so many matches to our socks.

The best game, however, was one created with the super-bouncy ball called a Super Ball. This ball not only had a lively bounce but was also the inspiration behind Lamar Hunt, owner of the Kansas City Chiefs, naming the NFL championship game the Super Bowl. Without either one of us being specialists in the field of physics, we figured out how to simulate baseball using the Super Ball and the wall on one side of our bedroom. One of us would throw the ball and make it hit the floor first, causing it to pop up in the air, simulating an infield pop-up in a baseball game. If the bottom of the wall was hit first, it would create a ground ball for the other to have to field cleanly. A missed pop-up or misplayed ground ball resulted in a base hit for the opponent. Normal baseball rules applied following all of that.

When one of us was "in the field," he would stand just in front of the sliding closet doors. These doors were designed to move right to left or vice versa, creating an opening for the closet, rather than the traditional door on hinges. The top part of the door had a roller kept in a track, and the bottoms of the doors were kept in place by a small, narrow piece of plastic placed strategically so that each door could not glide off track. Well, until a strong ground ball comes at you. Then, in backing up to make a play, the small, narrow piece of plastic gives way to 120 pounds of boy and the doors become swinging doors instead of sliding ones.

The first time this happened, Mark and I were stumped as to an explanation for the door breakage. So when asked by Dad, we gave one of the classic excuses for sin known to mankind.

"It just happened!"

Dad wasn't buying any of that.

Aaron used a similar excuse when he made an idol while his brother, Moses, was getting the Ten Commandments from God. He mentioned that he merely put some gold into a pot and melted it and a calf-shaped golden statue came out. Or, in other words, "It just happened!"

The difficulty with the line "It just happened" is that it never just happens. Sliding doors don't just become swinging doors without some sort of assistance. Despite the fact that the excuse never works, I am still quick to throw it out as a reason for my sin. I know this from personal experience.

My hidden sin for many years was associated with inappropriate dealings with the opposite sex. Now, I might say "they just happened," but in reality they were planned, connived, created, and carried out. At first I can rationalize there were innocent compliments being paid. Then I can continue to rationalize that I was just involved in harmless flirtation. When we talk, even around other people, a touch to the arm to make a point is shared. A hug is given and it's not the safe sideways hug. The embrace takes a little longer than most should or would. All of a sudden I find myself alone with a person. I find it easy to start telling her how inadequate and frustrating my wife is. She shares similar stories about her husband. As we talk there are "innocent" touches on the arm and leg. In that we work together on many church projects and programs, we easily reason that we just shared a "holy" kiss together. Finally a request is made for me to drop something off that she left at church when she knows she has the house to herself. I drive myself there and park away from the house in a secluded place and sneak into the house.

Of course, it just happened!

God wasn't buying any of that.

Months of groundwork with affirmation, flirting, confiding, and "innocent" touches. It all leads to something "just happening." Then the lies fly even harder. The second time around becomes easier. Sin creates a callousness to the conscience that allows a person to go farther and farther into darkness. All of a sudden you find that a pattern of sin has "just happened."

A similar situation occurred to one of our biblical characters. In the springtime, kings would normally go out and fight in war. One particular spring, David decided he would send Joab and the army out to fight the Ammonites without him. The army was victorious, but David stayed behind in Jerusalem.

One afternoon, after a nap, David took a stroll on the palace roof and happened to see a girl taking a bath while he was "looking over the city." He discovered who she was and sent for her to come see him in the palace.

That's when "it just happened."

You see, my namesake David had planned out some sort of trouble to take place. Otherwise he would have been with the army at war. It's my opinion he took a stroll on the palace roof because he knew he would catch some kind of sneak peak at a woman bathing at that time of day.

When the woman came up pregnant and her husband was off at war, where David should have been, David brought the man back home from the war so that a welcome-home party could make it look as if the baby were from the husband. Uriah, the husband, feeling a duty to suffer as his fellow soldiers were, refused to sleep with his wife. So David is left with the option of murder. He instructed Joab—who was where David should have been, with the army—to put Uriah on the front lines and then withdraw, leaving him to be slaughtered by the ensuing army.

The murder occurred, and when the report came back to David, he offered Joab condolences by saying something to the effect that those kinds of things "just happen" in war.

David and I would have been better off following Joseph's mode of operation in avoiding sin. Joseph, who had incited his brothers into the crime of selling him into slavery, was sold to the captain of the guard for the king of Egypt. God gave Joseph success in everything, and Potiphar noticed this and made Joseph his personal attendant. He gave Joseph charge over his entire household and all that he owned. The moment Joseph was put on the job, God started blessing Potiphar for Joseph's sake.

The story goes on that Potiphar's wife started looking at Joseph lustfully. Joseph turned her down over and over again. He avoided her and tried staying away from the trouble. Even though Joseph was eventually accused of a sin and punished for it, he knew, and more importantly God knew, of his innocence. God used the injustice as a way of getting Joseph into the position needed to save His people.

If I stay away from sliding doors, they never have a chance of becoming swinging doors. The difficulty with sin is that it is pleasing to the eye. The eyes see it, the heart desires it, and the mind starts rationalizing it. If I hang out on top of palace roofs I will encounter temptation. If I give in, it's not long before I wake up and realize "it just happened" again.

What plans are you making in advance that are going to "just happen?"

MICHAL: NOW THAT YOU CAN DANCE ... (2 SAMUEL 6:12–23)

I had a way of stirring the pot sometimes when I was in church work. Being a person of vision, I had a way of pushing people to an edge where they weren't quite comfortable.

Sometimes this occurred because I opted to lead the teenagers in a mission endeavor rather than taking them to a church camp or fun trip for their summer adventure. I know it sounds ludicrous to think that someone would not want missions being done. I think the folks that discussed the matter behind my back and in the church parking lot liked missions but did not want their own children on the front line, so to speak.

I also created a furor once when I worked with a Christian-based group toward a mission project in Great Britain. There was a battle going on at the time for control of the Southern Baptist Convention, and it had carried over into our congregation. The mission project was being sponsored by the "wrong" group in some people's minds. Rather than choosing a side, I tried to lead the church to do what God was leading them to do.

But that was not the worst pot I stirred.

I also pushed some folks to the edge in opening the doors of the recreation center to the general public in two different churches. We all want to say we're not prejudiced or bigoted, but sometimes it comes out anyway. I was questioned as to why someone that had a jewel stuck in her forehead would possibly want to take a crafts class in our church. There were numerous complaints about the ethnicities of people playing in our gym and in our fitness rooms.

But that was not the worst pot I stirred.

The worst possible pot I ever stirred was in allowing dance classes to be introduced to our recreation program in Memphis.

I'm not exactly sure when dance became one of the seven deadly sins in the Baptist Church, but it certainly was there. During high school I had asked the music minister why dancing was so forbidden among Baptists. He explained that the moves a girl made in dancing could make a boy fall into lust. I told him I could go there from watching a girl erase a wrong answer on a math test. I still couldn't see what was so wrong with the art form.

On my staff at Germantown Baptist, I had a very creative program leader that knew we could reach an entirely different audience with some expansion in programming. It included dance. Knowing the potential difficulties, I told her to proceed. In order to promote the upcoming new programs, we advertised in the weekly printout that was distributed to the church members upon entrance to the worship center. For some reason I've always know that piece to be called a bulletin. So the new programs started with square dancing. From square dancing we expanded to ballroom dancing. The leaders of the ballroom class even explained to me how they taught biblical principles of marriage in the ballroom techniques. Sounds good, right?

The murmuring began with a few groups of people and then started swelling up like crazy. A representative from one of the classes of complainers was designated to come see me. I explained the aspect of using these new programs to reach people that didn't go to church. The lady did not budge. I explained how godly principles were being shared in the classes. She did not care. So I told her dance is mentioned in the Bible, when King David celebrates before the Lord at the return of the ark of the covenant.

She looked me square in the eyes and said, "I don't care if it's in the Bible. I don't want to see it in my church's bulletin."

She proceeded to lecture me on the slippery slope I had put the church on. First it was those women in skin-tight leotards doing dance but calling it exercise. Then square dancing and ballroom dancing came in. She wrapped up her monologue by swearing that I would come up with pole dancing next and invite the girls from the Memphis strip clubs to come teach it.

Then I did it. Once again my mouth went faster than my mind, and I said, "No one will come do a striptease at this church without me seeing it first." I meant it to be funny, but it wasn't. The pastor didn't think so either after she told him. Perhaps someday I'll learn it's best to remain quiet.

Michal, one of David's wives, made a similar mistake in judgment. Michal had been given to David following his conquest over the Philistines. Later King Saul took her back and gave her to someone else. When Saul died, David reclaimed Michal as his wife. Her second husband followed weeping until he was told by one of David's men to go home. I imagine Michal may have wondered about the death of her father and if perhaps David had a hand in it.

After becoming king, David went to battle again with the Philistines and defeated them. The ark of the covenant was coming home! David worshipped in dance; he celebrated with the people of Israel. When he came home to bless his own family, his wife met him with dripping sarcasm. "How the king of Israel has distinguished himself today, disrobing in the sight of the slave girls of his servants as any vulgar fellow would."

It would have been best left unsaid. David pointed out the work of the Lord in his becoming king and reiterated that he would celebrate. Then the Bible points out she died without ever having a child.

Whether dance in the church is right or not, I must learn to communicate without sarcasm. What seems funny to my mind does not always translate in spoken word. Michal might have had a different outcome, as would I, with a soft word. Soft words can still be firm. They just don't have to hurt as much.

I did learn one lesson from it all. Two years later we were called by the Memphis entry into the XFL. It was a football league being created with a whole new sense of entertainment. The cheerleading squads for XFL teams were going to be quite risqué. One way to define them would be to say that they would be making the same moves as the Memphis strip club girls, with slightly more clothing on their bodies. They called us to request permission to hold tryouts in our gymnasium. I communicated on that request without sarcasm. I got directly to the point. I said, “No, we can’t do that.”

How about you? Would you like to have this dance?

SARAH: I'M KIND OF IN A HURRY HERE (GENESIS 15–16)

It was one of those mornings on which everything seems to take longer than it should. Regardless of the reason, I was running late for work. I decided to blend a fruit smoothie instead of taking the time for cereal or grabbing something on the way. I had just enough time to dump the fruit and juice into the blender and still get to work on time.

I dumped the frozen blueberries into the blender. I followed with a banana and some fresh strawberries. Then I poured in the orange juice. I put the top on the blender and ran it for a few seconds. Trying to keep from having to scrub the lid later, I removed it from the container, rinsed it off, and set it in the sink. I tried to lift the pitcher off the rotor but couldn't get it to maneuver correctly. I knew I was going to have to turn it slightly before the container would lift away. I decided to hold on to the base with one hand while turning the container and lifting with the other. That's when the trouble began.

I accidentally hit one of the buttons, releasing fruit smoothie into the atmosphere.

It landed all over the counter, the floor, the wall, and the refrigerator, and covered a good bit of my shirt. My dog took care of the floor duty, which would suffice until I returned home. I maximized my efforts by removing my shirt and using it as a rag to clean up the counter, refrigerator, and wall. It was going to have to be washed anyway, and I figured it made more sense than to dirty a towel.

I put on a new shirt and enjoyed a much smaller serving of a fruit smoothie on my way to work. Of course I exceeded the speed limit on the way to the office in an effort to make up lost time.

I decided that morning that one of the laws of the universe must be "The size of the mess is in direct proportion to the amount of a hurry one is in."

When you think about the law, it's accurate. Little babies spit up more on work clothes and Sunday outfits when there's no time to change clothes. Don't even get me started on leaky diapers under the same circumstances.

In my life it seems that when I'm in a hurry to get things done or see things happen, I tend to mess them up even more. I remember a phrase I heard once: "The hurrieder I go the behinder I get." It's very poor in spelling and grammar but quite appropriate in its meaning. I have no doubt my temptations and failures in highway speeding are directly a result of my being in a hurry to get somewhere. I can do the math in my head about how little time I actually save in traveling faster, but I can't convince my foot to lighten up.

I do the same thing in relationships. I want five-year-long relationships to be created immediately after having met someone I enjoy being around. I often wonder, *Why does time take so much time?* This hurried-up sense of life seems to always get me in trouble. I start to get in a hurry, and I attract speeding tickets and scare off people.

Luckily I'm not the first person in a hurry; nor will I be the last. I might not even be in the Hurried Hall of Fame. Abraham's wife, Sarah, was really good at being in a hurry as well. God had promised her and Abraham they would have a child after her childbearing years were gone. I have to admit, Sarah was patient for several years. Then she started believing the "hurrieder I go" statement. She came to the conclusion that God would not give her a child, despite the promise, and gave her servant to her husband and told him to have a baby with her.

Having been a husband, I realize that it doesn't always mean "go ahead" when a woman says "Go ahead." "Do whatever you'd like" does not mean "do whatever you'd like"! "Fine" does not mean "fine"! I reckon Abraham was wondering if it might be a trap, but Sarah convinced him this would count toward God's promise. Abraham, thinking as a man would think, ignored God's promise of a child through Sarah and slept with Hagar, the servant. As a result Hagar became pregnant. Sarah didn't realize she was pushing one of the blender buttons when she set up all of this.

Referring back to my comments about when a woman says "Go ahead," Sarah became angry and blamed Abraham when Hagar was walking around with a growing midsection. Gee, what a surprise.

I think that at the root of all sin is the idea that I can do this better than God. The first sin by Adam and Eve was tempting because they believed the fruit would make them just like God. They were in a hurry to be godly and figured the shortcut would do the trick. I still work on that same premise. The hurry I get into in life is a matter of my lack of trust to depend on God to fulfill life in His timing.

Sarah's hurry was the creation of another nation, which has been at war and conflict with her own son's peoples since that time. More conflicts have been recorded in history between the offspring of Ishmael and Isaac than any other groups of people. Thankfully most of my messes have not set up worldwide consequences. However, some of my hurried-up offerings have messed up a good number of people.

Like Sarah, I need to remember that it is in the waiting that my character is built. It is in the patience that I learn the dependence and trust in God I need to obtain the promise. Despite my rush, nothing is going to happen until God is ready for it to happen. I might as well stop and smell the roses.

Slow down. What's your hurry?

PETER: YOU CAN COUNT ON ME! (MATTHEW 26:31–35, 69–75)

The teenagers gathered on the staircase at one end of the building. It was the normal method of killing time before the Youth Bible Study period began. He would bring his guitar to the Wednesday-night activities at church and usually end up strumming a few hymns or choruses on the staircase. The girls our same age would gather around him and giggle and beg him to sing some more. "Play me one more song, Steve. Please?" Then more giggling would take place.

I sat on the staircase in the middle of the building. I usually had the elementary school kids around me, listening to me add my flavor to Bible stories. "Tell us another story, Dave. Please?"

I did some math on the situation and determined that if I just waited long enough I could date the elementary school girls that enjoyed my stories. Of course it would take thirty years to get there, but with my normal luck with the ladies, it made sense to wait. Steve had a lock on the girls of our age because of the guitar and musical talent. In school girls went after the athletes, and at church they went after the guitar players. The idea sounded sick when I was in tenth grade and they were in the second grade. It didn't sound quite as sick when I realized some of the women I'm dating in a single-again capacity would have been in the second grade then.

Musical ability had a monopoly on stage time in ministry. I noticed while growing up in the church that if a person had "talent" it meant he could sing. Somehow spiritual gifts were always manifested in musical ability. For someone like me, a public speaker, it would mean

I was not going to do anything in front of the crowd at church. There were always more opportunities to sing than there were to preach or speak.

All of this began to change when the church hired an activities director. He started showing us fun games, silly songs, and other ways a person could participate in leadership without singing. This man showed that us a talent or ability to be goofy could be used in ministry! The man was my mentor and my hero. He saw something in me and put me to work. My eventual call to ministry is mostly due to his influence in my life.

I went to speak with him once about using talents in ministry. I had noted that musical talent was readily used by the church but storytelling, comedy, public speaking, and administration were not. I bragged on my abilities and my desire to do more for the church. I pestered and bothered him in order to be able to do more in leadership. Don't get me wrong; my attitude was far from altruistic. I wanted to be on stage and get some of the glory the musically talented people were getting. I thrive on public affirmation and applause and saw the church as the way I could get both.

After months of my bragging, begging, and pleading, he put me in charge of something. He lined me up to help with a puppet show during an afternoon program with neighborhood children. I was to stand in front of the group of children and tell a story, then introduce the puppets for the show.

After all that time of bragging about what I could do and begging to do it, I never made it to the show. I had recently begun a relationship with a young lady, and she invited me over to her house for lunch prior to my engagement. When it was time to go, I ignored my duties and stayed with her. I "got busy" with my girlfriend and spent the afternoon smooching and hugging. She even reminded me several times that I needed to go, and I continued to tell her it would be okay if I was late and spent more time at her house while avoiding my responsibilities at church.

It was not okay to do so. I confessed to my mentor that I had been detained, without giving the truthful reason. He offered grace and let me know they had handled it fine without me. I knew then, and know now, that I set myself up by bragging about my greatness and let others down in looking out for myself.

Peter was good at bragging also. When told of the disciples all running away when Jesus would be taken, Peter responded, "Even if all others fall, I won't."

Then Jesus told Peter that he would not only fall away once but that he would also deny knowing Him three times. Peter was emphatic that even under the threat of death he would never disown Jesus. He knew that within his own abilities was a strength greater than that of all of the other disciples. It was as if he were telling Jesus that it was not only the musically talented disciples that could be in front.

We are all familiar with the story. The guards came to get Jesus, and the disciples ran away as fast as boys that just broke the neighbor's window in a front-yard baseball game. Peter, however, followed closely behind and arrived at a fire around the courtyard where Jesus was being tried. I have to applaud Peter here. He did get closer to the action than any of the other disciples. Yet, when approached about being a disciple or even knowing Jesus, Peter took the path of denial and lies.

Peter and I were good at the setup but lacking in the follow-through. I think a better path for me to take is to wait and trust God to provide the opportunities He desires for me to take. I'm not suggesting that I don't let people know of my gifts and abilities that allow me to assist in their ministry or project, but I am suggesting I should not brag and manipulate the situation in order to be used by God.

So what are you bragging about?

ACHAN: DAMAGE CONTROL (JOSHUA 7)

It was late on a Saturday night, and I crawled into bed. My wife immediately asked for passwords to my e-mail addresses. I mustered up some confidence in my voice as if I had nothing to hide and told her I could do that. A sense of panic came over me, as I knew there may be things I had not deleted just yet. I had been hiding a dark sin habit for some time.

On Sunday mornings I had to be at church earlier than she did, and I usually left the house before she was even awake. This Sunday morning proved to be the same. I took off feeling really good because I didn't have to open the e-mail accounts in her presence. I knew I could get to the office, erase the evidence, and minimize the trouble on the home front.

It's called damage control. It's a technique of defense and self-preservation. It was a trait I learned early in life. If you get caught doing something, admit to only that which the accuser has evidence of. Minimize the sin as much as possible. Avoid major consequences by admitting to lesser crimes than those you are actually guilty of. Divert and deflect the topic as best as you can. Answer questions with questions.

I opened up the e-mail accounts and went about deleting everything that could possibly incriminate me. I looked over each part of the e-mail website to make sure nothing would be left that could convict me. With that done, I could lie about what she had seen the day before, explaining that it was a pop-up ad that appeared on the screen, causing me to quickly exit.

I felt once again as if I had beaten the game. When you hide a lot of sin, you have to stay ahead of the game. I had heard confessions of men before me in similar sinful habits, and instead of invoking repentance, I increased resistance and tried to be smarter about how I hid my sin. A damage control mind-set keeps you sharp that way.

The message that day, of all things, had to be on one of the seven deadly sins. You guessed it; the message was on lust. What impeccable timing God has! It was as if God had orchestrated my having been caught on the night before a message on sexual purity. Knowing my wife had discovered some of my secret and hearing the pastor convey God's message of truth about sexual purity in marriage almost made me come clean on my own.

Almost is the key word.

You have to understand that once you start hiding the sin it becomes easier and easier to justify, rationalize, and accept the sin as a part of your life. Add to this the need I had to project an image of being a leader in the church and an all-around good guy. Also, it takes a great deal of trust to open up with someone about the reality of our sinful thoughts and deeds. In my case full confession also meant resignation and the loss of a job I loved and needed to take care of my family. I fought off the nudging of the Holy Spirit and believed the lies of the enemy and decided to take my chances elsewhere.

That afternoon was a quiet afternoon around the house. Before I left for the Sunday-evening service, I was asked for the information. I gave my wife the e-mail passwords and went to church. I was completely confident she'd find nothing, and I would have controlled the damage once again.

I got home, and my wife acted like nothing at all was wrong. We watched some television, and after our one son that remained at home went to bed, I wandered into the bedroom. My wife sat in a chair in the corner of the room, holding several sheets of paper. She then confronted me with page after page of incriminating e-mails.

They were the very e-mails that I had deleted that very morning, with time stamps indicating they had been printed following my deletion.

In the next few hours, I confessed to a few of the secrets regarding my sins, but not to all of them. I limited my confessions to the sins the e-mails proved. However, I did confess to enough sinful behavior that I was given the opportunity to resign from the church staff. Despite the pain I caused and the fact that my image was now tarnished, I still did not open up to confess all. Damage control was still in control.

In the next days I would reveal more and more as needed. I never tried to be fully open about anything, as I knew that being wholly truthful would not look "holy good."

Finally, with the help of a therapist at a two-week-long retreat for troubled pastors, the truth, the whole truth, and nothing but the truth came out. I choose not to go into details with people now, as it does neither them nor me any good to hash it out again. For the first time in a long time I could lay my head on my pillow and know that if someone was going to accept me for who I am, they could now do it with no pretense of who I pretended to be. It was freeing for me but frustrating and fearful for my wife.

When the children of Israel were making their trek toward their Promised Land, they had a few skirmishes and battles to fight. God was always clear as to what the nation was to do with survivors and the spoils.

When they had overtaken Jericho in a miracle of marching and music from trumpets, God had given strict instructions that the devoted things were not to be messed with. To do so would cause destruction of all the people. Furthermore, the precious metal items that were sacred to the Lord were to go directly into His treasury.

The nation was still celebrating the great victory over the mighty city of Jericho when Joshua sent a small army into Ai. The army should have been large enough, with three thousand men, to take the little city, but thirty-six of them died and the rest came running home. The people of Israel were shocked. Joshua hit the ground in prayer, wondering what might be happening. He was afraid they might win a big battle only to have God's people destroyed by little people in a little city.

God pointed out that someone was hiding sin in the community. Someone had messed with the devoted things from Jericho. I look back and still wonder how it is I think that if I hide the sin from you, then somehow God won't see it. Part of the damage control mind-set for me was to cheapen grace into a "get out of jail free" card.

God instructed Joshua to run through tribe by tribe, clan by clan, and family by family until the sin was discovered. In other words, everyone was to cough up his or her e-mail passwords. Please realize that when the announcement came out, the person that had actually taken the devoted things could have confessed right then and there. But he didn't. Damage control time! Maybe he considered that someone else did the same thing and that person would be punished instead. In fact, he or she would deserve it for taking the devoted items. It's not all that odd for a person to be more judgmental than usual toward those committing the same sin he is committing.

Finally, it was his turn. Achan stepped up, and Joshua asked Achan to give God praise and tell all he had done. Achan then confessed to all he had taken and where it was hidden. It was as if Joshua had the e-mails that Achan had deleted that morning to cover up his sin. Achan's sin was literally buried, as they found the stolen items underneath his tent.

My sin cost me my wife and a whole lot of strife, but it cost Achan his life. Achan and his family were taken out into a valley where they were put to death by stoning. Enough stones were used to completely bury all the people, along with their livestock and possessions. The stones were piled high enough that the area was even named the Valley of Achor. It served as a reminder to people to serve the one true God openly and honestly. This fact makes me appreciate and admire God's grace all the more. Instead of me being put to death, God put His Son to death in my place.

A phrase I heard lately helps in this situation a good bit. If we try to cover up our sin, God exposes it. If we expose our sin, God covers it up. Hidden sin does not do anybody any good. God gets no glory for that which we hide. Once we let others know of our hidden sin, then God is able to provide grace, and then the glory of God shines brightly.

What sin are you hiding? What damage are you trying to control?

AHITOPHEL: MY BAD VICE IS BAD ADVICE (2 SAMUEL 16:15–17:23)

I had gone to an attorney friend to get some things rearranged in my last will and testament. I had become romantically involved with a lady and was looking at changing my will to offer provisions for her and her daughter in the event of my untimely demise.

The attorney in question was a good friend and a follower of Jesus. We were members of the same church, although I had stopped attending while dating this woman. The attorney asked various questions, as he should have, about the status of the relationship with this change of benefits. He asked, "Do you plan to marry this woman?"

I told him that was a possibility. He then advised me of certain things and was going to draw up a sample will for me to review. In the draft he referred to the lady in question as my fiancée. This was a surprise to me as well as the lady. His explanation was that that term would benefit me better legally. He knows more than I do, so I let it stand. It sounded like good advice.

A couple of weeks later, I was in a conversation with someone on campus that attended this same church, and they commented on my recent engagement. It came about because she was trying to fix me up with another girl in the church, touting me as one of the "last good guys in Oxford," only to be told I was engaged. The shocked look on her face must have let her know it was an ugly rumor at that time. I said no formal engagement had taken place. I asked her where she had heard such a statement, and she said it was at church but added she was not sure where it had originated.

A couple of days following that discussion, one of the pastors of the church called me to congratulate me as well. When I asked him about the origin of the story, he said, "Now, it wasn't so much the breaking of a confidence as it was a prayer request."

I exploded at this comment. Some of the worst gossip sessions I've ever encountered were called prayer meetings. No one would just request prayer. We acted as if God were unaware of what we were going to request. No one would simply say, "Please pray for a couple I know that are having marriage difficulties." They would phrase the request this way instead: "Please pray for Ted and Alice. I heard she found out he's cheating on her. Someone else said that he said it was because of her alcoholism and cold behavior."

The pastor tried to convince me that it was done in innocence, but I was righteously indignant at this point. I shared that the news of my engagement was to be dealt with in the same way Mark Twain had dealt with the rumors of his death. I told the pastor, "The rumors of my demise are greatly exaggerated."

Eventually the relationship ended. I still thank God for that! Shortly after she was out of my life, I got the bill from my attorney friend. I discussed it with some people to get their advice. No one said to pay him. The advisors I sought claimed that he should feel lucky I was not taking him to court. I was ready for war! I even began advising others that if they were in a similar situation, they should hang the man out to dry.

Then, following that advice and acting out of bitterness and righteous indignation, I wrote him an e-mail accusing him of breaking confidentiality, and refusing to pay the bill. If he pressed on payment of the bill, I would take legal action on the breach of confidentiality. I was impressed that I had seen enough *Law and Order* episodes to frame such a letter.

His reply was to deny the breaking of confidentiality, but he also stated he would not seek payment for what was due. He rebuked me for not dealing with the matter in a spiritual manner. I felt justified in believing he must have been guilty or he would fight for the money. Oddly enough, while I am in my worst righteous indignation mood, I can judge others more poorly than usual as to whether they are being righteously indignant. I read his reply, and my advice at that point was to not respond and let it go. I had gotten what I wanted in regard to the money, and if he wanted to be higher and mightier and holier, so be it.

As you might guess, God did not give me a break on the matter. Sensing a relationship that needed mending, I was advised to scope out the sources of the original rumor of engagement. I was unable to link it to my attorney friend at all. I sent my friend a check to cover the bill, asked for forgiveness, and offered to pay whatever penalty or interest I might have accrued during my Judgmental Judy period. Fortunately the man forgave me and the penalties and interest. We were able to meet and restore our friendship. I have nothing but the deepest respect for this man and am honored to call him my friend.

I realize it could have turned out worse.

There was a man named Ahitophel. It did turn out worse for him. He was one of King David's counselors. After the sin with Bathsheba, David's son Absalom tried to take over the kingdom. Ahitophel decided to join the son in the takeover attempt. David heard of it and even prayed that God would make his advice foolish.

His advice? He told Absalom to sleep with all of David's concubines. Absalom did so in broad daylight. This was a part of the consequence God gave in response to David's sin. Nathan told David that since he slept with someone's wife in secret, someone would sleep with his women in public. So basically his advice to Absalom was to commit the same sin David had committed. Two wrongs never will make a right.

Then Ahitophel advised Absalom to attack David. Absalom checked with another advisor and got just the opposite recommendation. Hushai advised Absalom to avoid a fight, as David was an experienced warrior. When Ahitophel saw his advice was not heeded, he got his house in order and then committed suicide.

I'm grateful I did not put as much emphasis in my advice as Ahitophel did. I'm more grateful we didn't share the same fate. Oftentimes we advise others into committing the same sin that we are guilty of ourselves. I suppose it makes us feel better to bring in more failed people. Great care should be given as to whose advice to follow or ignore.

Whose advice are you following?

SAUL: COLLECTION OF SOUVENIRS (1 SAMUEL 13)

I had learned the prank from a former pastor. He had pulled it on an unsuspecting senior adult on one of their journeys. I decided it would be fun to pull it on one lady on our team that was building a church in Brazil. I pulled in a few key participants to assist me with the joke.

We were eating at one of the local restaurants one evening after a hard day of putting up cinder block walls. The director of the mission organization had arranged the meal for us and was our host for the evening. He was one of the people I had pulled in on the prank. The other was one of the dearest and sweetest ladies God ever created. We called her Mama Lois. Both she and her husband, Papa John, were very committed to our ministry. They were my main cooks for camps, ski trips, and mission endeavors. Mama Lois was to be the main reactor to the director's role in the prank.

The prank worked like this: I discreetly set a knife and a fork in the opening of the victim's purse, where it would slide down to the bottom. Then I had the director make an announcement. He said, "I know it's thrilling to be in a different part of the world doing God's work in missions. I hate to even have to comment on this, but we have found on previous trips that sometimes people like to take things back to the United States as souvenirs of their mission experience. Oddly enough, we have found people take, of all things, silverware from some of the restaurants we dine in."

When the announcement was made, Mama Lois pointed out that she had observed the victim placing something in her purse. She opened her purse and immediately became defensive, swearing she had not put the knife and fork in there. About that time I made eye contact with her and smiled. She knew she'd been had. This must have been a good memory for her because the following Christmas she gave me a beautifully wrapped gift that had a plastic fork and knife in it. I kept them as mementos for some time.

It's not rare to want to keep some mementos of a trip or game that was memorable. I still have the ticket stub to the 1980 World Series game to which Dad took me. If we have something, we can keep the memory alive in a different way. Even negative occurrences in life can have a particular item bring the situation back to the front of the mind and heart. I was once in a relationship with a lady that was not good. At one point I ended it, but she left her daughter's car seat in my apartment. When I'd see it in the spare bedroom, I would have to think about her. She knew I would have to get the car seat back to her at some point, and perhaps she thought the relationship could be mended at that time. I hate to admit it, but her plan worked the first time, but not the second.

There are times when God does not wish for us to keep a memento or a souvenir. There are some things we are not supposed to remember and keep track of. I had such a case like that. I had been hiding some sin and darkness in my life for some time. The skeletons finally decided to come out of the closet and visit people I knew and loved. It was not an easy time on my family at all.

Part of my restoration plan was to rid myself of things that would take me back to the hidden aspect of my sin. I did this successfully for a few months. The problem was that I didn't get rid of all the things in my mind. I reasoned that if some was left behind, it would make an even better story of God's miraculous work: "Not only did God restore me, but look at how strong I am now. I can resist these temptations on my own now!"

So, with my declaration of power, thoughts that led to inappropriate actions were coming to the forefront of my mind again like rapid-fire gunnery. I found myself going right back into hiding my difficulties so that people would think I had it all together. It was going to make a great story of grace even though I was not living in a way to honor the God of grace.

The problem for me was that keeping the memory of such things kept me from being completely purified from the situation. I rid myself of the tangible things that could lead me back to sin on the outside. I just didn't remove all the trouble spots on the inside. Eventually the lack of removing all the items led to even more trouble being created for my family with a divorce. I realize, and continue to learn, that while I don't control the thoughts that enter my head, I do have control over which ones can take up residence. I can't do that, however, without God's help.

King Saul experienced a situation similar to all of this. God had instructed the king to completely wipe out the Amalekites because of the trouble they gave Israel as they entered into the Promised Land. God specifically wanted the people gone as well as their livestock.

Saul, for some reason, didn't destroy Agag, the Amalekite king, and some of the livestock. Saul and his men went through the animals as if they were regular plunder and took only the finest of the sheep and cattle.

The prophet Samuel, who had delivered the "destroy everything" message, had already heard from God that the dictate had not been carried out completely. So Samuel went to find Saul. Just as I would do, Saul lied about carrying out God's command. He claimed to have carried it out completely. Samuel then asked why he heard sheep bleating and cattle lowing.

Saul claimed it would be great to use the best of the plunder as a sacrifice to God. He stated they had just brought back a few souvenirs, adding that it would be great to show the real power of God in that way. Unfortunately God had commanded what He desired in the first place—complete removal—and expected Saul to comply with the command. When reminded of the truth of God's command by Samuel, Saul again stated that he had complied with the Lord's desires. Saul finally confessed that he had made up his own mind out of the fear of what people would think. When he did this, he ended up disobeying God.

God was more concerned with the obedience from me and Saul than He was in our display of His power. What good is it to hang on to something to sacrifice to God when He wanted it gone in the first place? That's like a double slap to the face. When Saul finally came to grips with the truth, he admitted his sin. He asked for forgiveness in the hopes of worshiping with Samuel. Then, worried about his personal image in the same way as I was worried about mine, Saul asked Samuel to honor him before the elders and all of Israel. Instead of the public relations gig for Saul, Samuel had King Agag brought to him, and he executed him to carry out God's command. Saul and I have learned that when God wants something destroyed, the best thing to do is obey. God does not need my help to bring about glory for Himself.

What souvenir can open you up for more trouble?

REHOBOAM: THAT'S MORE LIKE IT (1 KINGS 12)

I usually listen to good advice, especially if I agree with it. If I happen to disagree, I am likely to manipulate or rationalize the direction in I wish to go anyway.

For about thirteen years I had some secret sin that inhabited and controlled my life. I found myself crossing lines and limits I never would have imagined crossing. In the midst of the darkness, I would often feel guilt and condemnation. This would lead to the normal idea of confession. The thing is, with my sin it would have meant the possible loss of my family and the sure loss of my job in the church.

I found it easy to talk in generalities with other ministers while we were attending conferences and workshops together. I would relay my situation as a person in my church and solicit the responses of fellow church leaders. I had projected such an image that no one at all suspected my stories were about me instead of someone else. In each case, everyone told my "friend" to face the music and confess and keep the sin from ruining his life further.

Of course, this was not the advice I wanted to hear.

I would go to others and find the same bit of advice in them. Everyone said the best thing to do was come clean with the wife and with the church and face the consequences accordingly. I simply did not want to go that route. I wanted to protect my family despite my continuing in a sinful manner that would destroy them. I wanted to protect my image as the minister that had it all together. I wanted to ensure that I would not lose my job and therefore my identity as a person. I had convinced myself I could compartmentalize my life and keep that particular part hidden.

I fell for the lie that no one had to know. The advice of letting others know never made sense to me. Yet, by believing that lie, I became more and more a slave to the sin. The more I became a slave, the more the lies convinced me of my freedoms. So the option of truth was not an option for me.

Finally I found some advice worth heeding. It was not from a scriptural or spiritual source at all. I heard it on a daytime talk show. The advice given was "Don't tell!" The advisor went further to explain that in confessing all you are doing is transferring your pain and guilt onto your spouse. Why in the world would anyone want to load that kind of pain upon someone they love? The best way to protect your spouse is to remain quiet. The advice continued, explaining that the pain and guilt are punishment enough without having to bring others into the mess.

This was what I had been looking for! Finally there was someone that understood the true issues here. It made so much sense to me. I needed to protect my family from my hurtful behavior, so I adopted this bit of advice.

I even investigated it further and found numerous psychologists, therapists, and counselors that all gave the same advice. None, of course, used any form of theology or Christian behavior in their theories. On the other hand, I had the advice I wanted and needed, and I continued to live in silence and in hiding. When thoughts hit my mind about confessing from all the earlier advice offerings, I would convince myself that I was doing the right thing in keeping things hidden. I ignored scriptural truth that would tell me otherwise and would stick to the talk show truth that allowed me to continue my sin in hiding.

The problem is, without facing the consequences of sin, the sin very rarely loses any power. An old adage a friend taught me goes like this: "If we cover our sin, God exposes it. If we expose our sin, God covers it."

So I found myself getting deeper and deeper into darkness.

I am a weird creature. I'm sure there are others reading this that would say they are members of the same club. I seek advice as long as it's what I originally wanted to hear. I appreciate sound advice as long as I can manipulate it into what benefits me the most.

Rehoboam faced a similar situation. Rehoboam was King Solomon's son and became the king when Solomon died. One of his first steps as king was to seek the advice of some elders on how to perform his tasks as king. The elders advised him to serve the people and make their load lighter than his father had done. The elders suggested showing a kind and merciful leadership they had not experienced with Solomon. The elders probably had at least heard of David's leadership and remembered it being more benevolent. The elders had also witnessed a Solomon that served the Lord, as well as the later years when he served false gods brought in by his many wives. Rehoboam sent the elders away and asked them to return in three days.

Rehoboam then asked some younger men what he should do. They advised him to make things even harder on the people. They lied to him about his strength and his worth in comparison to his father. They built him up by playing to his ego. They told him he had more power in a finger than Solomon did in his thigh. They projected an image of what a strong king would look like to Rehoboam, and kindness and mercy were not part of their description. They encouraged him to live up to that image they had created for a king.

The younger men were probably bucking for a promotion themselves. If they could convince Rehoboam to run with their idea, then they'd be taking over some of the advising positions the elders held presently. The younger men offered the advice they felt Rehoboam wanted to hear rather than what he needed to hear.

Rehoboam liked what he heard from the younger men and did just that. I have a suspicion he wanted to go that route in the first place. No one should be surprised that the people rebelled at the thought and, according to the Scripture, "the Israelites went home." Israel was in rebellion from that day on. Jeroboam led the rebellion and separated the kingdom into two parts. He took ten of the twelve tribes of people, and Rehoboam was left with Judah and parts of Benjamin.

Like Rehoboam, I listened to the wrong advice. A sin-filled life could have taken a new direction much sooner had I heeded the good advice. In the same way Israel suffered a split and long-term consequences, my wrong advice cost me a marriage and caused other long-term consequences.

I've often heard the phrase "Don't ask a question where you really don't want the answer." I think seeking advice is the same pattern. Unless I listen to both sides of the advice and really seek what God's advice would be, I am destined to manipulate the path toward what I wanted to do in the first place.

What advice do you seek?

JACOB: FIGHTING THE RIGHTS OF THE FIRSTBORN (GENESIS 25, 27)

The whole argument of birth order makes sense when you have children. In raising my own children, when James, the firstborn, would drop his pacifier, I would pick it up, boil some water, put the pacifier in the boiling water, take it out with a pair of tongs, let it cool and dry, and then put it back in his mouth. When Danno, the second son, dropped his pacifier, I would run hot water from the faucet and let it cool, then stick it back in his mouth. When poor Adam, who was the baby of the family, would drop his pacifier, I would simply pull the dog hairs off of it and stick it back in his mouth.

There are various views as to which is the best place to occupy in the birth order. Some view the oldest child as having difficulty due to being the test case for parents. Some view the youngest child as having the most difficulty, as a result of dealing with all the hand-me-downs and never getting anything new or original. I tend to view middle children as getting the worst deal. They still represent some test case scenarios, as they are usually totally different from the firstborn. They also get a good portion of the hand-me-downs. So in a sense they are treated with the penalties and prizes of both the oldest and the youngest.

I was a middle child. After reading my opinion above on birth order, I'm sure none of you are surprised at my views.

Most family photo albums end up being divided with 75 percent of the photos being of the firstborn, with the remaining children sharing the rest of the space. There are just certain rights given to the firstborn. In older cultures the firstborn's rights were quite significant. The firstborn sons usually took over the family business and took over the family when the father died. The inheritance given to the heirs would work out to the firstborn receiving twice as much as the others. In fact, much of the pressure of family that Jesus dealt with came about because He was not fulfilling His traditional role in their eyes as the firstborn.

In our culture the firstborn naturally gets a few breaks. They get to drive sooner, as they hit the magical driving age sooner. Graduation, certain camps, or sports that are age-driven, and movie viewing, seem to go with firstborn rights as well.

I suffered greatly at the rights of the firstborn. When the Walt Disney movie *Blackbeard's Ghost* first came out, my parents took my older brother and same-age cousin Brian to see it. I wanted to go but was not allowed to do so because Allen was older and I wasn't quite old enough yet. I was fourteen months younger, but that was "too young." Oddly enough, I never saw the movie until it came out on the Disney channel some twenty-five years later. It's a funny movie. I'm glad I finally saw it.

I remember other times when Allen got other aspects of preferential treatment. I always had to share a room with my younger brother, while Allen always got one of his own. Do you know the reason for Allen having his own room? You are correct! He was older!

Jacob was an interesting character. He was the second born of twin sons. Rebekah felt the twins jostling inside her belly as if they were competing as to who would be born first. Rebekah asked God what was going on and was told the older of the two boys would serve the younger. This was completely opposite of the culture's way of doing things. When the babies were delivered, Esau came first and Jacob was born with his hand holding Esau's heel. Even in the womb they fought for the firstborn rights. So the fraction of time between the two deliveries meant Esau, Jacob's older brother, was in line for the blessings from the father and double the inheritance.

Knowing brothers as I do, I can imagine some of the wrestling and verbal jousting that went on between these two as they were growing up. My own older brother used to use the fact that he was older as perfect logic as to why we should do things his way. I imagine Esau abused Jacob with the same logic. The story tells us that Esau loved the outdoors and Jacob preferred hanging around town. They were as different as most children from the same parents can be. I have a feeling both were vying for the attention from their parents, as most of us have.

In this, a truly dysfunctional family, you had the dad loving the oldest son the most and the mom favoring the youngest. Perhaps this was because she had heard the prophecy of the two boys from God. Jacob was much shrewder that I was. I harassed and tormented the firstborn of my household, but it never got me anything except more trouble. Jacob orchestrated ways to wrestle the firstborn rights away from his brother by offering him food when he was starving. He waited for Esau to come back from a long hunting trip with a pot of stew. When he discovered his older brother was starving and about to die, he sold the stew for his birthright. When it came time for the firstborn's blessing to be offered by the father, Jacob's mother helped him trick the old man out of the blessing as well.

With the blessing and the birthright, Jacob went on to be the next step in God's plan to form a nation. Oddly enough, when Jacob was offering the blessing to his son Joseph prior to his death, he placed Joseph's second son over the firstborn. Joseph even pointed this fact out to his dad, but he was rebuffed and told it was done that way on purpose.

In modern-day culture, I really can't whine about my older brother getting more than I did. Dad blessed us all equally, and when Dad died, each of us boys got something that was unique and special between us. Allen got the woodworking tools, Mark got the fly-tying materials, and I got the Gideon New Testament he received when he was baptized. Despite the culture, I still did my fair share of trying to wrestle with what firstborn rights I imagined Allen having. I should have learned, as Jacob and Joseph did, that God isn't as concerned with the order of our birth as he is in us receiving His second birth.

In being God's son, Jesus was the ultimate of the firstborn in our world. He had rights and privileges that are unfathomable to us. I'm talking about things that are even greater than getting to see a movie or drive a car first. Yet Paul writes in one of his letters that Jesus gave up all the rights as a firstborn in order to be like us. Jesus knew that the message of love, grace, and redemption had no credibility without Him becoming a real human being.

So while I whined and fought about my rights, Jesus taught me the simplicity of living in the moment of who God made me to be. In many ways, God sees each of us as His firstborn, offering us twice the inheritance and blessings.

I guess that ends my whining about being the middle kid!

NADAB AND ABIHU: INSTRUCTIONS ARE FOR AFTER YOU'VE SCREWED IT UP (LEVITICUS 10:1–5)

I had seen my own grandmother do it numerous times. In addition to that, I had observed my mother-in-law doing it with my children during their growing years. So I figured, how hard can it be to bake sugar cookies and decorate them for Christmas? I felt positive there were some instructions I could follow, but I felt equally as positive that I didn't need them. After all, what can a sheet of instructions tell me better than seeing it done by special people in my life?

The idea of baking Christmas cookies popped into my head because of a girl. It's amazing what men can think up when they need to win a girl's heart. This particular girl I had been out with a few times had a four-year-old daughter. On this particular date, I had invited the lady and her daughter to my apartment for dinner and the ceremonial Christmas-cookie-baking-and-decorating party. While it has been said the path to a man's heart is through his stomach, I knew that the path to a single mom's heart is through her children. So I really wanted to make an impression. I knew that I was still a child at heart and in some behaviors, so I assumed impressing a four-year-old wouldn't be a problem.

I purchased a collection of different ornamental cookie cutters. One was shaped like Santa Claus, one like a Christmas tree, another one a snowman, and one a star shape. They came in a collection in a stocking-shaped mesh bag. So it was Christmas the entire way. I put a bow on it and placed the child's name on a tag, or what I like to call "the toandfrom." The cutters were part of her Christmas gift, as was the opportunity to use them.

I had no idea how to make homemade sugar cookie dough, so I bought one of those tubes of cookie dough from the store. I remembered that Grandma and Mother-In-Law would lay out the dough and then cut out the shapes. So the little girl and I flattened it out just a bit on a large sheet of wax paper on my dining room table. Flour was scattered all over the wax paper, as well as the rest of the table and the floor. We put the cutters in place and formed various cookies for the baking. We placed the cut-out cookies on the cookie sheet. I had the oven preheated to the correct temperature, and we were ready to go. The first batch went into the oven. We then filled a second cookie sheet full and popped it into the oven as well.

While they were cooking, we prepared the icing, M&M's, sprinkles, and Red Hots candies for the decorating portion of the night. The smell of baking cookies filled the room, and the little girl was getting more and more excited as we waited for the oven timer to start beeping.

The beeping began, and we jumped to see the final product. I had a cookie cooling tray I had purchased along with the cutters so that we could cool the cookies properly before decorating. Everything was in place as we pulled open the oven door.

Much to our surprise, we didn't find any of the snowmen, Santa Clauses, Christmas trees, or stars. In the baking process the dough had risen and expanded, causing us to basically have a full sheet of cookie. It resembled a flat cake more than it did a cookie. There were faint lines where you could see that a cookie was trying to be a snowman but had become one with a Santa Claus. I still unsure as to who was the most disappointed that day between the three of us.

The mom stepped in to see the mess on the sheet and asked if I had followed any set of instructions. "Instructions?" I asked with a lost, wandering look on my face.

Apparently there was something different about the dough Grandma and Mother-In-Law made. I think the store-bought dough is made to rise and expand a bit more. I doubt very seriously too that we flattened the dough as much as the ladies in my life had done. I would have probably seen that if I had read any instructions on the ordeal.

Despite numerous failures in my life due to not reading instructions, I somehow still operate on the notion that instructions are for after you've already screwed up on a project. I know the right thing to do, and I know I can confirm it in the instructions. I just don't. Thankfully I am not alone in this behavioral trait.

Nadab and Abihu discovered the same thing when they didn't follow instructions completely. These two were the older sons of Aaron and were made part of the priestly family by God. Following the confirmation of the covenant of the law, our boys, along with Moses, Aaron, and seventy of the elders, went up the mountain and saw the God of Israel. It was said God did not raise His hand against these leaders and that they saw Him and ate and drank there.

The boys had been recruited by God Himself to serve as priests among the people. They had been consecrated as leaders of the people. A part of the service as a priest was to follow the strict instructions that were given by God on how certain parts of sacrifice and worship were to take place.

Aaron began the worship by following the instructions of sacrificing a bull and a ram for the sin offering and the burnt offering. A burnt offering was given, and the glory of the Lord appeared to all the people. Moses and Aaron went back into the Tent of Meeting, and when they came back out, a fire from God's presence came and consumed the offering. When this happened, the people shouted for joy and fell facedown on the ground as an act of worship.

Following this, Nadab and Abihu lit another fire in their censers and added incense to it. The fire they used had not been commanded by God. All of a sudden fire from the Lord did appear. It consumed Nadab and Abihu, and they died right there before the Lord.

Nadab and Abihu died, as did my relationship with the single mom. God had set things up in a certain way to separate the priests from the common people. God also wanted to set His people apart from others, so specific instructions on how to live and worship were given. Nadab and Abihu didn't follow those instructions and paid dearly for it. In many ways the relationship I had with the single mom did not follow God's instructions, and therefore it was doomed to death. The instructions are not there to limit what I can do but rather to teach me the best way to live. Nadab and Abihu tried to create the firework show without having the actual worship experience. The instructions were clear but were ignored. I fear that my worship planning often seeks the fireworks without the actual experience. Maybe I need to go read over the instructions again.

What instructions from God should you be reading and following?

SOLOMON: PREDECESSOR PROBLEMS? (1 KINGS 3:1–15)

Measuring up has always seemed to be a problem for me. I am the second of three boys born to my parents. Fourteen months separate me and my older brother; actually that should read "fourteen months and several intelligence quotient points." My older brother is one of those walking encyclopedias. If he read it, I imagine he's retained it.

Year after year, especially in high school, I would have to try to live up to the academic and intelligence standard my brother Allen had set for me. Year after year, teachers were disappointed that I was not like him. The only real thing I had going for me academically was that within a few days at the start of a school year, the teacher, having observed my behaviors, would move my desk up next to hers and tell me I was going to be her helper. I would overhear them say as they moved me to the front, "I'll put you up here, you little smart ..." Their voices would quiet before they could finish the sentence. I can only assume they were complimenting my intellectual abilities.

As much as I hated being the younger brother to one as smart as Allen, I have wondered how Jesus' siblings dealt with him. Allen is smart, but he was still a typical young man while growing up. He got in his fair share of trouble. Can you imagine following Jesus in school? You know His siblings had difficulty living up to His standards. Jesus' brothers and sisters were the first to be given the WWJD (What would Jesus do?) slogan. How nice would it be to be reminded that Jesus *always* turned in his homework on time, *always* cleaned His room without being asked, and was *always* respectful to His parents? Yes, it's always difficult to follow the successful and popular ones.

Years ago, when I became single again, I targeted divorced ladies as possible dates. I went out with a couple of widows and discovered that when a spouse is lost through death, the surviving spouse tends to glorify all the good the deceased did and minimize the bad. Divorced people tend to go the opposite route. That's why I targeted the divorced ones. I always figured that even I could look good when compared to some of the losers these girls had married and divorced. I knew there was no way I'd measure up with the good guys! It's always difficult to follow the successful and popular ones.

When I was involved with speech and debate tournaments in high school, part of my responsibilities included giving a humorous interpretation of a play or story. I remember sitting in a classroom, waiting for my turn to perform, and hearing the participant before me do a fabulous performance. I would look around to see if anyone else might want to go next instead of me. I never wanted to follow the really funny and talented persons. It's always difficult to follow the successful and popular ones.

Through my years of experience of working in churches, I have seen many successful and popular pastors and other staff move on to other ministry venues. For many of those churches, the next person in struggled to succeed with the Ghost of Staff Members Past haunting them. This is because it's always difficult to follow the successful and popular ones.

With this in mind, I had an idea for following a popular staff member in churches. I call it the "intentional interim." I would contract with a church to follow the particular pastor or staff member for a time period of one year. It would be crucial that the church pay the entire contract salary value up front. This will show its importance later. During that year I would preach boring and uninspired messages, skip important meetings, talk ugly in the pulpit about certain church members, and flirt with all the deacon's wives. Most churches would fire me after two weeks. That's why I would get my pay in advance.

After my short tenure, however, when the church is looking to hire a new pastor or staff member, they won't lament that he or she is not like Brother Bob. Instead they'll be thanking God he or she is not like David Waddell! While it's very difficult to take the place of someone that was successful or good, it isn't so hard to follow the other end of the spectrum.

In each of the jobs I've held, there was a predecessor that was incredibly successful and incredibly loved. In my main career positions, I have had to follow two Buddys, a Bobby, a Greg, a Sharon, a Frank, a Debbie, and a Stephanie. I always braced myself for the statement "That's not how so-and-so would have done it!" In each of these situations, I have had to guard my sarcastic tongue to not point out any of my predecessor's difficulties or shortcomings. Even following a popular leader, there are those that enjoy throwing the former leaders under the bus. I'm sorry to say that I have at times let my guard down and not always spoken as highly as I should have regarding these men and women.

Poor Solomon was in the same situation. He had to follow the most beloved king that ever existed. He followed his father, David, who was known as a man after God's own heart. Talk about having a tough act to follow. I think I may have had it easier with Allen or all of my job predecessors.

Despite following a popular king as well as taking over the family business, Solomon was God's choice to lead the building project of His temple. God had stated that David, as a warrior, had too much blood on his hands to lead the building of God's dwelling place. So the job was given to David's successor.

Early in Solomon's rule, God came and declared he would grant Solomon whatever he wished for. I assume there must have been some rules so that Solomon wouldn't do as I would do and wish for more wishes. Solomon recognized the kindness God had shown to his father, David, and acknowledged that God was continuing to show him the same kindness. At this point Solomon had already survived two kingdom takeover attempts by another of David's sons, Adonijah.

Solomon recognized his own humility and called himself a little child compared to David. The humility part may have been one of the things I could have worked at a little more in succeeding the people I followed. Then Solomon made his one request that God promised to grant him. He asked God for a discerning heart to distinguish between right and wrong. Wisdom, that's all he wished for.

God granted Solomon wisdom and discernment. He also gave him what he didn't request—honor and riches. God also promised that if Solomon followed the ways of his father, David, he would also have long life. Solomon passed the successor test! He spoke highly of his predecessor, and God honored him in new and amazing ways. Solomon became known as the wisest man to live. He was responsible for over 3,000 proverbs of wisdom. He wrote 1,005 songs. He also taught a good bit about animals, birds, reptiles, and fish. His fame spread all around the surrounding nations. David was not a forgotten king, but Solomon made a name for himself with his humility and his wisdom. He proved that by removing one's pride from the equation, one can follow the successful and popular ones.

Whose position are you now filling?

SAMARITAN WOMAN: DID I HEAR THAT CORRECTLY? (JOHN 4)

I had met her in August. Her parents moved to Springfield just prior to both of us beginning our college careers. She sat across the room during our Sunday school hour. She was cute, and unlike the other girls in the youth group, she had no idea how insane and crazy I was. At the close of our Bible study time, I approached her and introduced myself to her.

I saw her mostly in the Baptist Student Center following the introduction. I had taken on a part-time position as a minister of youth in a town about sixty miles from home. We would talk and occasionally get in a game of spades together. Spades was a popular game for me growing up. It was a major pastime of the speech and debate squad from high school, as well as students killing time in the Baptist Student Center.

It was getting to be near the end of the spring semester, and a couple of runs at relationships in college had played out, so I decided to ask this girl out. We went on our first date on a Friday and watched *All the President's Men*. It was a movie made from the best-selling book about President Nixon and the Watergate scandal. I know what you're thinking; I'm such a romantic!

I took off the next day for my weekend youth ministry job, so I didn't see her again until the following Monday. We got involved in a game of spades and were partners in the game. Throughout the entire game and the moments we were together after that, she kept repeating the same message. In a variety of methods and wordings, she would say, "My only night off is Thursday this week."

I swear she said it over twenty times during the hour we had between classes. Each time she said it, I heard the same subliminal message coming through: "Don't ask me to do anything on Thursday, because that's the only night I have off this week." Believe me, after about six of the comments I thought, *Baby, I will leave you alone. I promise!*

I have no doubt the females of our species that are reading this right now have made the judgment that I'm an idiot. You would be correct. I did not realize that when she said "I only have one night off work," she was really saying "When you ask me out, which I assume you will do from the numerous clues I'm giving you, you will know Thursday is the only day I can go."

Now, before you get too judgmental on my lack of reading the clues, you should know I've told this story to numerous people, both male and female. Each and every female has asked me whether I asked her out for Thursday, while each and every male has confirmed that I didn't ask her out for Thursday.

I was in a text messaging conversation with another lady recently. I could sense there might be some chemistry or magic starting with this budding relationship. She was not feeling well and asked me, "If I close my eyes, will you be here when I open them?"

I responded that she should try, and if the magic worked I would be there with her. She responded that she meant she was going to take a nap and was wondering if I could talk when she woke up.

I have this new theory about thunder. I don't believe it to be clouds bumping into each other in a storm. I think it might actually be God and the heavenly beings gathering together to listen to men and women try to communicate. They observe how clueless men are about women and how women don't understand our obviousness. The thunder is actually the heavenly laughter that is caused by our misunderstanding of each other.

Regardless of the differences in how we communicate, for me communication has always been ...

Well, you get the idea.

Communication is difficult for anyone to fully understand, whether a message is sent to the opposite sex or the same one. A message is sent in some sort of code, and the receiver must attempt to understand it.

Feedback guides the original messenger as to whether understanding has taken place or not. I have to make sure you understand me. The more difficult part of the process is trying to figure out what someone is telling me. It wears me out just to think about it.

I was told once by someone that I'm not a very good listener. I'm not sure what she really said, because I really wasn't paying much attention to her. Instead of listening, I'm usually formulating what I'm going to say to you once you stop talking. One of the pastors I worked with wanted me to improve my listening skills, so I was given a CD to listen to and learn from. Think about the irony of getting something to listen to in order to improve listening skills. I played the CD four times before getting everything I was supposed to from the introduction.

There is a story of a woman that had similar difficulties in communicating. It didn't matter what the topic would turn to; the woman would hear something else and respond accordingly. Jesus, on a trip through Samaria, stopped at a well for a drink of water. The disciples had all gone to find Him some food. Jesus met a woman that was coming for water long after most folks had filled up for the day. The timing of her water retrieval indicates she was, in some sense, a social outcast.

Jesus made a simple request for a drink of water. The woman wondered why He was even talking with her, because of their cultural differences. Jesus played off her reference to the differences between Samaritans and Jews and pointed out that if she knew who He was, she would be asking Him for water. She wondered how He'd get the water, since He had no bucket and rope to draw the water with. She further explained that the well had been visited by Jewish celebrities such as Jacob.

Jesus pulled the conversation back into something holy and redeeming and offered the woman some "living water." She thought that sounded great, because if she had that, she wouldn't have to lug around the great big pot of water every day. I have to admit, I do appreciate her logic in looking out for herself!

Jesus requested that she get her husband, but she denied having one. Jesus pointed out that there was truth in her statement and called out the husbands she'd had and noted that she was now living with a man without being married to him. She claimed He was a prophet and turned the conversation to the proper location of worship. Jesus gave her the proper motive of worship being done in spirit and in truth, and not necessarily being done in the right location.

Following His explanation, the woman pointed out that someday the Messiah would come and explain everything. Jesus pointed out to the woman that He was indeed the one whom she spoke of.

With every attempt to get to the crucial matters, the woman instead came up with something superficial to discuss. I can't really fault her, because I communicate with God in the same way. God may be telling me to do something on Thursday, and I'll hear the message in my own filter and in my own understanding. I will twist the message and rationalize it out until I have justified not doing exactly what God has requested of me. There's really not a lot of ambiguity in what God tells us to do. The ambiguity comes from the way I listen to the command. Perhaps I should stick to the topic of worshiping in spirit and in truth. How about you?

"I'm sorry. What was that you said?"

THE PEOPLE OF JESUS' TIME: WHAT WAS THAT NAME AGAIN? (MARK 8:27–30)

I heard a story once that Will Rogers was bet that he couldn't make Calvin Coolidge smile. Coolidge, as president of our great country, was a rather stoic individual. Will Rogers was going through a receiving line to shake hands with the president. When President Coolidge said hello to Mr. Rogers, Will commented, "I'm sorry, I didn't catch your name."

Coolidge not only smiled but also burst out in laughter.

One of the things I have prided myself on is remembering names. When I first started working in churches during college, I was given the advice to remember names. There is something special about having someone remember your name. I never wanted to say, "I can't remember your name, but your face is familiar."

When I would go to a new church to serve, I would get a copy of their picture directory. I always called it the "funny book." I would start putting names with faces. Sometimes I would know a person's name before I even met him or her. In one case I learned a lady's name in the book, but she had been married after the book was printed. Oddly enough, I still remember her maiden name as well as her married one to this day.

It got to be a game people would play with me as to how well I could remember everyone's name. I won the contests more times than not. I made it a goal to remember every child's name when we took them to camp. The last couple of years I was at Germantown

Baptist, we had anywhere from eighty to one hundred children at camp. It took the entire week, but I would get them all down. We established a contest of names in which I would tell the campers that I would know their names by the end of the week or else they could throw a pie in my face. I would call off every name, but the last one I would call would be one of the kids that needed to shine a little more than the others or needed to be a hero for a change. I would mess up on his or her name on purpose even though I'd been calling the child by name all week. The pies were usually just whipped cream in an aluminum pie pan, so in one sense it was still a win-win for me.

When I started teaching at the University of Mississippi, I was determined to do the same thing. Within two weeks I aimed to have all the names memorized to the point that I could call them out without the assistance of the class roll. I succeed at this every semester. In one class I had eighty students. Some doubted whether I could know them all by the end of the semester. Others told me to throw in the towel, as no one would really expect that to happen. By the final exam, I could call each of them by name.

The reason I brag about this is because God keeps me humble. Just when I think I'm the sharpest thing ever in name memory, I foul one up royally.

This happened during a search for a faculty member for our Exercise Science program within the department I worked for. One of the other colleagues on the recreation faculty asked me whether I was having dinner with the candidate that evening. I indicated that I was. I had not read the materials about him at that point, so I asked my colleague and friend as to his name. He said it was Barton Fink. It sounded familiar to me, so I figured I had heard it in a faculty meeting or a hallway discussion.

We get to the fancy restaurant to wine and dine the gentleman and try to determine whether we would think he would be a good fit for the department. I asked a few questions, as did the other folks at the table. Each time I would ask a question, I would be sure to use his name, Barton, as a way to show the informality of our faculty and impress him as to how good I am with names.

With each question I asked "Barton," he would pause and look at me as if I were crazy and then answer me. After the third question, he stopped and said, "My name is Michael, not Barton."

During this entire process, my friend that had called out the name "Barton" to begin with was having a rather entertaining and enjoyable evening at my expense. By the way, the reason "Barton Fink" sounded familiar is because he is a character in a movie of the same name. To make matters worse, there was a youngster by the name Michael Barton in one of my churches that was close to the age to one of my sons. One can see how easily I could get confused in this matter.

Recently I was asked to perform the memorial service for the grandfather of a friend of mine. I had met the man once but did not really know him at all. The family was very special to me, so I agreed to perform the service. I met with the family and got stories and tidbits about the man's life in order to formulate the message.

The man's name was very similar to that of another man I knew from a church I had once served. It apparently became difficult for my mind to differentiate between the two because I called the deceased by the wrong name throughout the memorial message. I know this because a dear lady tugged at the elbow of my suit jacket and let me know his real name. I asked what I had said, and she told me. I then asked her how many times I had called out the wrong name, and she promptly told me I had done so three times!

The following Sunday, I had that feeling someone was trying to get my attention. I turned to my right, and in the row behind me of the section next to me was one of my good friends. He looked at me and whispered, "I'm Gary Jenkins."

I acknowledged that and admitted that I knew that. This is when Gary pointed out that he had heard I was having difficulty with names. There's nothing like doing something humbling and actually having to learn humility with it.

Names are easy to confuse. When I was growing up, I was called by my younger brother's name as much as my own. I know that after a semester with a student, the name tends to leave me at times. I may see students during the next semester, but without the constancy of them having me call their names, the memory of their names disappears. Unfortunately I'm left thinking "The face is familiar, but what is the name?" The names Courtney and Christi blend together in my head. Jackson and Johnson apparently do too. I'm still confused about Michael and Barton as well.

The people that lived where Jesus lived had a similar problem. It seems that Jesus was making headlines wherever He went. Without a daily paper or the Internet, the word tended to travel around by word of mouth. People were hearing about people being healed, being fed, and being brought back from the dead. When they would try to figure out who was doing it, the confusion would come around.

Jesus took a moment once to ask the disciples as to whom everyone said He was. The answers came back that some thought Jesus was Elijah come back from the dead. Since Elijah had been taken to heaven in a fiery chariot, he never really died as far as anyone could tell. Based on Jesus' miracle power, it would be easy to confuse him with one of the original miracle workers, Elijah.

Others said He was John the Baptist. In that the two of them were cousins, there may have been a family trait that caused them to look somewhat similar. This is what my younger brother and I had to deal with. I was always glad my brother was so incredibly good looking!

Still others thought He was some other prophet. The name of Jesus had probably been bantered back and forth, but people believed what they wanted to believe about the other possibilities.

Jesus then asked the disciples who they thought He was. This is when Peter made the unbelievable declaration of faith in calling Jesus the Christ or the Messiah.

The others in the world, like me, were having difficulties with the correct name. Peter was quick to make sure all knew who Jesus really was. It was just a little while after this when Peter, following Jesus' resurrection to heaven, told people that they could not receive salvation with anyone else's name. Jesus is the only path to renewing our relationship with God.

I can't remember the face, but the name is familiar.

JUDAIZERS: NO EXTRA HOOPS AS OUR DEBT IS PAID IN FULL (ACTS 15:1–21)

I think my dad was typical of most dads. He was tightfisted when it came to finances. I used to listen to the Bill Cosby comedy routines about his dad and wonder how we must have been related. The money just didn't come out of the pocket or wallet easily.

Whenever my brothers or I needed to hit him up for a few bucks, we knew the Spanish Inquisition and Central Intelligence Agency had nothing on Dad in seeking information. We would have to come prepared with all of the who, what, when, where, and how in order to get enough money to buy a root beer at the game. Then we would hear the lecture about how long he would have had to work to get a similar amount when he was our age.

A question was posed to me in school once as we were discussing word problems in Math. The teacher asked me, "If your dad has five dollars and you asked him for three, how much would he have left?"

I replied, "Five dollars."

The teacher corrected me and told me I was wrong in that my dad would have only two dollars left. I snapped back that he would still have five dollars. She told me I didn't know my math.

I told her, "You don't know my dad!"

Trying to make her point she said, "Let's say he gave you the three dollars, what would you say then?"

"Then that wouldn't be my dad!"

He just didn't let go of money easily. I suppose it's a trait he handed down to me. My own sons referred to me as the Heat Nazi during those cold Missouri and Tennessee winters. Sometimes it would get to a "brutal" thirty degrees outside and they'd complain because I had the thermostat set at sixty-five. Oops, there goes my sarcasm. Plus I'm sounding like my dad.

When I graduated high school, dad gave me two options for my college career. I could go to any school anywhere I wanted. It was my choice. He gave me the option of paying for all my own tuition and books while living at home for free and attending Missouri State, or I could go elsewhere and pay my own tuition and living expenses and buy my own books. He must have raised me correctly, because I decided to accept the stigma of being in college and living at home to save some bucks.

While I was in college, my financial debt started to grow. I needed to buy a car in order to get to classes and work a part-time weekend youth ministry job in a town sixty miles from home. Dad loaned me the money to purchase a 1971 Gremlin. It had to be one of the ugliest cars ever made, but it did get me from point A to point B. I don't even remember Dad giving me a lecture at the passing of the dollars from his checkbook to the dealer. I assume that's because it was a loan.

Fast forward through a couple of wrecks in the Gremlin during the college years (and understand Dad paid for them and added it all to the loan). I was approaching graduation from college with a rather hefty loan due to my father. I had made efforts to pay off some of the loan, but you know how money goes. A date here, a trip with friends there, and all of a sudden you realize you haven't paid off a thing. Luckily the only interest Dad was charging was in hoping I'd become responsible enough to desire to pay off my debts. I wasn't really doing that well in that area.

I approached my college graduation night. The world awaited me. I had a new wife and had been accepted into seminary for my graduate work. I knew money would be tight, but that is life. I walked through the line and got the diploma case and shook the hands of the university president. Yet this huge debt clouded some of the dreams and excitement in my heart.

I approached my dad following the "Pomp and Circumstance" finish of the ceremony, and he told me, "Your graduation present is that your debt is forgiven. Consider it paid in full."

Who is this man, and what has he done with my father? I wondered.

Forgiven. Paid in full. Despite all my studies and theological understanding, it didn't make sense. I was given a gift of grace. I had received something I hadn't earned, and I didn't have to pay the penalty of what I had earned. Dad wanted me to be able to start my life with a clean slate. No residue of any past debt would haunt me.

It's the same gift offered to us by our Heavenly Father. In my life I have created debts, left scars in the hearts of people I love, and generally screwed up some lives. I have created this huge debt of wrongdoing penalties, and all I hear my Heavenly Father saying are the same words I heard my dad say: "Your debt is forgiven. Consider it paid in full."

Here's the crazy part. Throughout the rest of my dad's life, I wanted to pay him back for the debt he had forgiven. Silly, right? I kept creating the haunting residue of debt and was never comfortable just accepting the gift. I felt this insane sense of responsibility to do something to earn his favor. I was trying to prove myself worthy of the gift he gave me because he felt I was worthy to receive it.

Talk about your vicious cycle. Yet I find myself on the "treadmill of approval" with God all the time. If I work harder, try harder, and stay better, then I can pay off part of the debt He has already paid in full.

The early church had to deal with this a good bit. There was a movement by some of the Jewish believers that felt Gentile converts should go through the Jewish ritual of circumcision prior to being able to accept Christ as their savior. These folks were called Judaizers. The addition of an extra hoop to jump through was causing trouble in the church. The mind-set of making someone Jewish prior to that person being able to follow Christ was putting people right back in a performance-based salvation. Paul argued that the law never set the Jews free, so it didn't make sense for them to burden the Gentiles with it. If we were to return to the law, following Christ would be more about what I do rather than what Jesus did. What the Judaizers were suggesting was just like what I did with Dad. I accepted the gift freely and then made myself a slave in order to pay off what I no longer owed.

There were times my dad would hear something I'd say or observe something I was doing and he would shake his head and say, "You ain't right." I wonder when I try to please God with Judaizer efforts to "buy" grace if He's not thinking the same thing.

Grace is given. Your debt is forgiven. Paid in full. Enjoy life with a clean slate.

SOLOMON: IT'S THE "HOWEVER" THAT HAUNTS US (1 KINGS 11:1–10)

I had a very nice life and résumé built. In the matter of just forty-five years of my life, I was right where I wanted to be. People knew me and respected me.

I was just about to celebrate the twenty-fifth year of being married. I arranged an anniversary trip for us to go to Scotland that March while my wife would be off for spring break. I had three sons: two in college and one a freshman in high school. These were excellent sons that caused little if any trouble in their upbringing.

My wife and I received numerous accolades as to how well behaved the boys were and what good young men they were. I was often asked our secret in raising such good boys. I always responded that we prayed a lot, they had a great mom, and they were never fed the off-brand frozen waffles. We always bought a popular brand-name waffle for the toaster. I always figured there was something in the batter of the brand-name waffles that the generic folks didn't put in theirs. Whatever the reason, they were great kids.

We were the models of Christian family and marriage and child rearing. People would ask us how to deal with things like Santa Claus, rock music, and Harry Potter. People would point us out and use us as an example of what we had together with the love, the laughter, and the fun we had in life.

Career wise, I had graduated with a leisure studies degree from Missouri State. This university has a good reputation for developing great leaders in the field of recreation administration. I went on to Southwestern Baptist Seminary in Fort Worth and graduated in two full years with a master's in religious education. Of the six Southern Baptist seminaries, this one had the greatest capacity for training men and women for careers in church recreation. Once I graduated from seminary, I served in churches that were recognized as flagship churches in their communities. The first three were "First Baptist" by name, which usually indicates a church is one of the first or largest churches in the community. One of those three was the church where the call to the ministry began in Springfield, Missouri. From there I was able to move to one of the top recognized churches in the entire Southern Baptist Convention in the Memphis area.

I was respected by my wife, my sons, my church, and a nation of church leaders I worked with in conferences and in networking opportunities. Life was good, and I was at the top of my world. Then the however hit.

"However" is a word that usually takes the reader or listener in another direction than the one in which he or she was originally headed. My "however" was evidence of a dark and sinful life that exposed itself and nearly ruined me. I lost the trust and respect of a wife. The marriage was never able to rebound or rekindle from that point and eventually ended in divorce. I lost the respect of my three sons and continue to work toward rebuilding that with each of them. I resigned my position of leadership in the church and struggled emotionally to find satisfaction in a new career path. It took me over three years to get into another suitable career. It took over ten years before I took on any realm of leadership in a church.

In the story of Solomon, there is a section that explains all Solomon had going for him. I couldn't even come close to the level in life he had achieved. Solomon was the son of the most honored and revered kings in the world. He wrote amazing proverbs and even gave us the raciest part of the Scriptures, where he describes his love for a lady. He owned gold, silver, horses, livestock, chariots, weapons, and land. He was known for his amazing wisdom. People would actually travel to Jerusalem to sit under him and listen to his wisdom. He built the temple and equipped it with all the things God desired for His dwelling place. He had an amazing palace and furnished it with all the finest in the land.

Then the story gives the "however." It is the "however" that gets us into the most trouble. It states, "King Solomon, however, loved many foreign women."

Solomon was given the same charge as his father, King David, had been given: follow God and His ways, and the kingdom will remain with you and your family forever. One of the charges that was always given in the Old Testament stories was that Jews were never to marry outside their religious and cultural boundaries. In other words, they were not to marry anyone that was not Jewish. There were times when God wavered from this Himself, as with a Moabite woman named Ruth marrying a Hebrew named Boaz, but for the most part the purity of the race was deemed important. God knew the heart of a man and knew he would be easily swayed by the eyelashes and soft voice of the fairer sex. Just ask some of the heroes of the faith, such as Judah, Solomon, and David.

Solomon, however, ignored that decree and married them anyway. A few verses later, the count had been done. The total number included seven hundred wives and three hundred concubines. That's one thousand women to deal with at home. I don't know how he did it. I don't mean to be ugly, but life is difficult enough when trying to keep one woman happy. How did Solomon keep a thousand of them happy? With the simplest math, that allows you to schedule three women per day to be a husband for.

Let's do some more math. Multiply whether you are just to listen or to fix a problem by one thousand. Multiply toilet lid closing by one thousand. Multiply crying for no reason by one thousand. Multiply chick flicks, white wine, and chocolate by one thousand. In roses alone, a Valentine's Day dozen means 12,000 buds!

We all know David did a few things that were pretty evil as well. In fact, David had difficulty with the ladies himself. The difference is that David repented and would set about being obedient from that point. Solomon, instead of repenting, simply added more and more women, gods, and idols to the mix.

The problem for Solomon, much like me, was that the women influenced and enticed him to do that which he knew was wrong to do. They turned his heart toward their false gods and caused him to do evil in God's eyes. He did, as I did, make the choices to disobey, but the scene was set by someone committed to diverting him from the truth. Solomon built high places and shrines for some of the false gods. I'm quite sure that some of this was done in order to appease some of his wives and keep peace among a group of his wives vying for his attention.

Solomon lost the respect and the trust of the people. Eventually he died and his throne was given to his son Rehoboam. He, however, was given only one tribe to rule over. The others were given by God to one of Solomon's adversaries.

I was really good at projecting an image of having life all together. Unfortunately, images cannot stand up to a "however." Solomon and I both had opportunities to turn from our ways, but we chose the path of protecting our image rather than facing our sin. However, it doesn't have to end with a bad finish. There is hope beyond the "however" in our lives.

What's the "however" in your life?

DAVID: HARD BOILED AND OVER EASY (2 SAMUEL 11–13:22)

The news had just broken. One of the most noted television evangelists was caught in a scandalous act. The year was 1988. Prior to being caught with a prostitute, the evangelist had been on the other side of the judgment, calling out Jim Baker and Marvin Gorman, other noted television evangelists, in their own particular similar scandals.

I remember being rather judgmental about this situation myself. The punishment given to Swaggart by the Assembly of God powers was a mere three-month sabbatical during which he was free to preach in the world, but not in the United States. The punishment raised the eyebrows of several evangelicals. The assumption was that the $14 million given to the assembly might have played into the decision. I figured he should bite the bullet like any other Southern Baptist minister would and resign. Not only was the punishment light, but Swaggart refused to accept it and ended up leaving the Assembly of God.

Despite having some similar baggage in my closet, I became very outspoken about the punishment given and the fact that Swaggart avoided it. I thought his own church would do more than they did, but they offered "cheap grace" and let him keep preaching despite the sin. I was outraged when his church ignored the act and behaved as if nothing had happened. How do we become national news and then go back to normal?

Fast forward a few years to 2009 and we find another famous person in a similar scandal. Tiger Woods was found to be having affairs with numerous women. I didn't have the same amount of judgment in this case. A lot of that was because in between all those fast-forwarded years, I myself was discovered to be involved in the same types of scandalous behaviors. Before I was found out, I found it easy to hit Swaggart hard. After surviving the scandal, I found myself more merciful toward similar sinners. I didn't want anyone to have to suffer the same consequences I did. I actually sympathized with and defended Tiger Woods using some of the same rationalizations I had used to use to justify my own sin. Very simply, it looked like this: When my sin was hidden, my judgment on others regarding similar sins was harsh. When my sin was known, my judgment on others regarding similar sins was nonexistent.

Prior to my own discovery, in some sick manner, I enjoyed the fact that others were caught in the same sin. I reveled in their punishment. In a way, I took on their punishment as a way of trying to manage my own addiction and sin. So when people like Jimmy Swaggart and Bill Clinton bit the bullet, I was there, ready to throw the first stone. Like many others, I would have had to drop my stone to the ground based on Jesus' standards for rock throwing.

After my own punishment, I would try to neglect or ignore the guilty party, because the consequences that others face bring up too much pain from my own consequences. I didn't wish to talk about it over and over again. The topic was too painful. Like most that live in the pain of consequences, I was ready to move back to a more normal life. I even despised movies that featured adultery, for that very reason. Even after all the years that have passed since that day, there still are people that will mention the day when all my sin was exposed. Some people just can't let go of things.

It wasn't all that much different for my namesake king in the Bible. David was told a story by Nathan the Prophet about a man that had much livestock stealing the one lamb of another in order to prepare a meal for a traveler. David, in hearing this was outraged. He was ready to have the man put to death. That is until the prophet Nathan told David that he was "the man." David then had to deal with the reality of his own sin and consequences. David, who had many wives, not only took the wife of another man but also put that man to death to cover up the sin, which had resulted in a pregnancy.

One of the consequences of that sin was that David's family turned out to be a lot like him. We hear about this quite often, where the cycle of sin or behavior is handed from one generation to the next. His firstborn son with Ahinoam was Amnon. By being David's firstborn son, he was in line for the throne one day. That is, until he acted like his father.

At one point Amnon developed some lustful feelings for his half-sister Tamar. Instead of asking for her in marriage, which probably would have been granted, he sought the advice of a friend. The friend plotted with Amnon to get her alone so Amnon could have his way with her. Amnon followed the advice and followed through with the plans, eventually raping his half-sister. Once the act was done, Amnon despised her and sent her away. In those days that meant Tamar would basically live like a widow in her father's home. No marriage and no children would come into her life.

When King David was told of the situation, the storyteller in 2 Samuel states that he was angry. But that's it. No punishment was given. No shotgun wedding was held. The girl was seen as unfit, and Amnon was to go on with life as normal.

David did nothing but get angry.

At least with his own sin he didn't leave Bathsheba as a widow. He took her on as one of his wives. But in the case of his son's sin, he tossed his own daughter aside as if nothing had happened. Perhaps David saw too much of himself in Tiger Woods, rather Amnon, and chose not to relive his own painful consequences. He might have even hoped his son would not have to pay the same price for his sin.

As the story unfolded, there was someone completely outraged by the situation. Absalom was Tamar's full brother and lived for two years while determined to make Amnon pay for what he did to his sister. Amnon was eventually killed by his half-brother Absalom, in response to the rape. Absalom couldn't let it go, and it ended up ruining his life as well. The disgust of the lack of punishment also led Absalom to try to take the throne from his father. In so doing, Absalom slept with David's concubines in public as a way of demonstrating his coup for the kingdom. The cycle of murder and adultery that was birthed by David's sin now continued on through the generations to follow.

We see it continue in the stories of so many of the kings of Judah that assumed the throne.

I think it's easy for me to get outraged when it is my sin that remains hidden. I find it equally as easy to want to wish the consequences away for those, like me, that had their skeletons discovered. The greatest joy I have is that my sons have committed to let the cycle die with me. I admire them for this commitment, and I advise them to guard their hearts. Sin is sneaky.

So what sin are you hardest on? Which one outrages you most? Is there a reason for that we need to discuss? What cycle do you need to not ride?

PALTI: FEAR MAKES EVERYTHING BIGGER (NUMBERS 13)

I've had a fair share of time on camera. Two of the churches I served were on a weekly broadcast. So when I led in prayer or did a children's sermon, I was broadcast to the entire viewing area. Recently I began teaching classes at the University of Mississippi, where I am filmed and broadcast to our remote campuses.

I've always heard that the camera adds twenty pounds. I didn't realize it took a couple of inches off the hairline as well. Somehow when I look in the mirror I don't see myself getting any larger, but when the camera captures my image, I somehow gain fifty pounds.

I always get tickled at the funny mirrors used by some carnivals and fairs. The mirror is shaped in such a way that one's body looks short and fat or tall and skinny. I want to get one of the latter mirrors for my house!

I remember the first time I visited the church I attended as a child. The hallways that once seemed so large to me were tight and small.

Sometimes things seem larger to us than they really are. Our vision gets distorted by cameras, funny mirrors, and tricky memories. These items don't have anything on one aspect of making things look bigger than they are. This aspect can grow faster than anything until life itself has made us become a wimpy, scared kid hiding in the corner.

I speak of fear.

I had to be about five years old when I discovered the monster just up the street. I encountered the fearsome beast in the mornings as I would walk to the bus stop that took me to kindergarten. The moment

I would step out my front door and get close to the street, I would hear its vicious bark.

Up to this point in my life, I was familiar with dogs, but I don't recall much about them. Our family had one briefly around that time, but I don't remember much about it. I do remember the dog being friendly with a cute little pink tongue that would try to lick me on the face.

This monster of a dog was nothing like that. It was not cute; it was frightening. It didn't try to lick me, but I felt it would tear me apart and eat me if it could. It was huge and had fur that would stand up on its back. It didn't have a cute little pink tongue and instead had a huge black tongue that would show itself every time the dog barked. It was the first time I'd ever seen a chow. To me it looked like a miniature lion.

When I would step out onto the street headed toward the bus stop, that dog would come running to the fence and bark at me. Seeing a gnarling grin of nothing but dog teeth along with the sound of a vicious bark was more than this little boy could handle. Despite my parents telling me the dog couldn't get to me through the fence, I was not convinced. All it took was another run to the fence, and I was living in fear once again. I found myself frozen when the dog made his runs. I couldn't move. I was stuck in my fear. The dog got larger and larger to me. The more I feared it, the more fearsome it became. I finally got over it when my parents convinced me to laugh at the dog instead of being scared. It took some work, but finally the dog grew tired of not seeing my fear and gave up on me walking by his yard.

We see this so clearly in the report brought back from the spies sent out to look over the Promised Land in Canaan. Twelve spies, one from each tribe, went out to view the land before leading the entire nation into it. Two spies came back confident that God could deliver the enemy into their hands. Ten spies allowed a bit of fear to get into their system.

Caleb said, "We should go take possession of the land, for we can certainly do it." No doubt Caleb was recalling the miraculous move from Egypt, and he placed his confidence in his God rather than in his abilities. The vicious barking sound of the dogs was not going to keep this guy from getting to his bus stop, the Promised Land.

Ten of the spies saw things differently. Caleb looked with faith; these ten looked with fear. They saw the fangs and big black tongue of the enemy and were frozen in their tracks. Palti was one of those spies. I chose his name out of the ten because he was from the tribe of Benjamin, which King Saul later reported to be the least of the tribes in Israel. Perhaps Palti started a legacy of fear in his tribe.

Palti and company spoke of the land and the way it flowed with "milk and honey." Then they immediately went on to describe the power of the people living there. They talked about how fortified the cities were. Although they had beaten the best army known to man, the Egyptians, these ten men couldn't possibly see the defeat of a nation that was weaker than the one they'd already beaten.

Following the shooting down of Caleb for exhibiting faith rather than fear, the people went further with their fear, speaking of the size of the people living there. By the time the story was finished, the Israelites were as little as grasshoppers in the sight of these people. They had grown even larger during the return trip and discussion with God's people.

What is it about fear that makes it larger than life? I know the fear of unemployment is one of the causes for Americans to return over a billion dollars' worth of vacation days. I know the fear of public speaking can create butterflies in one's stomach, and the butterflies will actually go to war with one another. The fear of death keeps some people from enjoying life. The fear of getting hurt again causes some to withdraw and not attempt new relationships. The fear of the unknown keeps some people in bad situations and relationships because the knowledge of something bad seems safer than the unknown.

So what can we tell Palti, my five-year-old self, and others that live in fear of something?

Should we, as Joshua and Caleb did, exhibit a little faith instead? Did you know the phrase "Fear not" or "Do not be afraid" occurs over one hundred times in the Bible? I think God is trying to give us a message. The words of Christ that come to mind are in John 14:27: "Peace I leave with you, my peace I give you ... Do not let your hearts be troubled and do not be afraid."

What humongous dog is barking at you today?

ESAU: CIVIL DISOBEDIENCE (GENESIS 28:1–9)

Limits and boundaries are always confusing to me. Close, as I understand it, counts only in hand grenades and kissing. There are lines, and we are not to color outside them. There are lines, and we are not supposed to cross them. There are lines, and we are not to hit the ball outside of them.

Records are made to be broken, but rules are to be kept. Civilizations rely upon this kind of order. Cultures die without them. There must be a strict adherence to the law if we are to live together.

Sometimes, however, I like to bend the rules, cross the lines, and hit the ball out of bounds and call it fair. I like to brag about it too when I beat the system. It has a nice defiant ring to it.

It's because I'm a rebel at heart. It's not a coincidence that I teach at a school with the nickname Rebels. I've been one all my life. Tell me there's to be no talking in school, and I'll figure out how to pass notes. Tell me I'm to go a certain speed on the highway, and I'll push it over by between five and nine miles per hour. I know, by doing the math, that I'm not saving but thirty or forty seconds of time, but there's some weird sense of accomplishment we get out of doing things we are not supposed to do.

The Bible refers to this as our sin nature. While growing up I learned about the two different kinds of sins. One is commission and the other is omission. My favorite definition of those two terms was from a little boy that said "Commission is the sins we commit, and omission is the sins we want to commit but haven't yet."

In actuality, the former means doing things we know to be wrong but do anyway. The latter means committing sins while not knowing they may be sins. I have a history of commission sins. My driving record indicates this with numerous speeding violations. Recently I purchased a car with cruise control, so I hope to shorten the commissioned speed traps.

As I look back on my history of commission sins, I realize that not only am I a rebel but I also commit some of my sins as a way of proving to others that I don't have to follow the rules. It's as if my sin screams out, "I don't have to follow your rules! Watch!" If a schoolteacher told me a certain way of getting something done, I'd spend more time trying to prove I could do it my way. I suppose I could add stubbornness to combine with the rebellion. I was defiant, disobedient, and rebellious, but I did it in sort of a civil manner.

During a time in my life when I was hiding some sinful behaviors, I would set up things in life to fail in order to give me permission to carry out my sin. For example, if my wife would be unloving or what I considered uncaring, it gave me the right to look at a particular website or plan to act out inappropriately during my next out-of-town trip. If the pastor was deemed unfair or unjust in a decision regarding me, it gave me permission to sneak in a beer break during hospital visitation day or to spike my soft drink with bourbon in a staff meeting.

Of course, my rebellious stance could never be known. That would destroy the "good and godly guy" image I had worked on for so many years. So all of my rebellion and acting out was like the joke about the preacher that called in sick one Sunday morning so he could sneak into another town to play golf. St. Peter pointed it out to God and asked what should be done about it. On the next hole, the pastor teed off on a long par-five hole. As he hit the ball, he saw it fly high into the air and travel farther than he had ever hit one. It bounced once on the ground, and a squirrel scooped it up in his mouth and went running toward the pond. All of a sudden, a hawk snatched the squirrel and flew circles in the air while the pastor hurried himself to follow. The hawk carried the squirrel to the outer portion of the green and released it. The squirrel landed on the ground, ran a few steps, and spit out the golf ball on the green, where a gust of wind came from out of nowhere and rolled the ball into the hole for a hole in one. Peter, somewhat disgusted, turned to God and asked Him why He had performed such a miracle for a pastor that was sinning. God replied, "Who is he going to tell?"

I'm acting in inappropriate ways to prove I can, and at the same time I can't tell anyone how much of a rebel I am. When all the truth about my ways came out and I shared some of the reasoning, it sounded even sillier and more stupid than I would have imagined.

Esau and I seem to be a lot alike. Esau was swindled out of his birthright and blessing from being the oldest son in the family by his few-seconds-younger twin brother, Jacob. He also must have kept his wrongdoing a secret, because when it came time for the blessing to be given, Isaac prepared Esau for the task. Nice to know I'm not the only image projector protector. Jacob, with the help of his mother, tricked his father into giving him the blessings of the firstborn.

Esau's way of getting even with everyone was to do something his father, Isaac, had told Jacob not to do—marry a Canaanite woman. Already having two disapproved wives, Esau went to his dad's half-brother Ismael, knowing how it would spitefully displease Isaac, and got one of his daughters to marry him. So not only was he being defiantly disobedient but, in a civil manner, he was also accomplishing the deed with the brother that could have rightfully claimed firstborn rights away from Isaac. The nephew and uncle had that in common.

Esau differed from me slightly, as he performed his disobedience right in front of everyone. Despite it being against God's wishes as well, Esau chose to stick it to the man (his dad in this case) in disobeying the commandment given to his brother.

In addition to the commission and omission, I would suggest another category be given, and that would be the sin that also carries the note of defiance to it. This is sin, much like mine and Esau's, that has the message attached that we know it to be wrong but still do it as a way of letting God know that we are in charge of our own lives.

Of course, as you know, God does have the last word. Esau and I have stories of untold trouble from our defiant acts. Esau's descendants include the Edomite people and the Amalekites, both of which cause problems for Jacob's heirs throughout the Old Testament stories.

What's your disobedience saying?

THE RICH RULER: SOMETIMES I BE HERO ... SOMETIMES I BE GOAT (MATTHEW 19:16–30)

For a long time, sports has had a love/hate relationship between the notions of competition and cooperation. The creators of the New Games Foundation in the 1970s, team-building events, and programs like Upward Sports have attempted to divert competition away from sports, games, and contests. The aim was to get away from the emphasis on the level of performance and concentrate on the enjoyment of the experience.

It hasn't worked completely.

Competition in our world is still ever present. Competition itself is not sinful. Like most things in life, the way we handle it is what determines the right and the wrong of the issue. Life, as in games, ends up with winners and losers. A baseball player in the 1960s would describe his on-field performance with the simple phrase "Sometimes I be hero ... sometimes I be goat."

I have never seen this issue played out as well as it is in the following of college and professional sports. Before you claim me as being judgmental, please understand that I am still struggling with this myself. The tendency to turn young men and women into gods is unbelievable in our culture.

A few years ago, as I was walking into one of my classes, a cornerback on the Ole Miss football team came up to me. He asked if I had seen their game against the arch rivals, Mississippi State, the previous weekend. I shared that I had not seen it, because I was flying back from Phoenix following a visit with my oldest son and his family.

He proceeded to tell me how badly they had been beaten and how poorly the people in the university and community were treating them. I told him that surely the world did not judge him and his teammates' worth solely on the team's performance on the field. He looked me straight in the eyes and said, "Oh yes they do."

I had seen this kind of behavior before.

In the early 1980s, I worked at a church in southeast Texas. High school football in Texas can be added to the fanaticism of the college and pro games. I entered a grocery store and saw two men that appeared to be in their fifties verbally accosting a young man. The young man was the third-string sophomore quarterback for our local high school football team. He had been called into duty that season when the first two quarterbacks were injured. He led us to a winning record and in the final game created a showdown. If we won, we would go to the state playoffs. If the rival won, they would go.

We lost.

The two older men were giving the poor kid fits. They were trying to make him the goat and blame the lack of the playoffs on him. I interrupted them and asked them to leave the young man alone. The two men then turned on me. While I was listening to them tell me what I didn't know and where I could stick certain things, I saw the young man mouthing "Thank you" as he tiptoed away from the scene.

I was reminded that I'd seen in numerous game situations that people who never played the game and often have little understanding of the game are ready to curse a group of young men and women for not keeping them happy. How in the world have we gotten to the point where we judge a person based on his or her performance? Oh wait, it's wired into our DNA.

From the day Adam and Eve took a bite of forbidden fruit, we have been on a treadmill of performance reviews to gain God's favor. We feel as though if we act just right and behave correctly, then God's blessings will be poured out upon us. Our performances can't answer the question of why bad things happen to good people, other than to imagine that the people suffering bad things must not be as good as we thought. Perhaps they have committed some hidden sin that no one knows about.

I have made this performance-based theology an art form. For years I hid a pattern of sinful behavior and darkness. This behavior, combined with a mind-set of performance, created much turmoil in my spirit. How can I, if I am truly a follower of Jesus, do such things? So instead of seeking God in the matter, I would attempt to create new plans or programs in the church to take care of a lost and hurting world. I felt that if I increased my performance of the good, it would undo the consequences of the bad. It's not the way God works. I found ways to make it work in my mind, but never in my heart.

So when I would think an impure thought, it would lead me to create a new program to reach people. Depending on the level of thought or sin, I might even offer to help out with the junior high boys' class or team. If I were to act out inappropriately on an out-of-town trip, it might lead to creating an after-school program for needy children and families. Some of the best and brightest ideas I had in ministry were founded in my heart as a "pay it back" theology. After all, it's pure physics: for each sinful action, I created an equal and opposite Christian reaction. I'm just thankful that what I meant for payback, God used for good. My on-field performance had to be that good to provide the feeling of approval and affirmation. I wanted to appear to be the hero rather than the goat.

Jesus encountered a young man with the same thought process I had—*If I do enough right things and avoid enough wrong things, it will gain me the ultimate right place.* The young man was a ruler of some sort and came to Jesus to ask Him what had to be done in order to gain eternal life. Please note Jesus didn't refer the young man to the Great Commandment of loving the Lord your God with all your heart, mind, and strength. Instead Jesus offered him the last five commandments: don't steal, don't lie, don't commit adultery, don't murder, and honor your mom and dad. Jesus read this man correctly as a performance-based performer.

The young man apparently was pretty good at the performance-based image protection gig, because he claimed he had done all of those things since childhood. Now, I've been on both sides of the honor your mother and father commandment. I know there were times when I wasn't even remotely close to honoring them with my attitudes, actions, or words. I know my own three sons have thought their dad was insane and losing it. So I doubt this man kept all of those commandments as stated. I would have lied about the others as well, or at the very least diverted the conversation to the lusting and hating avenues Jesus gave in the Sermon on the Mount. I do anything to avoid the truth coming out.

When Jesus offered him the solution of giving away everything that was keeping the performance going, the man walked away. Apparently he didn't want to lose the control of how to gain God's favor. I know how that feels, in that it seems to make more sense if I can pay it back somehow.

The main problem with the performance-based judgment is that it turns us into players, actors, and actresses. We pretend to be better than we are in the hopes of fooling an all-knowing and all-seeing God. We posture ourselves to convince others we've got it all together.

This may have been the reason Jesus told the young man to get rid of everything that kept the performance in mind. As long as the man had his riches, he was not going to walk off the field or stage of his performance. Jesus knows that until we rid ourselves of the performance mind-set, we'll have no need of Him. And really, all He wants is us—the "me" that is really me, with all of my flaws, losses, defeats, stupidity, and imagined glory. He just wants me. He wants you too. I think I'm finally catching on.

What field, court, or stage are you on today?

THE POTTER: HERE LET ME FIX THAT MESS (JEREMIAH 18:1–6)

The first time I saw the process done was at an amusement park. Sixty miles south of Springfield in the Branson, Missouri, area was the amazing place called Silver Dollar City. A friend of mine referred to it, perhaps more accurately, as Steal Your Dollar City.

The theme of the park was late-1800s southwest Missouri. It featured a variety of rides as well as visits from sheriffs, bank robbers, townspeople, and the vigilante group called the Baldknobbers. It contained the normal aspects of an amusement park with rides, gift shops, and all sorts of dining selections. The unique aspect of the park was the features including old-time crafts and skills needed for survival. One could learn how to make lye soap, pull taffy, salt cure or smoke cure meat, weave, quilt, blow glass, make candy, and other assorted crafts. They even had a candle-making place, but they only worked on wick ends!

It was a great place to take a date, and later in life when I returned to Springfield, it became a great place to spend a day as a family. My favorite rides in the park were the funnel cake ride, the homemade peanut brittle ride, and the fried pork rind ride.

One intriguing thing I saw, while there with a date during my college years, was an artist making a vase out of clay on a potter's wheel. I had heard of a potter's wheel before in the Bible, but thought nothing more of it. Then I observed this master. He piled a lump of wet clay in the middle of the stone wheel. Then he started kicking his legs over and over again, spinning a wheel under his feet. With a push of his foot, the wheel holding the clay began to spin at an equal speed. He would form the clay with his hands while continuing to spin the wheel at the proper speed with his legs.

I couldn't believe this guy! I have trouble walking and chewing gum at the same time! This will become clearer to you as I get further in the story. Before we knew it, a beautiful shaped vase stood before us. He slowed down the spin, pulled the vase off the wheel with some wire, and set it on a counter to dry some more before firing it in a kiln. I stood there amazed at what I had just seen.

A couple of years later, my mom went back to college, and part of her course work was in pottery. She learned, as had this man in Silver Dollar City, to form things out of clay with her bare hands. She did upgrade on one aspect. She had an electrical wheel. It was spun by an accelerator pedal similar to what you would see in an automobile.

Mom became quite the potter! I'm the fortunate one, however, in that God seems to put women in my life that enjoy her pottery. Two ladies that I've worked with over the years have several pieces from her collection. A lady friend, whom I pursued in my heart, has numerous pieces as well. When I visit Mom I'm always amazed at her new ideas and her creativity in forming things out of mud. I always bring a variety of items home for gifts.

A couple of years ago, I decided it was time for me to learn how to do this. I saw a brief portion of the movie *Ghost* in which Patrick Swayze comes back and works the potter's wheel with Demi Moore. With the experience I'd gained in watching the guy at Silver Dollar City and Patrick Swayze, I figured I was ready for the first lesson. So I sat in the chair with the wheel in front of me. Mom indicated where the accelerator was and showed me how to operate it. She told me it had a hair trigger touch to it. That means it doesn't take much to make it spin at the desired speed. She worked with me to get it spinning at the proper speed and seemed satisfied when I achieved the goal.

She asked me what I wanted to make, and I told her I wanted to form a pot—something of a size that would be suitable for baked beans, soup, or a vegetable dish. She then dropped the appropriate amount of clay on the wheel. I got the wheel spinning at the correct speed, and she told me to form my hands around the clay and start to form a circle. I applied pressure to the clay, and all of a sudden the wheel slowed down. My concentration on the clay had made me lose the effectiveness of my right foot. Now the lump of clay looked like a wizard's hat of sorts with a round bottom and a leaning pointed top.

We tried again, and a similar slowdown occurred when I started to press in on the clay. Mom warned me not to lose the spinning speed, so I planted my foot and revved it up a bit too much. Some of the clay decided to go airborne and land in various places in the garage. We worked on the spinning speed again and then applied pressure. Once again the speed slowed as my concentration went elsewhere. When this happened, I gunned the pedal and more clay took off spinning, landing in various sites.

At this point Mom recommended I make a cereal bowl instead. She had that same look of frustration I had seen countless times while growing up. She pointed out that a cereal bowl is much easier than a huge pot. So we tried again, only to come up with the same results. Tiring of my ineptness, she stepped away and told me to practice on my own for just a moment. I started to get the feel of it, and after a few more trials I was actually seeing a bowl shape up in my hands. She taught me how to put my hand inside it and thin out walls. My cereal bowl was looking dandy! I couldn't wait to introduce it to Toucan Sam and Cap'n Crunch when I got home.

I let the wheel slow down and looked at my bowl with great pride. Mom took some wire and ran it under the bowl to set it free from the wheel. The wire helped maintain the shape of the bottom of the piece while it was being removed.

As she lifted the piece, she commented, "Well, maybe you can use it as a planter."

My cereal bowl had a hole in the bottom that a quarter could easily pass through at any angle. She was looking at me through the hole when she made her comment. Apparently when I was spinning to do the wall-thinning trick, I had set my fingers too low and actually moved the clay away from the bottom of the bowl, pressing it up the side. The nice part of this was that the hole made the caving wall of one side seem insignificant. At that point, I did the only humane thing possible and put the "planter" in her pile of scrap clay that could be recycled.

I feel certain Mom made a beautiful cup or vase out of that same piece of marred clay at a later date. While I messed up making anything good out of the clay, the potter could take my leftover mess and turn it into a masterpiece.

The verses in Jeremiah 18:3–6 suddenly made more sense to me. "So I went down to the potter's house and I saw him working at the wheel. But the pot he was shaping from the clay was marred in his hands; so the potter formed it into another pot shaping it as seemed best to him. Then the word of the Lord came to me; 'O house of Israel, can I not do with you as this potter does?' declares the Lord. 'Like clay in the hand of the potter, so are you in my hand, O house of Israel.'"

I think a good many of us could say that we are that piece of clay in God's hands on the Potter's wheel. I can recall numerous times that God has taken this lump of mud named David Waddell, which has been marred and misshaped, only to form it into what seemed best to Him. All of the marring that takes place in our lives gives God the opportunity to reshape us into what He's already designed and called us to do. This is why we find ourselves where we are. It was certainly no surprise to God.

Want to take a spin?

HAM: LOOK AT HIM! LOOK AT HIM! (GENESIS 9:18–27)

He was one of the giants in the field of church recreation. He was in charge of a major program in a large church in a metropolitan area. As a college and seminary student, I had observed this man around his peers at a yearly recreation workshop. After I landed a job at a church in southeast Texas, I learned this man was moving to another church that would be somewhat close to mine.

What happened next was a complete surprise to me. He reached out to me. He wasn't one of those guys that have a circle of friends and exclude others. He taught me a valuable lesson in that he thought I could be of value to him. He quickly became a hero, a guide, and a role model for me. He befriended me to the point where I was hanging out with him and his gang at the conferences. We would even enjoy sneaking a wine cooler or beer into our time together. To this day I'm not sure whether I enjoyed the beer more or the thought that I was getting away with something I wasn't supposed to be doing.

It was during one of the yearly conferences that I saw the director of church recreation for Southern Baptists talking with my friend. As I walked by, my friend told him, "You should include Waddell in your idea."

The idea was to send numerous church recreation ministers to Alaska to work with smaller churches in ways they could use sports, crafts, drama, and socials as a way of inviting the community into their church. I was recruited on the spot because of my friend's recommendation. It was the one and only time I've been to the largest state in the Union. It was also the first of many projects I was invited to assist with on a national level. So my friend elevated me to a higher position of influence by getting me involved with the Alaskan project. Ironically, my friend was unable to help out himself.

A few years later, I moved from that area, but we kept the friendship going with occasional phone calls and would continue to see each other at the yearly recreation conferences. I had a new crowd I was hanging with at the conferences, so we would still chat, but we weren't hanging around as we used to do.

One year I was standing around talking to some friends at one of these conferences when I saw my friend walking down the sidewalk of the cabin dorm rooms used for the conferences. Walking with him was a lady from a church in a different state. I knew of her and the work she did in recreation ministry. She walked into a room. My friend did the "look around" to see if anyone was watching and then went into the room himself. I pointed it out to my friends standing with me so that all of us could get a look at what my friend was doing. We all commented on how bad that looked. One person suggested it certainly couldn't be what it looked like. I recognize in my heart, with my own sinful lust, that if it were me it would be exactly what it looked like.

I should explain that during this span of time I was getting involved in a much darker sin habit than sneaking a beer. I used the conferences as a way of getting involved with the sin, feeling safer because the chances of not getting caught were good when I was miles away from home.

I know that the right thing to do, according to the Scriptures, would be to confront the friend with his alleged sin. I also remembered Jimmy Swaggart doing this to another television evangelist before getting busted himself. So instead of facing my own sin in another person, I chose the path of least resistance and pointed it out to others standing with me. There's a weird sense of judgment about my own sin that takes place when another person's similar sin can be brought out into the open.

So on that day and subsequent days and years, I saw my friend behaving as if nothing was going on, when I knew that it was. I never confronted, but I continued to talk about it with other church recreation ministers. Even after the truth came out about my friend and this lady and they had to deal with broken homes and wrecked churches, I did nothing to console or comfort him. My own sin hounded me too much to do so.

Following the great flood, Noah became a farmer, planted some grapes, and made some wine. With the wine he got drunk one night and laid down in the middle of a room stark naked. There is much speculation about what went on during Noah's nakedness. Needless to say, the writer of Genesis chose not to tell us, other than stating he was naked.

Noah's son Ham saw the nakedness, and instead of confronting his dad and covering up the nakedness, Ham decided to go tell his brothers. There's something sinfully enjoyable about talking about someone else's sin. I know I would gladly discuss your sin over my sin any day!

The other brothers decided to deal with the situation rather than talk about it. They got a blanket, and with each one holding one corner, the boys backed in and covered their dad so as to not see him in his nakedness. They even turned their heads so that they wouldn't see what was happening. The next morning, Noah discovered what happened and became really ticked at Ham. Noah ended up cursing his son to be a servant to his brothers for the rest of time.

I'm not sure why Ham did what he did. I have a feeling he and I are a lot alike and Ham was exposing a sin in his dad because he probably had some similar sin in his own heart. He knew that if the attention was on Noah's sin, then his would stay protected. I exposed my friend and let others know of his sin, all the while covering up and burying so much more sin myself.

Oddly enough, the story of the curse of Canaan was used for years by a group of people that believed in enslaving a certain people in our country. In the same way, our own nakedness of sin was exposed as the misinterpretation of this curse was used to demean and abuse people.

Years later, after my own sin had been exposed, my friend sought me out to console me. Confessions were made, and forgiveness was offered. He continues to be one of my best friends and is serving once again in church leadership. He remains a hero and guide to me.

Speculation can take place, but we'll never know what could have happened had I confronted the sin instead of telling others. Luckily my friend didn't give me the same curse Noah gave to Ham's son Canaan. Even still, I live with a bit of a regretful curse that I could have made a difference had I chosen another path.

What are you seeing your friends do?

SANBALLAT: I MESS YOU TERRIBLY (NEHEMIAH 2, 4, 6)

He was one of the most active morning worship attendees we had. You could always see him in the back of the auditorium with a scowl on his face. He never seemed to be happy, but he was faithfully in attendance.

He was not recognized as a part of the regular power structure of the church. The mere existence of power structures in the church made the list of things I wished they'd taught me in the seminary. In every church there are a few people that actually run things. Because of financial gifts, longevity of membership, or other traits, the people of the church have given them the power to influence the direction of the church. Unfortunately the qualifications of membership in a power structure didn't always coincide with Biblical qualifications of leadership.

This man didn't seem to be vocal in that realm, yet for some unknown reason he still yielded a great deal of influence. I heard years later that he was also known to use all sorts of harassment techniques to divert pastors and church staff into changing their plans. It was his technique of messing with their minds and hearts. If he could frustrate them enough, they'd divert from one direction and possibly do what this guy thought they should be doing instead.

Some time later I ran into this guy. It had been seven or eight years since I had been in the church, but they were already working with their third pastor in five years. This man shared with me that he had worked with all four pastors of this church over the last thirty years and that every one of them was an idiot. I asked him what the common denominator was during those years of leadership. He didn't catch on, so I pointed out that if all four of them were idiots, perhaps the one doing the labeling was the problem rather than all four pastors. He still did not catch on, so I left it alone after that. I have to admit, I did enjoy messing with his mind for a change.

There's something sinfully fun about diverting the plans and leadership of others. Why is it in our DNA to mess with people like this? I know I always did this in a somewhat sarcastic manner. I went to one staff meeting in Springfield where the pastor shared a word of encouragement through a business cliché. "Gentlemen," he said, "we're going to start working smarter rather than harder."

I knew what he meant and where he was going, but it sounded so cliché that I couldn't help but mess with him. I asked what that meant. The pastor simply repeated the cliché. So I acted in complete and total confusion and started picking the statement apart as to what it meant for us on staff. One of the others chimed in with a joyful statement about not having to work hard anymore. Finally, in frustration, the pastor diverted us to another topic.

During my first tenure as a full-time staff member, the pastor that hired me left to go to another church to serve. We brought in his replacement, and in my youthful immaturity I had a more difficult time working with this man. My work seemed to always be under scrutiny, and the simplest of complaints given to him about me were treated as if they were major job-ending difficulties. Sensing he did not have my back, I questioned his plans and halfheartedly carried them out. It was when the emphasis of my job changed three times in four months that I saw the handwriting on the wall. I needed to leave.

During the span of time I was trying to leave, I never outwardly rebelled against him, but I would ask questions or make statements with doubt in my voice to influence others to think twice about following his leadership. When questions came up about him, I was not quick to defend his integrity but left it open with a roll of my eyes or a shrug of my shoulders to communicate whatever such a gesture would.

When I finally found a new church to serve in, I tried to go quietly, but the damage was done. In some people's eyes I had served to create questions in their mind about him. I had messed things up for this man to work effectively with some in the church.

I hate to admit it, but one of the characters in the Bible has that same characteristic in him. Nehemiah was attempting to rebuild the wall around Jerusalem. He gained the king's favor in doing so, but another group of people saw nothing but trouble with a rebuilt wall and went about trying to sabotage the work. The chief troublemaker, and my likeness in the story, was Sanballat.

Sanballat first tried sarcasm, asking if they would build with stones that were already knocked down and burned. He referred to them as "feeble Jews" and asked if they might offer sacrifices or be able to build the wall in a single day. Perhaps this was a punch at the story of creation, in which huge things happen in a single day. None of the sarcastic barbs slowed down the building efforts. I figure he didn't shrug his shoulders or roll his eyes effectively enough, because the Jews kept building.

Even when the wall was completed, Sanballat kept after the efforts to disrupt the work. The doors for the gates had yet to be hung, so Sanballat sent a total of four notes with an invitation for Nehemiah to leave the work and come meet with him and his associates. Nehemiah answered each request with a note that he could not leave the work to come meet with him. The fifth note Sanballat sent included the rumor that the Jews were going to rebel against the king. Nehemiah denied the rumor and went back to the work God had given him to do.

My oldest son told me he and his pastor had a conversation about Sanballat and compared him to El Guapo in the movie *¡Three Amigos!*. Prior to the big battle in the end, one of the Amigos, in a crowd-rallying speech, indicates that all people have an El Guapo in their life. El Guapo was the notorious criminal that was oppressing this local community. The Amigo stated that for some their El Guapo might be poor self-esteem or a lack of education. Of course, for them their El Guapo was a mean guy that wanted to kill them.

Nehemiah and the Jews could use the name Sanballat instead. It seems that no matter what we try to do for God or in God's service, there seems to be a Sanballat getting in the way. I know I can think of numerous people I would swear served as a Sanballat in my life.

Unfortunately there have been times in my life where I was the Sanballat for someone else.

Fortunately my Sanballat work did not deter the pastor in my first church from doing what God led him to do. In fact, God used the man in leadership for several more years without me helping him one way or the other. I was able to see him a few years ago when the church held their one hundredth anniversary as a church. I admitted to him that he was a far better leader than I had ever given him credit for in those years. It was fun getting to hear from people in the church how much of a blessing he had been to them and their families.

Who are you messing with?

ADAM: BUSTED!
(GENESIS 3:1–19)

It was work, but it was one of the areas I enjoyed working in most. In three of the four churches I worked at, I had the joy of working with the senior adults and their recreational events. One of the things we tried to do was take an extended trip every year or every other year. I was able to take them to see all sorts of sights in different areas of our country. Niagara Falls, Washington, DC, Disney World, and the Statue of Liberty are just a few of the places I've escorted the children over age sixty.

It's difficult enough to keep five people happy on a family trip. Multiply that by nine and try keeping forty-five people contented. Some liked to shop, some liked to sit and people watch, and all of them enjoyed eating. On the journeys, I discovered a great place for people to do all three—the wonderful shopping mall that is located in so many communities. The bus can drop them off in one place and park in a remote part of the parking lot. The group can pace themselves accordingly inside the mall. Usually there would be a cafeteria for the folks, while some risk takers would hit the Corn Dog 7 franchise. The shopaholics in the group would start drooling, and the men in the group would start groaning. I would usually plan to stay a little longer in a war museum or the Baseball Hall of Fame to even things out among them.

During the time at the mall, I would usually find a place to eat and walk around in the event someone needed me. I might find a bookstore and read portions out of their sports section or comedy section. On one particular trip I found myself in the middle of the mall, standing while talking to some of the men in our group. Like typical husbands in a mall, they had deserted their wives to find some sense of male sanity in the area. So I decided to engage them in conversation. While one was talking, I noticed out of the corner of my eye a rather attractive-looking lady coming toward us. She was one of those fair-skinned, redheaded, lightly freckled, blue-eyed girls with the right amount of curves. Well, as much as I could tell, anyway; I wasn't really looking at her that closely.

There is an attribute that men think they have that they don't really have. Regardless, it is impossible to convince them otherwise. That attribute is the ability to think we can look at a beautiful woman and not get caught doing it. We turn our seats, reposition ourselves, or act like we have a crick in our neck in order to gain a better view. I know this because once while getting coffee with my wife she commented on how much I must have enjoyed looking at the well built lady dressed in a really tight dark blue sweater decorated with white polka dots and a tight-fitting denim dress with high-heeled leather-strapped sandals who was getting coffee at the same time. Of course I deny it to this day, as I'm quite sure I barely noticed her. I told this story once to a lady friend who told me I was not only busted, but hipped and figured as well!

As the men in the mall were talking, my eyes picked up the beauty of this lady, and apparently I was more enamored with the look than even I realized. I turned my body as one man continued to speak in order to make it look like I was more interested in what he had to say. In reality I was positioning myself to get a better view of the beauty. My eyes followed as much as they could before my neck took things over and moved to watch the shape of this woman fade from my view. As I turned back to the group of men, I realized no one was talking anymore. They were all looking at me with sneaky-looking smiles on their faces. To break the ice I said, "I'm sorry, what was that you said?"

One of the men smiled even brighter and said, "It's okay, Dave. We saw her too."

Busted!

I tried to talk my way out of it, but I could tell a few of these guys had been there, done that, and gotten the T-shirt. No matter how I stuttered or stammered, their sneaky little smiles communicated the same thing to me: "Busted!"

I might as well admit it now; when I refer to people watching, 95 percent of the watching is actually girl watching. It's about the same when I go bird watching, car watching, or boat watching too. It wouldn't take me long in any of the shopping malls to find the best place to people watch. I remembered a friend once told me that Billy Graham said if you are driving and you notice the beauty of a girl, then it's not lust. However, if you circle around the block to see her again, you've probably crossed the line. A lady I worked with briefly in a consulting role told me a story of how her boyfriend did the same thing to her while having dinner. Sometimes it is the beauty I discover. Other times I circle back around the block to discover it's the other thing. It's a trait that has led to much more difficulty in my life than a few old men busting me.

I have no idea what makes me think that no one is watching when I make such obvious contortions and twists with my body in order to see the beauty that is coming toward me. When sin enters the picture, the lies abound about a good many things.

Adam, the first man God created, found this out the hard way. Actually he was the first one to find this out. God had given a very clear definition of what could be done and what wasn't to be done. In true human fashion Adam desired what he didn't have more than all that he did have. Right there with you, Adam!

In the story it says the woman struck up a conversation with the serpent. The serpent convinced her that God's threat of death was a lie and that the fruit would actually open up her eyes to truth. Adam, who was right there with her, ate the fruit with the woman. The moment they ate the forbidden fruit, their eyes were opened and they realized they were naked.

Busted!

In another normal human trait, they tried to hide from God and cover up the sin. Blame was born as Adam blamed the sin on "that woman you made for me" and the woman blamed the serpent. No matter how they stuttered or how they stammered, God had that look on His face that we don't like seeing.

Busted!

The story of sin was birthed because someone saw that it was "pleasant to the eyes." In the book of James, it is stated that the path to sin begins in our desires. We see something we want, and regardless of what we know, we aim to get it. So in a sense, when it comes to sin, we find exactly what we are looking for.

Which way are you looking?

ZACCHAEUS: "A WEE LITTLE MAN WAS HE" SYNDROME (LUKE 19:1–10)

The whistle hung from my neck and lay on my chest. I had borrowed a black-and-white striped shirt from the hanging closet in the recreation center's equipment room. I had a stern look on my face. I was ready to take charge.

I was a substitute basketball official.

On this particular Saturday, we were not missing one official; we were missing both of the ones scheduled to call the older elementary boys' basketball game. Being the part-time recreation assistant, it was my duty to do whatever I could to get the game started on time. My friend Tom, who had played competitively on his junior high team, was going to fill in as one of the referees. I lined up someone to watch the center and control the equipment room so that I could assist as well.

I had never been to any course or workshop about how to officiate a basketball game. I was a fan and had watched numerous games, so I felt qualified. I knew from my observations that a referee had to be tough and controlling. Otherwise bedlam would be sure to break out.

Tom tossed the opening game jump ball into the air, and the game was on. I immediately switched into what I would call a Dr. Jekyll-and–Coach Hyde personality turn. I called violations that should have been ignored. I missed some calls because they traveled while I was counting off a possible three-second-in-the-lane violation. I was using my loud authoritarian voice on these poor fourth-grade boys. I was going to show them who was in charge!

This was not the first time I used an authoritarian whistle. In fourth grade I was the stair monitor for North Rock Creek Elementary School. I was equally as hard on stair walkers as I was on basketball players. I figured I had to exhibit my power in a strong way in order to be respected.

At the first time-out, Tom came up to me and encouraged me to ease it up a bit. He claimed I was going overboard with my sense of authority. He was correct. I was suffering from what some call short person syndrome, or SPS.

SPS is a form of what's called the compensation theory. This is when people select certain leisure practices to bolster areas of life in which they feel inadequate. An example of this is a cubicle worker who enjoys some risky adventures, such as skydiving. Sin choices seem to follow the same pattern; the lies convince us that the counterfeit will address our need of affirmation, love, recognition, self-esteem, etc. So in that realm, SPS occurs when someone that has been blessed with a lack of height and feels that he or she is not recognized or respected because of that tries to make up for it in other realms of life. I usually tried through sarcasm and humor, but with a whistle around my neck, I became the sheriff of wherever I was. In fourth grade it was stairs. On this particular day it was basketball.

Short person syndrome is a close relative of another disorder called shouldn't be in authority syndrome, or SBIAS. It seems security companies and the Transportation Security Administration attract those with SBIAS. People that never had, or in some cases should not have, authority in their lives enjoy the power rush that occurs by being able to boss people around. I also call it the Barney Fife syndrome, named after the wimpy deputy on *The Andy Griffith Show*. Barney rarely got respect, but he enjoyed it when the law was upheld. He was not allowed to keep a loaded gun, so Sheriff Andy made him carry his only bullet in his pocket. He's the classic example of what a bumbling legalist would look like. He was prepared to write a ticket or shoot someone for the slightest of infractions.

Luke tells a story that is not found in the other Gospels about a man with SPS. Or in his case we could call it the WLMWH disorder.

Those that remember the song from childhood about Zacchaeus know that stands for "wee little man was he."

Luke refers to him as being a tax collector. Or, as Zacchaeus, suffering deeply with WLMWH disorder, would point out, he was the chief tax collector. Now, before you start cursing and rehearsing about our own Internal Revenue Service, you should understand how it worked in that day. Zacchaeus was demanding, with the Romans' blessings, more from people than the taxes actually demanded. The Romans hired tax collectors and just wanted their designated tax share. Anything gained above that could be kept by the tax collector. Zacchaeus apparently was milking the system fairly well, to the detriment of even his own Jewish people. I have no doubt he was getting even with a few tellers of short jokes as well as lining his pockets with unfair taxes.

Luke's story refers to his size because, in order to see Jesus, Zach had to climb a sycamore tree so that he could actually see Jesus coming down the street. Our little short man must have heard about Jesus and the way he befriended all people. I have no doubt that Zach, like the rest of us, desired a bit of affirmation so someone would appreciate him for who he was. Jesus saw him and invited himself to spend the day at Zach's place. This, of course, raised the eyebrows of a good many "religious" people in the area. Tax collectors were the worst kind of sinners to the religious leaders of that day.

While spending time with Jesus, Zach made an alarming decision. He chose to give half of what he owned to the poor and committed to pay anyone he had cheated four times the amount originally extracted. Jesus even commented, "Today salvation has come to this house, because this man, too, is a son of Abraham. For the Son of Man came to seek and to save what was lost."

I love the insertion Jesus gave calling Zach a son of Abraham. That probably sent the religious leaders into all sorts of compensation theory actions! That day Zacchaeus discovered that the best way to deal with his self-inflicted inadequacies was to line himself up with the Jesus-given adequacies. God made Zach and me the way we are on purpose. If God had wanted me to be taller, I would have been taller. Instead He gifted, wired, and shaped me exactly the way I am supposed to be. The SPS has transformed into a much healthier condition of truth made by God through the death and resurrection of His Son. For me it's called DICJ, otherwise known as the David in Christ Jesus truth. Substitute your own name, and you can have the same truth in your life.

What disorder can Jesus transform for you?

BEN-HADAD: TRASH TALKING KING (1 KINGS 20)

The driveway served as the battlefield in a way. On one side of the driveway was the front yard, in which stood two Bartlett pear trees. On the other side was the object used to determine the winner in many skirmishes with my oldest son. It stood over ten feet high and had a huge block of plastic attached to it. On the plastic shield was a round metal frame where a net hung underneath a ring.

It was our basketball goal.

Starting when James was in sixth or seventh grade, we began a basketball battle between the old and the young—or, if you will, the experienced and the novice. I had been a victim and a victor in a good many one-on-one games in my life. Where my height might have proved to be a disadvantage, my lack of speed ensured defeat would occur a lot.

When we started playing, James was a little shorter than I was, and a good bit lighter. I could easily back him down and turn around to make an easy shot. Not wanting to destroy his spirit, I would generally try other shots or other moves and make the games a bit more competitive. We kept a running tally of wins and losses for Waddell bragging rights. With my weight advantage and experience in playing the game, I built up a fairly good win–loss record. Despite his failures and struggles, the young man never gave up. He was also quite good at what has become known as trash talk.

Most of the fun of having an ongoing game like this with a son is the connection the game gives you at other times. I'd get home from work, and he might be practicing his shot on the driveway. I'd start to head inside, tired from a hard day at work (I know that no one will buy the "hard day" line), and James would say, "You got a game in you, old man?" or "Think you can take me today?"

Clothes would be changed, and the game would ensue. As the buck, or alpha male, there was no way I was going to let his trash talk win. Don't think for a minute the trash talk was a one-way street. Often when he would throw down the gauntlet, I would reply with a cutting and funny comeback that was equally as trashy.

Trash talk has become a norm in sports these days. I utilized it with my son and also in numerous lunch basketball games at church. It was fun coming up with unique and creative ways to talk trash in a Christ-centered activity. It can be done!

There was a point where my game became more trash talk than action. James grew taller than me and somehow got stronger. I tried to back him down for an easy shot and discovered I was trying to move a brick wall. James' talent and abilities easily shot past my level of expertise, and I saw my winning record fade away quickly. Whereas I never wanted to destroy James' spirit by continually beating him, James, when he started winning, did not share that same level of compassion and mercy. This led to a whole new level of trash talk.

One year James had come back from college for the weekend. On a Sunday afternoon we decided to play a best-of-three series. I had not played in a while, so it didn't surprise me when I was a little out of shape during the first game. My legs seemed to ache, and it was hard to breathe, but I attributed that to being out of shape. In the second game I was hitting every shot I put up and won the game, pushing the final game. After a short rest we played again, and James easily cruised to victory.

The next day, I went to see my doctor, thinking I had my normal winter sinus infection. Upon further review, the doctor sent me to the hospital. I was experiencing my first round of atrial fibrillation. This is where part of the heart works and the other part just quivers. Medication and a procedure called cardioversion got my heart back in rhythm.

While I was still in the hospital, James came back into town to see me. I couldn't help myself. "James," I said, "you do know that you lost a basketball game on Sunday to a man that had only half of his heart working?"

The trash talk continues to this day. The difficulty with most trash talk is that it points out my abilities and talents and leaves little for the glory of God working through the situation.

King Ahab, King of Israel during the time of the prophet Elijah, got involved in a bit of a trash talk battle. Ben-Hadad, king of Aram, sent word to Ahab: "your silver and gold are mine, and the best of your wives and children are mine."

Ahab, showing a bit of cowardice, gave Ben-Hadad what he requested. Not completely satisfied, Ben-Hadad sent another note claiming he would come and clean out Ahab's entire palace. Ahab consulted his elders, who told him not to give in this time. Upon hearing this, Ben-Hadad went into trash talk mode. "May the gods deal with me, be it ever so severely, if enough dust remains in Samaria to give each of my men a handful."

Not to be outdone, Ahab replied, "One who puts on his armor should not boast like one who takes it off."

James and I have nothing on this pair!

Then a third trash talker came into play. A prophet of the Lord told Ahab that Ben-Hadad's vast army would be put into Ahab's hands. Not only that, but God would provide the victory through the young officers of the provincial command. Sure enough, the young officers struck down the opponents and got them running.

Some of Ben-Hadad's advisors claimed this was because the God of Israel was a god of the hills. If they battled them on the plains, they reasoned, the outcome would be different. God took their overconfidence and once again declared victory would belong to Israel. The Aramean soldiers fled like crazy at the onslaught brought about by God. The trash talking Ben-Hadad went to Ahab and begged for his life. Ahab granted it even though God had determined he was to die. So a prophet, sounding as if he were trash talking, told Ahab that his life would be forfeited because he did not take Ben-Hadad's life.

I suppose it is part of our nature to brag and talk big about what we can do. It is in the trash talk that I rely mostly on my own abilities and my own talents to accomplish a task. You'll note that when God stepped into the battle, Ahab found no need to trash talk the fellow king. God fought the battle and took on the trash talk for him. I hope to learn the same lesson.

With that in mind, do you think you can take me?

CAIN: IN A PINCH (GENESIS 4)

It was a tradition in our family that a person celebrating a birthday would receive a birthday spanking. These were not delivered with any force whatsoever, as was the custom with regular disciplinary spankings. One swat would occur for every year the recipient had been alive, and at the end Mom and Dad would say, "And a pinch to grow on!"

You could run, but you could not hide forever when it was time for the ceremonial spanking. It served as a rite of passage, so to speak. One would not really be a year older without the sanctity of the birthday spanking.

On my seventh birthday, I had no reason not to expect the same treatment. This birthday, however, turned out just a little bit different. I had developed a sense of wonder about matches. Dad was a regular smoker, so he would strike matches to light his cigarettes. It may sound weird, but I enjoyed the sulfuric smell that occurred when the match was lit. Now that I was seven, it was time to plot a way to sneak some of Dad's matches and hide in the basement and light a few. I knew that one of my friends across the street had a similar curiosity and would join me in my quest.

I recall playing a game where we would light a match and hold it until we just had to let go. The person with the shortest leftover stick would win. In another bout, we would make the striking of the match one fluid motion, releasing the match so it would go flying into a chalk circle on the floor. We also attempted to see how long one of us could keep a flame going by lighting another match before the one we were holding would die out.

Then it happened. My mother, who never seemed to come to the basement except on laundry days, came to the basement. As I noticed her presence, I was holding a lit match in my hands. She gave me "the look"—that trait that mothers have that communicates displeasure so well. Mom asked what was going on, and despite the evidence of a burned match held in between my thumb and fingers, I screamed out, "I don't know!"

Mom saw the evidence of burned matches on the floor and looked back at me again. Then, without hardly any hesitation on my part, I hollered, "I didn't do it!"

It's surprising what will come out of my mouth when I am in a pinch, caught with my hand in the cookie jar! I never seem to own up to my actions or behavior. For some reason the lies and rationalizations seem to want to come out first.

In a typical feeling of invulnerability, my friend and I had not considered the fact that the sulfuric smell of the match would carry upstairs. We had not thought through the pinch created by the consequences of playing with matches either. I can only imagine God was protecting us from our own stupidity. He does that when we're in a pinch.

Needless to say, we had been discovered. We were busted. My defense, now that I look back, was rather weak. It was the fear of Mom that caused me to blurt out "I don't know" and "I didn't do it." Knowing I was busted, I also tried the "it just happened" line, but she wasn't buying any of that either. Apparently she had not heard of the self-lighting matches that had been created and jumped into our hands.

My friend was sent home with the threat that his mother would be called. I was escorted upstairs to my room, where I received a different kind of birthday spanking. She didn't stop at seven; nor did she give me a pinch to grow on.

You might think I would have learned my lesson at age seven, but I have not. When confronted with sin and disobedience to this day, my defense mechanisms quickly revert to the approach of "I don't know," "I didn't do it," and "It just happened," which never works. For some reason my initial reaction is to lie, divert, or deflect. I know the consequences seem worse with the cover-up, but I just can't convince myself. Even President Clinton realized after his own little cover-up that the best thing to do is just be honest in the beginning. Stan Laurel, a comic actor in early movies, both silent and speaking, got the old honesty adage wrong when he said, "Honesty is the best politics!" On the other hand, he might actually have something there!

The first natural-born person to ever live seemed to have the same difficulty I have. Cain was the first son born to Adam and Eve after they had to leave the garden because of their own round of lies, diversions, and deflections in their own sin. Cain got a younger brother not too long after that, and sibling rivalry was born along with this brother, Abel. Cain was a farmer, and Abel became a shepherd. When it came time to give God an offering, Cain gave some of his grain while Abel gave the best of his sheep for a sacrifice. God was pleased with the attitude and the gift Abel gave. This drove Cain absolutely nuts!

One day, while out in the field, Cain decided to play with some matches of a sort and murdered his brother. In the same way as the sulfuric smell rose out of the basement, the cries of Abel's blood went up to heaven. Cain apparently assumed God never came down to earth to visit anymore. When God did show up, He asked Cain where He could find his brother.

Cain found himself in a bit of a pinch and responded, "I don't know." He then asked if he was his "brother's keeper." I have to admit he did quite well in the "lie, deflect, and divert" method.

I've heard married men say that when their wives ask them a question, their wives already know the answer when they ask it. It seems God established this trait long before the women tried it. When Adam sinned, God asked him why he was hiding. When Cain got rid of his brother, God asked about where He could find him. Both times, God knew the answer before asking the question. Like me, both Adam and Cain decided to lie about, divert, or deflect the question rather than coming right out with the truth.

When James wrote his letter to the twelve tribes, he pointed out how sin takes root in us. It begins with evil desire, which is followed by enticement. After desire conceives, it gives birth to sin. Sin, when it is fully grown, finds death. I'm sure I don't see "I don't know" or "it just happened" in the definition.

John takes it a step further and tells us that when we "confess our sins to him, he is faithful and just to forgive us our sins and to cleanse us from all wickedness."

Perhaps a better method of dealing with this matter is to replace the diverting and deflecting and make some decent decisions. When I do make an error or sin, I should own up to it and not try to create a story to save my image or reputation. It never fails that the "smell of sulfur" will go upstairs, where my sin is discovered despite how well I try to cover it up. As Mark Twain once said, "Tell the truth and you don't have to remember anything."

And that's the pinch to grow on!

MC HAMMERED: BEYOND EXPECTATIONS (JOHN 2:1–11)

It was one of those staff teams where you didn't have to be crazy to work with the others, but it certainly helped. A new senior pastor was now on the job, and to establish good relationships outside the office, he would have us all go to lunch together. The church would pick up the tab, so of course I was in favor of going!

This was a staff that also liked to play pranks on each other. Troy, the music minister, would remove my office chair when I had to run elsewhere in the building. He would move it to the restroom, choir loft, or even the second-floor youth Sunday school rooms. I would have to go on a facility search to find it. The pattern of pranks had been set by the previous senior pastor, who could have easily earned a doctor of prankology diploma.

The former pastor was the one that taught me the "stolen silverware" trick to play on innocent travelers on mission trips or senior adult trips. His most well-known trick was when he put a life-size cardboard cutout in the janitor's closet knowing it would scare our custodian, Jesse, nearly to death. That trick backfired, however, when a call was made to the local police by a suspicious neighbor who thought she saw someone in the church late at night. The practice in situations like that was to have the pastor open up every door in the church so the police could check the place out. In that it was in the middle of the night, the pastor forgot about his prank that waited for Jesse the next morning. That poor cardboard cutout almost took a couple of rounds because of the surprise it caused when that door was opened.

We found ourselves in a Mexican restaurant for a get-to-know-you-better luncheon. Between ministers and secretaries, we found ourselves at a table for eight. I was seated next to the pastor, and Troy was next to me.

I leaned over to Troy and suggested a prank to play on the pastor. I explained to him that I'd get up, giving the excuse that I needed to go to the bathroom. While away, I'd tell the server that we were going to play a joke on one in our party and ask her to bring the pastor a nonalcoholic margarita. I told Troy, to remove suspicion, that he could also "go to the bathroom" and tell her when it needed to be delivered. The pastor, of course, would balk at the sight of an alcoholic beverage, but I'd pick it up and guzzle it down. Troy agreed it will be a great trick. So I got up and arranged the prank with the server.

When the meal was wrapping up, Troy excused himself for a moment. When Troy came back, he gave me a slight grin and a wink. I thought to myself, *The game is on!*

The server set the margarita in front of the pastor. The expected response is even better than we could have imagined. The fear of someone seeing an alcoholic drink in front of him had the pastor scribing a resignation letter in his head.

That was my cue! I leaned over and said, "Let me get rid of the evidence!" I slammed the drink back and had it gone in a matter of seconds.

Then the reaction began. My tongue and throat felt as though they were on fire. I felt a warmth coming from my stomach and rising quickly toward my head. My eyes felt as though they were crossing. I felt a little dizzy and lightheaded. I hadn't had a reaction like that since I was in college. That was the last time I'd had a drink like this one. My eyes, now bloodshot and filling with tears, looked at Troy. His slight grin had turned into a Cheshire cat grin. Immediately upon making eye contact, he burst into full laughter. This was not what I had been expecting in this prank. I turned to the pastor and noticed that he was in full laughter as well. So was everyone else at the table.

When the laughter finally subsided, Troy confessed that while I was "in the bathroom" he told the pastor about our prank. The pastor suggested the change from a nonalcoholic drink to a double shot of tequila in the margarita, turning the trick onto me. Everyone at the table was in on the prank. When Troy went to tell the server that it was time to bring the drink based on my original plan, he told her to change the makeup of the drink.

I couldn't tell if my red face was due to embarrassment or tequila.

Can you imagine expecting one thing and getting another? There was a master of ceremonies at a wedding once that did just that. Some friends of Mary, the mother of Jesus, were getting married in Cana. The master of ceremonies, or MC, would judge the wedded couple based on how well the reception or party was conducted. A poor reception, and the couple would be social outcasts. This young couple really wanted to put on a good show for the MC.

Unfortunately the party was in full swing and nowhere near the end when the couple ran out of wine. Having planned numerous social events in my life, I know this can be embarrassing. Parties die for the lack of refreshments. In this case, the couples had more problems than just party planning.

Mary, realizing the social embarrassment at hand, told Jesus about the problem. Jesus told her it wasn't His time yet for such acts. Mary, despite Jesus' claim, told the servants to do whatever Jesus told them to do. He instructed them to fill up some jugs with water and serve the MC with that.

Mary acted out of faith in what she knew her Son could do. The servants were simply following orders. I can imagine the looks on their faces when they got more than they expected as well. They put water in the jugs and ended up serving wine when they dipped a ladle into the jugs. It would have been fun to see the looks on the faces of the servers when a rich aroma of wine rose to their senses upon the raising of the ladle.

The MC, already full of earlier samples of wine, tasted the wine created by Jesus and made a declaration that was bound to serve the couple in the community for a long time. He said, "A host always serves the best wine first, then, when everyone has had a lot to drink, he brings out the less expensive wine. But you have kept the best until now."

Crisis averted. The couple had saved face in Jesus' first miracle.

Jesus does what He is best at doing in exceeding expectations. Despite numerous examples of God performing wonderful and miraculous acts, I still have low expectations of what He can do for me and through me. I go through life expecting a plain margarita when God wants to light me up for so much more. I expect to keep drinking the same old wine, but the God of creation wants me to experience the best wine He has to offer.

I should learn this lesson with more ease than I have been learning it. When my sons were born, I asked for good wives for them. God gave them great wives. I asked God for good grandchildren, and He gave me grandkids that set records for greatness. I asked God for restoration in my career, and He has offered me an unbelievable path at influencing tomorrow's leaders.

So why do I still put the glass to my mouth expecting only lemon juice? More times than not, my low expectations are to control my level of disappointment. If I don't ask the really great girl out, then she can't reject me. If I don't seek the best opportunity to serve, they can't tell me I'm no good. A friend once told me that faith, to her, meant expecting the very best and not figuring disappointment in the picture.

Jesus told his followers that they would see even greater samples of God's redemptive work than He had done. I think I'll start expecting the wine to be the very best.

More wine? Or would you rather have a nonalcoholic margarita?

DAVID: SILENCE ISN'T ALL THAT GOLDEN (2 SAMUEL 11–12)

I had just returned home from a long day at work. Operating a recreation center for a church seemed to be a never-ending job. Although I might be away from the center, I was still in charge. At times, my staff would have to call me and ask my opinion or seek a direction on how to deal with a certain situation. Many of these years were before the invention of cell phones and call-waiting services.

Most nights there would be no interruptions of my evening at home with my family. Occasionally a call would come in that would require me to go back up to the center to deal with situations. I hated doing that. I am the kind of guy that just wanted to stay home with my family when I got home to them. Needless to say I developed a fear of ringing phones. In the evening, when the phone would ring, I would hesitate before I answered it, saying a little prayer in hopes that it was not work-related. Most of the time, the call was for the wife or one of the boys. Still, whenever the bell rang, I would panic that I would have to go back to work.

The fear of receiving that phone call waned in comparison to others I was afraid of. For many years I hid a dark and sinful part of my life from others. I usually kept a good bit of myself secret from those I met in this hidden sin. I didn't want them to know they were sinning with a church leader. Besides, I never wanted them to know enough about me that they could make trouble for me. I felt I was doing quite well at hiding the sin and hiding my identity.

I was standing in the kitchen talking to my wife on that day after the long workday. The phone rang. The momentary panic regarding the recreation center hit, but I answered it anyway. The call was not from the recreation center; instead it was from a lady I had met while out of town for a workshop. A new sense of panic came over me. I could feel the blood rushing to my head. *How in the world am I going to do damage control on this one?* I thought. I did feel a bit of relief that I, and not my wife, had answered the phone.

The lady asked how I was doing and how my day had been. Despite whatever her questions were, I tried answering in ways that would make it sound as though the recreation center had called for information. She continued to try to keep the conversation going, but after I gave more recreation center–related answers, she finally said good bye and hung up the phone. My heart was racing at that point. I was scared out of my wits at the idea of it being discovered that I wasn't as pure as I seemed.

I apparently did a good enough job with my lying and diversion, because my wife thought it was the recreation center and didn't even ask about it. Even still, my heart felt so heavy about my sin coming to find me at home. Two thoughts consumed my mind that night. The first was "be sure your sins will find you out." The second was ways to be more careful the next time I sinned to be sure that this didn't happen again.

The next day, I called my friend from a pay phone to find out a few things for myself. I used pay phones, of course, so there would be no paper trail or way to catch me. I thought I was so smart. It seemed she had gotten my name from the hotel where I had stayed during my time in her town. She had then placed a simple call to 411 and obtained my home phone number. She apologized for the call, knowing that I was a married man. It didn't matter; the damage was done. I immediately thought of others I had sinned with and wondered whether I would be hearing from them. The irony of this close call was that it wasn't enough to make me stop in my sin. It only made me more careful and thoughtful as I planned out my next sinful adventure. You see, close calls don't stop sinful behavior. Close calls give the enemy more ammunition to fire away at lies to get you right back into trouble.

Getting caught provides a better chance of creating an atmosphere of change. God knew this and years later made sure my sins did find me out.

From that time on, my time at home was always disturbed by any incoming phone call. My heart seemed to skip a beat and feel so heavy until I could hear the call wasn't about my sin. I lived in a paranoid state, never knowing when the shoe would drop and I would be found out. Oh, it wasn't just phone calls. It was looks over my shoulder, parking in remote places so my car couldn't be seen, and creating alternate e-mail addresses, all designed to keep my sin in silence. I can't even begin to describe the panic I would experience when my wife would say "We need to talk" or ask "Can we talk?" I was always scared that the sin I kept in silence had somehow been found out. My heart rate would jump each time she innocently desired to speak about other issues.

David, my namesake in the Bible, had some of these feelings himself. After he plotted and planned a way to get another man's wife into his bed, he had to plot and plan a way to get rid of the other man. While his army was off fighting, David took a stroll on his roof and saw a woman bathing. He inquired as to who it was and found it was Bathsheba, the wife of Uriah the Hittite. David sent for her and slept with her.

While it wasn't a phone call, David did get a message that Bathsheba was pregnant. Now with her husband off at war, and with a number of people knowing she had been in the palace, David had to get busy in covering up future potential messages coming in. David connived a plan to get Uriah home. David knew that if Uriah would sleep with his wife, he could cover up his own sin. Unfortunately the man did not play along.

On the first occasion, David invited Uriah home from the war and gave him the night off to go home and wash his feet.

David got the message that Uriah did not go home.

Uriah, it seems, chose to sleep at the entrance to the palace with the servants. So, in other words, there were witnesses that no relations were had by the husband and wife. David got on Uriah for not going home. Uriah pointed out that the ark of the covenant lived in a tent, as did all his fellow soldiers, and that he could not take comfort being at home while knowing all that. That was not the phone call David wanted to receive.

David knew the baby could start showing at any time, and he couldn't afford that phone call if he were to continue covering the sin. So the next night, David invited Uriah to a banquet and got him well fed and drunk. David sent him home only to receive the message that once again Uriah had slept at the palace gate.

David ended up killing the man in his own attempts at damage control. He told Joab, the commander of the army, to put Uriah on the front line and then retreat, leaving him by himself to fight the enemy. Of course Uriah was killed immediately.

The prophet Nathan came to visit David. I imagine David was feeling smug about the cover-up of his sin. No one would know, and no one had to know. Yet, in his heart, David had to feel a little bit of anguish over the possibility of Nathan knowing something. Hiding sin makes everyone suspicious and suspect. Nathan told David a story of a poor man with one lamb and a rich man with flocks of sheep and cattle. When the rich man had a visitor, he decided to take the poor man's lamb for the feast rather than kill one of his own.

David, in his anger, declared that the man must die. That is until Nathan told him, "You are the man!" In the same way my sin found me out, David had to deal with his as well.

David writes in Psalm 32 of how his heart felt during the time he kept quiet about all of his hidden sin: "When I kept silent, my bones wasted away through my groaning all the day long. For day and night your hand was heavy on me."

It was the silence in my heart that made me fear the phone call or conversation. David and I discovered that sin kept in silence wears away at the soul. There was no rest or peace in life, for we were always scared of being found out. For King David it was the prophet Nathan who exposed the sin. For me it was deleted e-mails that somehow reappeared in my inbox.

What are you being silent about?

REHOBOAM: GOOD TIMES AND BAD (2 CHRONICLES 11:1–17)

The excitement had built up for nine months. It seemed to have been even longer. In fact, it was longer, because my firstborn did not come on his due date. He decided he had a good life going on in the womb and was not planning on coming out. Our doctor sent us home from a visit on a Friday with instructions that if the little rascal didn't pop out in the next few days, we would induce labor.

The follow-up visit was on Monday, the second of August. I wanted to go ahead and induce that day so he could have an 8/2/82 birthday. Had he come out on his own, the doctor wouldn't have argued, but he protested against inducing on that day. I'm pretty sure by this point the mama wanted to induce immediately. Since we were inducing, we could pick the day to go in to the hospital. The expectant mother, who had not seen her own feet for months, opted for the next day. My mother's birthday was on the fourth of August, and I had a brief thought of waiting until then. But better judgment and the fear of what a desperate pregnant woman could do to me made me remain quiet. So on August 3, we were hooking up the expectant mom and giving her the drug that would chase my child out of the comfort zone.

Everything seemed to be going well. We were in our fourth year of marriage when we decided to try to start a family. College and seminary were behind us, and I was employed by a church, so it seemed logical to get things rolling. Once the decision was made, it didn't take long for the pregnancy to become a reality. We read as many books as we could and attended all the child-birthing classes and doctor visits to get us to the last day. In the classes, they advised me, as her partner, that to get her relaxed or breathing properly, I might have to actually get right in her face and breathe with her.

The excitement was at its peak when the process began, and we planned for my firstborn to have his coming-out party. Prayer, worship, and my dependence on God took a bit of a backseat through the process. What with all the other stuff going on—and it was going so well—I suppose I didn't see the need.

My prayers to God came back strong during the labor and delivery. No one told me that labor pains bring about demon possession in a woman. We were told in the classes that the dad / significant other / partner could eat but the expectant mother could not. So I packed a lunch for the long, laborious ordeal. Hindsight tells me now that a tuna fish sandwich may not have been the best choice for lunch. Especially in light of me trying to get her to breath with me in the taught pattern designed to lessen labor pains. "Get that tuna breath out of my face!" she screamed. It sounded loud enough that I figured security would be on the scene any minute.

The child was born. It was a son, and we named him after me with "junior" attached to the end. "Joy," "happiness," and "elation" do not adequately describe how I was feeling. In what I can only describe as a macho attitude, I was proud to have a son that could carry on the Waddell name. I know it sounds silly to some, and I can't explain why, but it meant a lot to me. My mom designed a birth announcement, claiming we had a "new slugger" in the lineup. She drew a baby in diapers with a Kansas City Royals helmet on his head. Life was good.

Then, in a follow-up visit with the pediatrician, we discovered James had a slight heart murmur. The doctor tried not to alarm us, but it didn't work. We were soon on our way to Houston, Texas, to visit with a specialized pediatric cardiologist to figure out what was wrong and how, if possible, to fix it.

You can imagine I was humbled and on my knees. I knew I needed a miracle, and I begged for one. The two-hour drive to Houston was quiet between my wife and me, but it was plenty noisy between us and God. When things had been going well, I hadn't given prayer a second thought. Now that things were not so joyous and happy, I found myself needing God's help more.

When we got to Houston, they connected all sorts of wires and things to my newborn baby. The doctors asked us to make him stop crying. I couldn't even make myself stop crying. Numerous tests were done, and we awaited an answer. While waiting, we observed so many other babies in worse shape than our son. When we got the final answer, it was, in so many words, "Hurry up and wait." There was a chance the boy would outgrow it or the heart would compensate for it somehow. Follow-up visits were scheduled, and we were sent home. The ride home was as equally as quiet. I was mix of emotions myself. I found myself praising God for the report and at the same time getting angry at God for letting it happen. I prayed, seeking a miracle for the heart, and also started trying to figure out what I could do to make it better.

The good news of this story is that James' heart learned to do whatever it had to do to overcome the situation. He is a strong young man with kids of his own at this time. I am still amazed at how desperate I am when in need and how forgetful I am when things are good.

Rehoboam had the same thing going for him. The son of Solomon took over as king of Judah and Benjamin. Rehoboam had already made an error in trying to be tougher than his dad. This led ten of the twelve tribes to break off and make Jeroboam their king. Now Rehoboam found himself ready to go to battle against those ten tribes now known as Israel. When the word of the Lord commanded Rehoboam to not fight his brothers, he obeyed and instead fortified Judah. God honored him, and even the priests and Levites abandoned their own fields and flocks to join him in Judah.

Things seemed to be looking really good for Rehoboam. He lived in the same way his grandfather David had lived. The people were worshiping God again. God blessed Rehoboam with wives and children. Things were looking great.

Then, after he had become strong, he abandoned the law of the Lord. His disobedience and lack of loyalty led to Egypt attacking and capturing some of the fortified cities. Things were suddenly not looking so good.

A prophet came to tell Rehoboam that he had abandoned the Lord. Upon hearing this, the leaders humbled themselves. God chose not to destroy them and promised deliverance to come soon. God did, however, make them subject to the Egyptian king so they could learn the difference between serving God and serving the kings of other lands. Because Rehoboam humbled himself before the Lord, His anger was turned from him and he was spared.

Like Rehoboam, I tend to live a roller-coaster life. When times have been bad career wise, I have sought Him diligently. When marriage troubles hit, I sought His face numerous times each day. When I want a particular relationship to work, desire better work conditions, or just rattle off whatever makes me uncomfortable, I seek God's blessing. When I have exactly what I want in life, I tend to forget the wonders He has performed and stay limited to the measly things I have accomplished.

How are things? Good?

SOLOMON: I SHOULD HAVE LISTENED TO MYSELF (1 KINGS 11:1–6)

My years of hidden sin had led to the eventual death of my marriage. While I was working through the grief of that event, my mother made a comment to me. In regard to dating again, she said, "I hope you can find a really nice girl."

I knew what she meant. She didn't just mean "nice." She was leaning on the Scripture about being unequally yoked. Paul warned about it in his letter to the church of Corinth. Jesus talked about the fact that a man will serve only one master. Jesus referred to money or faith, but anything could take the place of money in mastering a person. Mom wanted me to find someone that would bolster my faith rather than blowing it. I knew she was correct. I now wish I had listened to her and myself.

For me, the recipe for disaster was a pretty girl in the restaurant where my friends and I were dining. She had just picked up the last banana pudding that was available at the dessert bar. I was recovering from some surgery on my left foot and still wore one of those big black boots on that leg and was required to use one crutch to avoid putting too much weight on the foot just yet. As she turned with the plate, I reached to grab it and said, "Thank you."

She was shocked at first but then offered it to me. I told her I was just joking and played jokingly on her sympathy toward me being on one crutch. We both laughed and went our separate ways. As she was leaving the cafeteria she walked by my table, and I asked her what her name was in the event I needed to file a complaint regarding the Americans with Disabilities Act about her taking the last banana pudding. Knowing that I had already joked about my one-crutch condition, she replied with a sarcastic quip about me chasing after her on one crutch to find out where she worked if I was that interested in knowing her. My friends at the table with me laughed like crazy and commented on my wonderful ways with the opposite sex.

I frequently ate at this particular restaurant but never saw her there again. Later I discovered she was a temporary staff member in a nearby office. The path to my newfound knowledge was that another worker in that office was a friend of mine who not only knew Banana Pudding Girl but was also good friends with her. My one-crutch aspect had been discussed during a break, and my friend knew it had to be me because of that detail and the humorous interaction.

In the preliminary days and dates of getting to know this girl, everything seemed to be going fine. She was appreciative of the fact that I got along with her daughter and that I was thoughtful and considerate. She wondered how in the world I could ever be divorced as well as why I hadn't remarried yet. I must admit all of that made me feel really good. Even after sharing some of the reasons for the divorce, she sugarcoated it into one of the best rationalizations I've ever heard. None of it was true, but I enjoyed believing it just the same.

We dated on and off for about a year and a half. I decided I was determined to make the relationship work and went all in. I didn't realize it at first, but looking back at it I see that I started making little decisions that impacted me spiritually. In the moment it all looked innocent, but in the long run it had disastrous consequences for me. We might take a weekend trip to enjoy free hotels at one of the casinos located about an hour and a half from home. Relaxation, indoor swimming, and free meals were awarded to this lady for merely losing ten times that same amount of money on previous trips. So the three of us would make the trip and enjoy the weekend. *Missing one Sunday of church isn't that bad,* I would rationalize. She would even mention going to church with me, but when it came around to the following Sunday, I found other things to occupy our time.

Then there would be a weekend devoted to getting my house up to shape. Do-it-yourself projects would have me working at home and missing another Sunday of worship. Throw in a trip here and a sleep-in there, and I found myself racking up a number of weeks since being in a church service.

Then the bad news hit. She was experiencing some financial difficulties and was about to be evicted from her apartment. Instead of seeking information as to what got her into financial trouble, I decided to be the shining white armored knight and swooped in to save the damsel in distress. Despite knowing better, I invited her and her daughter to live in my new house with me. Every voice in my head was telling me to turn from a decision to house this girl, but I chose not to listen. I believed I was strong enough to fight off any temptation and deal with any issue that might arise. Imagine me beating my chest right about then in a false sense of self-confidence.

That's when the real trouble began. Again, despite having "been there" and having "done that" in my life, I started walking down the same path of destruction. I pushed family and friends away and found myself being more and more tightly wound into a situation that was not honoring God. Both friends and family were concerned for me, but I didn't listen to any advice at all, neither from them nor from the voices in my heart telling me God's truth.

For the next year I experienced stress and trouble with this relationship. Prayers then became stronger. I was typical of Old Testament Israel in saying, "I have messed up and deserve this punishment, but please rescue me now!"

Through a series of events, I was finally able to move away from this situation. Friends have asked me how I ever got into the situation to begin with. The answer is simple. I didn't listen to my own advice, which I could take directly from the Scriptures. What starts off as a small justification grows into a more powerful life direction. I wade into what seems like safe ocean water and discover a powerful wave has consumed me.

Solomon was the third and final king of the united Kingdom of Israel. He followed his father, David, to the throne. He got there despite some interference and trouble brewed up by some of David's other sons, but nonetheless, in keeping God's promise, Solomon was put on the throne. God promised him that for the sake of his father, David, there would always be one of his sons on the throne. God also promised that if Solomon would keep His laws as his father, David, had done, he would be blessed beyond recognition.

When Solomon was granted one wish by God he didn't request riches or land. He asked for wisdom in order to rule God's people. God granted him wisdom and then rewarded his humility with unbelievable riches.

Solomon had some good years until a family trait came to catch up with him. He apparently didn't learn the lesson about troubles that accrue from improper dealings with the opposite sex from his father, David. Solomon, despite the warning from God to not marry people outside of Israel, took a good many wives from all over the world. I'm sure all of them made sense politically at the time. Each one of the ladies probably told Solomon, as my girlfriend did to me, everything he wanted to hear. They lured him in with their beauty and charm. It made good sense to Solomon to marry each one. In all, Solomon ended up with over three hundred wives. If you folks think keeping up with one spouse is trouble, think about poor Solomon!

Even though Solomon wrote many of the wise sayings in the Bible, he didn't listen to his own advice when it came to women. He warned of the ways of evil women and their outer beauty leading a man astray, similar to sheep going to be butchered. I can always envision myself being in line with a woman at one end and me bleating all the way to the chopping block, thinking I'm having fun while I'm actually facing my eventual death.

Solomon eventually gave in to their requests to bring some of their own gods into Israel and into the temple. He knew the law, and he knew better, but he still gave in to their requests. I can only surmise that he did so to keep peace in the family or to keep them all smiling. The evidence of the other gods and the influence of his wives eventually led Solomon away from worshiping the true God. After Solomon had been king for forty years, God took his life and Solomon's son Rehoboam became king.

Rehoboam eventually lost ten of the twelve tribes of Israel as a result of Solomon's wayward ways at the end and his own decisions to not rid the land of the idols. Thankfully God has given me one more chance to get it right.

The enemy is not a fool. He knows exactly what my weak spot is and can easily set me up for failure. Like Solomon, I caved to keep a person happy even though I knew it was not what God wanted for me. Like Solomon, much of my pain in that relationship was brought about because I didn't follow my own advice and that of my mother in looking for a "really nice girl."

What should you be hearing from yourself?

SECURITY-MINDED DISCIPLES: HALT! WHO GOES THERE? (MATTHEW 19:13–15)

I jokingly talk about others with the Barney Fife syndrome, or BFS. It's a condition in which someone has authority but shouldn't. The syndrome was coined as such from the skinny deputy on *The Andy Griffith Show.* He was pretty much inept, but Sheriff Andy kept him around, trying to make him into a good lawman. Barney would write a ticket for anything and everything. He enjoyed pushing around his authority even though most of the folks in town acted as though he had none.

The people suffering from BFS, like Barney, are quick to raise their voice or get rough. They cannot handle having their authority or position questioned. They have a keen sense of duty to the cause of security and peace. I have accused security companies and the Transportation Security Administration of hiring people with BFS.

It wasn't until a particular concert was in town that I realized I suffer from the above-mentioned disorder.

Having put some time in churches in the area of youth ministry, loud concerts were not a new experience for me. When I moved to First Baptist in Springfield, Missouri, the church had a youth minister, and my job duties were strictly in the area of recreation ministry. Although I had no direct responsibility for teenagers, I was usually placed in charge of their mission trips and volunteered to assist in various other programs because my sons were in the group. So most of the time, in youth events, I played the role of volunteer dad and helped out wherever I could.

Several of the churches in the area were working cooperatively toward bringing in a concert band for the kids of the city. It was kind of fun, because up to that point I had never really seen my Baptist church get involved with Methodists, Catholics, Presbyterians, and Lutherans. It was usually hard enough in my past experiences just to get different Baptists to work together! The band was selected, which raised the spirit and excitement of teenagers in all the churches. We were bringing in the Newsboys.

Music never has been my forte. I like listening to it, but I will flunk every exam when I have to actually name a song or the group that sang the song. So when the Newsboys were announced, someone had to tell me the names of some of their songs. Then they hummed a few bars of the song and I realized who it was we were bringing into town. I kind of got excited myself.

There was going to be a huge need for volunteers, so being the dad that I am, I stepped forward for my assignment. I was given the choice of working security at the backstage door or putting in earplugs and monitoring the kids that wanted to rush the stage. Being the lazy man that I am, I figured the easier night was going to be at the backstage door. This door led to one of the streets through the Missouri State campus. I also did not want to be that close to the blaring music.

On the night of the concert, I took my place at the back door. Real security people gave me my job duties, which were fairly easy. I was told to not let anyone in the door unless he or she was wearing one of the concert personnel nametags. I was given one of those as well. I wanted desperately to use the "Badges? We don't need no stinking badges" line, but I have discovered that real security people, as well as those with BFS, rarely have a sense of humor.

The time went slowly. After about a half hour, I hadn't had anyone try to sneak in during my watch. I don't even recall anyone walking by the place. Finally, about an hour before the concert was to start, I got a little bit of action. People were approaching my door, but I noticed they all had their badges in place. Being the good security person I am, I let them through with a word of greeting. Under my breath, I was practicing my "You can't come in this way" speech. I went from an authoritative "Halt, who goes there" to the more polite "I'm so sorry, you can't enter through these doors."

Then I saw the young man approaching the door. At first glance I noticed he was not wearing a badge. His hair was done in sort of a punk look. He was wearing clothing that did not look like anything the good Baptist children were wearing to my church. I figured he was a concert crasher for sure. I stopped him at the door and asked how I might help him. He shared with me he needed to get inside the coliseum. The battle was on!

I informed him that without a badge like the one I was wearing, no one could get into this place. I was very firm and authoritative with my approach. Just as I figured I had this guy right where I wanted him, he said, "What if I'm in the band?"

I didn't know the names of their songs and recognized them only when someone would hum or play one of them. There was no way I was going to recognize a band member when I'd never seen them before. Before I could save face, the regular security guy dropped by and asked what the difficulty was. I explained to the guy that this man did not have a badge. That's when the security guy said, "You do know he's a member of the band, right?"

I admitted I did not and that I had gotten carried away with my authority. I had nearly kept a person away from the very place where he was needed. When I get to thinking about it, I'd done it before as well. There have been incidents in which I didn't want someone knowing about a particular event at church because I wanted to enjoy it selfishly and not have to worry about that person hanging with me. Here was an event that might bring someone closer to God, and I was playing security guard. It's a good thing my "bullet" was in my pocket!

At other times, I have offered advice that was more works-oriented than grace-filled. Quite often, whether consciously or subconsciously, I keep people away from the place where they can get the answers they seek in life.

Some of the disciples were right there with me!

Jesus had just finished speaking to a crowd, and some of the parents were trying to get their kids to meet Jesus. The only thing that stood in their way was a group of badge-wearing disciples. I'm sure they had in their minds that they were protecting Jesus from being bothered by these little rug rats. So the disciples, suffering with the BFS, took it upon themselves to make sure the children did not get into the coliseum. The disciples rebuked the parents for bringing them up there. They were not going to get close to Jesus.

Jesus caught on to what they were doing and got on the BFS-suffering disciples. He let them know quickly to let the children come to Him. In fact, Jesus pointed out that the kingdom of heaven actually belongs to the little ones. He reminded us as well that we have to approach God like a little child would. We just have to get around the tough security people!

What is it with me and the disciples in this situation that makes us want to protect Jesus and end up keeping people from meeting Him? The lesson I can learn from this is to keep the doors open and let the children of God get to the place where they need to be. Jesus can handle it from here!

Halt! Who goes there?

JACOB: CELEBRATING THE PAST OVER (GENESIS 31–33)

The promises of God are spread all throughout the Scriptures. Assurances are given that God is with me and will take care of my needs. Jesus said, “Don’t be afraid of those who want to kill your body; they cannot touch your soul.”

I don’t believe I’ve ever really faced someone that would actually kill my body, but I feel certain that I gave some people in my life the ability to kill my future career or relational opportunities.

Following the discovery of hidden sin in my life and the resignation from my leadership position in the church, I was assigned to a committee tasked with preparing me for restoration to the ministry. We worked on things such as Scripture memorization, honest confession, and avoiding the traps that had caught me in the past. As a part of the honest confession, it was their desire that I be open with future employers as to why I resigned from the church and the reason for my unemployment status.

I felt as though I were the character in Nathaniel Hawthorne’s book *The Scarlet Letter.* You can imagine the looks I received when a potential employer looked at the reason I left my last job and saw “adultery” or “moral failure” listed.

I felt as though a cloud were hanging over me, like the old cartoon character in the comic strip *Li’l Abner.* Paranoia developed as I was be passed over for jobs I felt qualified to do. When I would meet with my team, one of the questions I would always be asked was whether I was being open and honest with my wife and with potential employers about my situation.

It's not abnormal for the party that has been caught in the sin to want to put things behind him or her as quickly as possible. I couldn't seem to do that fast enough. I would see church members in public and feel as though they were saying, "There's *that* guy. He had it all and threw it away for the pleasures of sin."

Through some intensive counseling and supportive families, we worked through a lot of the aspects of our situation. For a couple of years we seemed to be progressing toward a healthy restoration in marriage. I found myself back in a leadership position in recreation in a faith-based retirement community. Unfortunately, we returned to some of the behaviors that had gotten us in trouble in the first place, and we decided the best thing to do was divorce.

Now I have divorce to add to the list. It took place three years after the revelation of my sin but seemed to bring the three-year-old news back to the forefront. Once again I felt like "*that* guy."

I lived in fear that an attorney would use the information of my sin against me. I wondered if the restoration team would ever use it in a similar way. I knew a church member or someone close to the situation could offer an opinion and possibly kill any chance I had in the future.

Despite the knowledge that God could put my life back together after divorce, I still lived in the fear of the murder others could cause with their knowledge of my sin. Despite having the assurance that God puts lives back together after major failures, I put more fear in the stories and less faith in the God of restoration. All I could imagine was finally getting into a close relationship with another woman only to have her know someone from my past and get all the sordid information. This would, of course, be the final nail in that relationship coffin!

Shortly before the divorce was finalized, I moved to Oxford, Mississippi, to begin my career as an instructor with Ole Miss. I thought maybe this would be my chance to avoid my ties to the past until I kept seeing people I knew from Germantown Baptist that now lived in Oxford or whose kids were attending the university. I again lived in fear of someone talking too much. I had not accepted the past as a part of my story. Despite God's assurances, I still wanted to project and protect the "good guy" image.

I even pursued one Oxford woman who, shortly after meeting me, asked me if I had ever worked at Germantown Baptist Church. My initial thought was, *Oh great! I finally find a really great girl, and she has to find out about my story.* The woman had a sister that attended the church. Fortunately she remembered the good things about my ministry rather than the way I ended it.

So what is up with this fear of the past? Why do I feel as though it seeks me out and desires to kill me again? I seek my friend Jacob to help me find an answer. Jacob was a sneaky and ornery kind of guy. Sounds just like me! He was born with a twin brother, Esau. Even in the womb he and his brother tussled and wrestled. Esau became firstborn though birth. Jacob came out holding on to Esau's heel. Even in the womb there was some sibling rivalry going on. His own mother helped him trick his dad out of a blessing. He also swindled his older brother out of the rights of the firstborn.

Shortly after deceiving his father and brother out of the proper blessing, Jacob knew Esau was going to be ticked. In fact, Esau stated that once his dad died, he would kill his brother. Jacob's mother caught wind of this and sent him to live with her brother.

On his journey to his uncle's house, Jacob had a dream in which God restated the promise he made to Abraham and assured Jacob that he was playing a role in the creation of a nation. God assured Jacob that He would be with him until the promise came to be. In a way, God used the trickery and deception of Jacob to further His plans for the creation of a nation that followed Him.

Jacob hooked up with his uncle Laban and, in the years to follow, fell in love with one of his uncle's daughters. Laban, having a few tricks up his sleeve, conned Jacob into marrying the oldest daughter first and swindled another contract for work out of Jacob for the girl he actually loved. Numerous children were born to Jacob, and finally he set out away from Laban to claim the land that was part of God's promise to his grandfather, Abraham. Jacob, in his normal manner, left in such a way that he ended up fearing his own father-in-law. Although he left with just that which was his own, the mistrust he had for Laban caused him to sneak away without announcing his departure. Unbeknownst to Jacob, his wife, Rachel, had taken Laban's idol gods. So Laban headed off to find his son-in-law.

Poor Jacob. So far the list of people wanting revenge from him consisted of his own brother and his own father-in-law. This had to make family oriented holidays difficult.

On the journey Laban caught up, and all ended up well. Jacob, however knew it was time to meet his brother, Esau. Despite the knowledge of a promise of God that he would be the father of a nation, Jacob was worried that Esau would kill him. He held more fear of his brother than he did faith in his God. Jacob sent messengers ahead to contact Esau. The messengers returned to tell Jacob that Esau was on his way to see him and had four hundred men with him. I think we all know that Jacob took that to mean his brother was bringing an army. So, to play it safe, Jacob sent all sorts of gifts in advance. Then he divided his family and flocks into two groups, with the reasoning that if Esau killed one group the other would still live. He was trying to soften up his brother's heart rather than depend on the promise of God.

When Esau finally met up with Jacob, they shared an embrace and a kiss. All that worried Jacob about the past was actually over. What Jacob did not realize was that God was working in Esau's heart for forgiveness. Esau, much like my ex-wife and others I hurt in my life, did not hold a grudge so much as he just wanted to get on with his life. God had blessed Esau with family and flocks, similar to the way in which Jacob had been blessed. I know Jacob had to live a little easier knowing no one was out to get him anymore.

People like Jacob and me get to the point where we learn that the ugly parts of our past are as much a part of our story as the glorious moments. The ugliness of deception and betrayal is part of the story of God's grace in our lives. It's not something to be proud of, but it's not something we have to run away from either. In fact, God uses the good, the bad, and the ugly of our lives to get us where He wants us to be.

What in your past have you been running from?

JOSEPH: WHAT IF I STOP SAYING "WHAT IF"? (MATTHEW 1:18–25)

The resignation was announced on the first Sunday of the month of March. A few days later the church flew my wife and me to a specialized retreat center in the mountains of Colorado. The place specialized in working with ministerial staff struggling with some aspect of their calling. Mine was due to a long period of hidden sin and darkness in my life. I was resigning from a position that was somewhat the envy of church recreation leaders in the country. I felt as though I were going from the penthouse to the outhouse in a matter of the few moments it took me to read my resignation.

One of the things the pastor shared with the church in each service where my resignation had been shared was that I would need help finding a new job when I got back from the retreat. The church was going to pay me through the end of May, but after that I needed a way to take care of my family. Out of a church of over six thousand attendees on that day, one job offer came through to me. It was from a good friend that ran a small construction business that specialized in building fences. I would be building fences. One friend pointed out the irony that a man needing boundaries in his life would land a job building fences, which create boundaries for property. I was petty enough at that time that I did not enjoy the irony.

Let me assure you that I have never been mistaken for a handyman. In church-building mission projects I would usually be assigned to trash detail, providing concrete, or blowing up balloons for the kids. The work crew that assisted my friend would vouch for this lack of "handymanliness." One man, Joel, tried to teach me how to use the nail gun. He was holding two pieces of wood together, and I was to nail them together. Operating the gun took more finesse than power. The trigger was held down, and then you would strike the piece of wood in a quick fashion and withdraw the gun from that point at the same rate of speed. It was very similar to how I've seen karate demonstrated in breaking boards.

Joel gave up his teaching career with me that day when the nail brushed the edge of the skin between his thumb and pointer finger. If I had been filmed, the footage could have been sold as a modern-day remake of silent movie slapstick humor. I smashed hands with fence posts, knocked coworkers over by turning quickly while carrying fence posts on my shoulder, and came close to running a hand saw over a man's finger. The saw was not supposed to be digital in that sense.

I started work in April and continued through August. In the hot and humid summer of Memphis, I had a continuous theme of "what if?" running through my head. Sometimes it had to do with being increasingly sneakier and conniving in hiding my sin. What if I hadn't left a paper trail? What if I had been more diligent at deleting things off the home computer? But then I remembered that the sin was discovered by my wife, who read e-mails that had been previously deleted from the account. God took care of that what-if rather abruptly.

The next popular what-if had to do with the first time I tinkered with and was tempted by the life of sin. What if I had said no and run, as Joseph did with Potiphar's wife? What if I had stayed away from the places that drew me in so easily? What if I had been stronger in fighting the temptation? What if I had been open and honest about the difficulty early on and had gotten the help I needed? I had numerous opportunities to do the right thing, but I chose not to until it was in the what-if stage.

The what-ifs don't stop with just regret. My visionary tactics had me asking "what if?" as to what I would be doing in my former ministry if God had restored me. I wondered if I would ever serve in a church again. What if no one thinks people change? Similar what-ifs started to play in my heart again as my wife proceeded with divorce plans. Sometimes when I'm with my sons and their families, I wonder, *What if their Mom and I were still together, making this visit together?*

I am not even close to being the what-if champion. Most of the what-ifs in my life have been created by my own doing. The what-if champion has to be Joseph, the earthly father of Jesus. Everywhere I look in his life creates a what-if scenario.

I never thought about it until a preacher mentioned it a few years ago. Joseph, had the Jewish nation not fallen into captivity centuries before, would have been king of Judah. He would have been in the line of David that was promised by God to always be in the position to reign and rule over God's chosen people. Joseph would have been living in the palace with all the riches and glory of a king. Instead he found himself working with wood. Barely making a living making tables and chairs and the occasional wooden fence post, he went from having the life of a lord to shaping a table leg on a lathe. I hope Joseph was better than I am at working with tools and wood.

What if the people had not rebelled against God? What if his forefathers had not led the nation into idolatry? What if Josiah's reforms had stuck and God had removed the consequences of previous acts of disobedience and infidelity? Instead of using a rule, Joseph would be in rule over all the people. I know I had days when I lived in the what-if mind-set while working with wood. I feel Joseph had those same kind of days.

Then, as if it couldn't get worse, Joseph discovered his fiancée was pregnant though he had not been with her. He opted to simply put her away quietly in such a way that she would not experience as much humiliation and shame as she otherwise might. According to Scripture she was to be stoned to death, but Joseph opted for a more grace-filled choice. Mary said the baby was from God, and Joseph had a dream that confirmed this point. So in marrying her, the shame and humiliation fell upon him instead. From that time on, he would face the what-ifs of the people who doubted the origin of this child.

I know these what-ifs had to bombard this man for the rest of his life. He lived in small towns. Most of us have an understanding of living in a small town and having everybody know your business. Any time someone in town snickered as he walked by, he had to wonder,

What if it wasn't a miracle or the dream was just a dream and not a messenger from God? Whenever someone inquires as to who Jesus' real father is or doubts the angelic stories, the temptation for the what-ifs have to come flying right back into the picture. After all, why would Joseph be so accepting when no one else I know would be 100 percent perfect in that realm?

What is it about the what-ifs that drive us into repeatedly asking the question? I know some of the issue is the image I can project. I want to be known as the obedient follower even when I know I am not. The root of sin can be found in the what-ifs. The what-if states that my plan is better than God's plan. I play it out in my head that if I could simply go back and change a decision or an action, then I could be worthy of God's love. Living in the what-if mind-set keeps me from giving God glory through the story. Living in the what-if mind-set keeps the emphasis on me and my efforts rather than seeing how God has worked and is working in my life.

Perhaps I need a new direction for my what-ifs. Instead I should ask, "What if I were to trust God that He has me right where He wants me today?" or "What if I were to accept that all that has happened to me is a part of my story of God's redemptive work in my life?"

The direction of our what-ifs will determine whether we live in regret or in revelation.

What if ...

CPSIA information can be obtained
at www.ICGtesting.com
Printed in the USA
FSHW011205311019
63602FS